The
Rights and
Responsibilities
of the
Modern
University

THE
RIGHTS AND
RESPONSIBILITIES
OF THE
MODERN
UNIVERSITY

WHO ASSUMES THE RISKS
OF COLLEGE LIFE?

Robert D. Bickel and Peter F. Lake

CAROLINA ACADEMIC PRESS
Durham, North Carolina

ISBN 0-89089-675-5
LCCN 99-60461

Carolina Academic Press
700 Kent Street
Durham, NC 27701
Telephone (919) 489-7486
Fax (919) 493-5668
www.cap-press.com

Printed in the United States of America

To Marilyn and Lea

Contents

Preface

During my eight years as a university attorney, and more than twenty years of teaching education law, I have observed what I believe to be an unnecessary struggle to properly define the joint responsibility of the university, its students, and to some extent parents, regarding the safety and quality of college life. It is my fundamental belief that the law—both judicial decisions and legislative enactment—should recognize that an unreasonably unsafe learning environment is not an appropriate learning environment. The college or university, students, and parents must understand that students who come to college—at age 18 or so—directly from a family setting characterized by dependency and parenting, are not yet fully prepared for the freedoms of an adult life without the continued active intervention of family and the active guidance of the university. Our colleague, Gary Pavela, describes the challenge as "complementing freedom with structure for the student within the context of university life."

Several years ago, I took this idea to my colleague Peter Lake. Together we examined the body of texts, caselaw, and commentary, and, with support from Dr. Don Gehring of Bowling Green State University (providing for a summer teaching and writing opportunity for me), we developed the first of two articles on the subject. That work expanded, during a period of three years, to a series of lectures, seminars, and brief papers presented at various annual meetings of educational associations and special workshops at the University of Notre Dame, the University of Montana, the National Conference on Law and Higher Education, the annual meetings of the National Association of College and University Attorneys and the International Association of Campus Law Enforcement Administrators, and elsewhere. The result has been this book, presenting our view that prior notions of university law have failed to accurately reflect the shared legal responsibility of colleges and universities, and their students for student safety.

Our views have been described as controversial by some university attorneys, and some in both higher education law and university administration see our observations as calling for a return to in loco parentis—an era of autocratic university control. We admit to generating a debate for the purpose of clarifying and redefining university/student relations in the legal sense. What we seek is not a return to the days of autocratic control of students by universities but the replacement of a failed approach to the management of risks that threaten student safety and the security of the learning environment.

Many people have inspired and contributed to the development of this book by way of countless formal and informal discussions, seminars, and debates. I am especially appreciative of the support of our colleagues Gary Pavela, Ed Stoner, Peter Ruger, George Shur, Joe Buchanan, Beverly Ledbetter, Art Broadhurst, and Jeff Chasen, Pamela Bernard, Sheila Bell, Joel Epstein, Paul Ward, Jim Beasley, Mike Shanahan, and Jan Majewski. I also wish to thank the faculty and editorial staff of the Journal of College and University Law, and especially Professors John Robinson and "Tex" Dutile, and Brien Crotty, for their active involvement in the publishing of our views and for inviting us to lecture on this subject at the Notre Dame Law School. I also genuinely appreciate the support of Stetson University and my colleagues at its College of Law who encouraged our research. Finally, we give special thanks to our research assistants, Melissa Jagger and Holly Burke, for their careful work in checking our sources, to Sharon Gisclair, who spent countless hours with this manuscript, to Pamela Burdett, our reference librarian, and to Barbara Lernihan, Connie Evans, Louise Petren, Susan Stinson, Marge Masters, and Shannon Mullins for their patience and superior secretarial skills that made the production of this manuscript possible.

Robert D. Bickel
October, 1998

Several years ago, Bob Bickel walked into my office for one of our frequent "two people who teach torts" chats. Bob had always supported my interests in tort duty and rescue doctrines, and cases like *Tarasoff v. Board of Regents* (the seminal duty to warn a victim of a foreseeable attacker case). I knew of his stature in the university law community, but I saw only the obvious connections between my work and his. Bob said that I should become more involved with university law issues and that I would enjoy the field and the people involved in it a great deal. I like Bob so much as a person and a friend that in an act of faith, I agreed to do a few things with him.

Bob was animated from the start by two points in particular. First, he kept pushing me on the idea that tort "duty" law was the key to the future of modern university law. Second, he insisted that a series of problematical decisions had been the result of a misreading of the cases involving the 1960's civil rights movement on campus. We both share a deep affection for American universities, and I could detect that Bob was concerned that the law was somehow on the brink of facilitating the erosion of community and safety in institutions of higher learning.

In retrospect, Bob's intuitions—formed by years and years of devoted (often selfless) service to the field—emerged to me as profound insights regarding the law of higher education and tort law generally. As we began to write law review articles and travel to more colleges and more professional meetings, the themes of this book became apparent to us.

Writing the book was greatly facilitated by the conjunction of our sabbaticals in 1998 which gave us the time and opportunity to complete this book. The book was made possible by the diligent work of our faculty support staff (led by Connie Evans), particularly Sharon Gisclair and Barbara Lernihan, and with the assistance of Louise Petren, Susan Stinson, Marge Masters, and Shannon Mullins. My handwriting is particularly atrocious (I am still not good with computers) and their work was often akin to that of dedicated Egyptologists. Many people have supported us in our endeavors. Bob has thanked many of them in his Preface, but I would like to express particular gratitude to Joel Epstein, Greg McCann, Ray Goldstone, Art Broadhurst, Jeff Chasen, David Aronofsky, Mike Shanahan, Adam Oler, and Keith Sipe. My research assistant Melissa Jagger deserves special recognition for her dedicated and invaluable help on the book; Labor Day 1998 was aptly named for her. I would like to remember my mentor when I was in practice in New York City at Cahill Gordon & Reindel, Michael J. Tierney, who taught me most of my lawyering skills. I must express a very special gratitude to my parents Chester and Mary, who worked so hard to insure that I received the education I needed to make a project like this possible: there were many sleepless nights and early mornings, and many financial sacrifices along the way. Also, I will always remember that Coyote was my constant companion through the long spring days I spent writing and revising the manuscript. Most of all, I must thank Bob himself: he has been my greatest facilitator and one of those few great friends of a lifetime. It is my most earnest desire that this book become a lasting tribute to his lifelong efforts to improve the law, and safety on American college and university campuses.

Peter F. Lake
October 1998

The Rights and Responsibilities of the Modern University

I

Introduction — Toward a Balancing of Rights and Responsibilities on Campus

Modern American universities often evoke images of laureled sanctuaries where higher learning is facilitated in a unique and particularly safe environment. Yet, college education is filled with potential safety risks for students. The media now reports regularly about criminal attacks on students on campus, injuries to students on field trips and in study abroad programs, injuries from defective premises, and of course, Greek life incidents and alcohol problems on and off campus.[1] The incidents reported

---

1. Since the early 1980's, literally dozens of articles have been written in prominent newspapers, education news publications, and association journals about the growing risk of criminal intrusion and student assault on college campuses, fraternity (and in some instances sorority) hazing, alcohol related student injury and death, and the potential liability of the college or university. *See, e.g.,* E.T. Buchanan, "Alcohol on Campus and Possible Liability," NASPA JOURNAL, Vol. 21 (Fall 1983) 2; S. Janosik, "Liquor Law Liability on the College Campus: When Are We Responsible?" NASPA JOURNAL, Vol. 21 (Fall 1983) 21; Z. Ingalls, "Colleges in Growing Danger from Drinking-related Lawsuits Experts Say," THE CHRONICLE, Vol. 30 (Mar. 1985) 11; D. Gregory, "Alcohol Consumption by College Students and Related Liability Issues," 14 J. OF LAW AND EDUC. 43 (1985); T. Meyer, "Fight Against Hazing Rituals Rages on Campuses and in State Legislatures," THE CHRONICLE, Vol. 32 (Mar. 1986); D. Richmond, "Putting an End to Fraternity Hazing," NASPA JOURNAL, Vol. 24 (Spring 1987) 48; C. Fields, "Colleges Weigh Liability in Alcohol and Sexual Harassment," THE CHRONICLE, Vol. 34 (Feb. 1988) A13; D. Wright, "Violence on Campus," AMERICAN SCHOOL AND UNIVERSITY, Vol. 60 (June 1988) 37; M. Collison, "National Interfraternity Conference to Weigh Alternatives to Pledge System in an Effort to Halt Hazing Excesses," THE CHRONICLE, Vol. 35 (Dec. 1988) A25; M. Collison, "Two National Fraternities Plan to Eliminate Pledging in Campaign Against Alcohol Abuse and Hazing," THE CHRONICLE, Vol. 36 (Sept. 1989) A1; D. Richmond, "The Legal Implications of Fraternity Hazing," NASPA JOURNAL, Vol. 26 (Summer 1989) 300; D. Richmond, "Crime on Campus: When Is a University Liable?" NASPA JOURNAL, Vol. 17 (Summer 1990) 324; S. Dodge, "Campus Crime Linked to Students' Use of Drugs and Alcohol," THE CHRONICLE, Vol. 36 (Jan. 1990) A33; A. Nicholls, "A Sense of Security," TIMES EDUCATIONAL SUPPLEMENT, No. 4089 (Nov. 1994); C. Shea,

by the major media are only a fraction of the problem. Student safety has become a core issue for modern universities.

"Wall of Silence," THE CHRONICLE, Vol. 40 (June 1994) A25; R. Fossey, M. Smith, "Institutional Liability for Campus Rapes: The Emerging Law," 24 J. LAW AND EDUC. 377 (1995); H. Wechsler, "Secondary Effects of Binge Drinking on College Campuses," Higher Education Center for Alcohol and Other Drug Prevention, Educational Development Center (1996); P. Finn, "Preventing Alcohol-Related Problems on Campus: Acquaintance Rape," Higher Education Center for Alcohol and Other Drug Prevention, Education Development Center, Inc. (1996). http://www.edc.org/hec/ S. Walton, "Social Host Liability: Risks for Fraternities and Student Hosts," NASPA JOURNAL, Vol. 34 (Fall, 1996) 29; O. Chadley, "Campus Crime and Personal Safety in Libraries," COLLEGE AND RESEARCH LIBRARIES, Vol. 57 (Jul. 1996) 385; J. Asagba, "Campus Violence: A Case Study of Residence Halls," COLLEGE STUDENT JOURNAL, Vol. 30 (June 1996) 158; T. Lenski, H. Meyers, D. Hunter, "Understanding Students' Intentions to Use Safety Precautions," NASPA JOURNAL, Vol. 33 (Winter 1996) 82; T. Cornwell, "One Million Weapons on US Campuses," TIMES HIGHER EDUCATION SUPPLEMENT, No. 1287 (Jul. 1997) 9; E. Bennett-Johnson, "The Emergence of American Crime and Violence on the College and University Campus," COLLEGE STUDENT JOURNAL, Vol. 31 (Mar. 1997); J. Marcus, "Court Opens Lid on Campus Crime," TIMES HIGHER EDUCATION SUPPLEMENT, No. 1291 (Aug. 1997) 9; J. Selingo, "Alabama Appeals Court Allows Former Pledge to Sue Fraternity for Alleged Hazing," THE CHRONICLE, Vol. 44 (Dec. 1997) A42; T. Cornwell, "Student Dies in Fraternity Revels," TIMES HIGHER EDUCATION SUPPLEMENT, No. 1296 (Sept. 1997) 9; M. Geraghty, "Hazing Incidents at Sororities Alarm Colleges," THE CHRONICLE, Vol. 43 (June 1997) A37; B. Gose, "Efforts to End Fraternity Hazing Have Largely Failed, Critics Charge," THE CHRONICLE, Vol. 43 (Apr. 1997) A37. David Satcher, the U.S. Surgeon General, has stated that alcohol is "a serious problem with our young people at every age, but especially on college campuses, as we see more binge drinking." Leo Reisberg, *Some Experts Say Colleges Share the Responsibility for the Recent Riots* [by students, over alcohol], CHRONICLE OF HIGHER EDUCATION, May 15, 1998, at 48. In reaction to all of this, Congress has enacted legislation affecting the handling of student records and crime reporting by colleges and universities. Most recently, the failure of colleges and universities to deal successfully with abusive alcohol problems led to the enactment of Section 119 of PL 105-244, 112 STAT. 1581, 1596 (to be codified at 20 U.S.C. § 1011h), as a part of the Higher Education Amendments of 1998, providing, *inter alia*, that colleges and universities must increase initiatives to reduce binge drinking on American campuses. Declaring that colleges and universities must make significant efforts to change the culture of alcohol consumption on campuses, Congress requires the appointment of campus task forces to examine student and academic life, and to make recommendations to reduce alcohol and other drug-related problems. The law expresses Congress' concern for illegal consumption of alcohol and drugs, and seeks an effective code of disciplinary sanctions for students who violate campus drug and alcohol policies, as well as a co-operative effort by colleges and local businesses to reduce illegal consumption of alcohol, and alcohol abuse by students on and off campus. The continued attention of the national media and Congress to the problems of campus crime, alcohol-related student injury and death, and the effectiveness of student disciplinary policies supports the assertion that prior legal paradigms have failed to properly reflect the rights and responsibilities of the modern college/university, and its students, in matters of student life and student safety.

There are some basic causes of danger on college and university campuses. First, many of the young men and women who move to the college campus and/or a college town are living "on their own" for the first time in their lives. Colleges often house large concentrations of these young men and women in densely populated dormitories. Many of these dormitories—now residence halls—are decades old and were first designed and occupied in an era when crime on campus was not a major concern to administrators, students, or parents. A significant number of today's students continue to reside in halls that were designed without the benefit of safety features that are common by today's standards. Retrofitting old dormitories can only do so much. Colleges have a tendency to allocate resources to educational and other endeavors first, not to maintenance of student housing. Campus housing culture thus is vulnerable to criminal intrusion. Second, a typical campus is occupied by students who are, for the most part, very young and who enjoy substantial freedom. For many students, campus life is different from the more protected lifestyle of high school or home, and presents new experiences of fraternity or sorority life, an intense social environment, unique and more powerful peer pressures, etc. Third, the campus itself is often an amalgam of old buildings and newer ones, put to a variety of uses—*e.g.*, science laboratories, sport and recreational facilities, art studios, residences, parking garages and lots, arenas etc. Operation of facilities brings with it standard risks that other similar operations face. Fourth, for many college students campus life seems safer than it is partly because they may assume that most other students are harmless like themselves. This illusion of safety is its own kind of danger. Fifth, American college campuses have experienced a surge in dangers associated with alcohol cultures that they all too often seem to breed. In combination with the other risk factors, alcohol use by students can create special dangers. These are not the only sources of danger but are among the most significant risk factors on campuses today.

Unfortunately, all indications are that the dangers of college and university life will increase. Insurance statistics show steady, and in some cases alarming, rates of growth in college student injury claims. The growth may continue: students who have experienced the culture of violence, incivility and intoxicants occurring in K-12 education are on their way to college. And the rise in travel abroad and externship programs, for instance, also greatly increases risk to student safety.[2] With potential danger to our col-

---

2. Consider three recent events. In March 1996, four students were killed in a bus accident in India. The parents sued the university, *inter alia,* claiming that dangerous roads and an inadequate driver were to blame. In May 1997, a group of students from the University of New Mexico was ambushed in Ecuador by gunmen who killed the wife of a

leges on the rise, we need answers more than ever on how to make college life safer. How should we fairly and reasonably allocate the rights and responsibilities of students and universities to make campuses safe?

Paradoxically, at the time of greatest need, the law of higher education relating to the allocation of risk and responsibilities is most complex and confusing. Obviously, there is much more to creating safe and productive learning environments than legal rules. However, university law has had and will have a major impact on university safety and ultimately on the effectiveness of a college's educational program. Higher education law co-creates the foundations of the university environment and apportions the rights and responsibilities of the participants in university life. Legal archetypes and images, as we shall see, serve to focus the imagination of university culture. That imagination is remarkably powerful. Legal images and rules can radically alter parameters of risk and can foster a range of effects on university culture from dictatorial style control of student life, to disorder, danger, and administrative disempowerment. For example, if courts tell students that they are "consumers" completely free of university "control" and are destined to drink, they will begin to believe and act on that message, to the point of rioting when campuses ban alcohol. Even seemingly harmless ideas like treating a university as a business can be troubling. Radical consumerism and bottom-line administrative mentalities can disserve safety and fracture any sense of shared responsibility for safety on campus. Ultimately, the university is both a creator of and a mirror of society itself. The law can help to make the image in the mirror brighter, or darker.

At present, university safety law does not send entirely clear messages on how responsibility for student safety is and should be allocated. Parents and prospective students see college catalogs filled with serene, almost monastic pictures of campus life, pictures of scholarly faculty and diligent students in libraries, laboratories, and office settings, and visual images of sophisticated extra curricular activities and a high quality of life. University lawyers and administrators, however, are well aware of the dangers of student injury and the (potential) litigation that comes from it.[3]

---

professor. In January 1998, five St. Mary's College of Maryland students were raped in Guatemala.

The *Washington Post* recently reported that "the number of U.S. college students receiving academic credit in overseas programs has nearly doubled from 48,483 in 1985-86 to 89,242 in 1995-96 the latest year for which figures are available, according to the Institute for International Education." Amy Argetsinger & Valerie Strauss, *Educators Wary After Overseas Attacks Boom in Foreign Travel Poses Risks, Colleges and Missionaries Say,* WASHINGTON POST, Jan. 20, 1998, at B1.

3. *See* Perry A. Zerkel, *The Volume of Higher Education Litigation: An Update,* 126 ED. LAW. REP. 21 (1998) (noting increases in university litigation.)

University administrators (often highly educated) are told to do their jobs and exercise responsibility for student affairs—but will be criticized if they have inappropriately "assumed duties" to students. Their jobs are on the line with each decision they make. They often live in a world with classic "catch 22s"; the typical college administrator often feels both frustrated and disempowered by law. The law of student safety itself—principally case decisions—is often a complex, confusing maze.

The complexity and confusion in university law is the natural and direct result of the revolutions in university law and culture in the post World War II era. Since World War II, and particularly since the 1960s, university law has changed dramatically from images of university authority to images emphasizing student *freedom*.

Most commentators and courts believe that the American university stood for the most part *in loco parentis*[4] (in the place of a parent) to its students before 1960 (being somewhat arbitrary in the dates). In Chapter II we discuss the era in detail, although the basic idea of a university *in loco parentis* is easy to grasp—simply imagine parental, sometimes even paramilitary style, *control* of student life and affairs. Dean Wormer, of fictional "Faber University" in the movie *Animal House*, comically portrays, to a surprisingly large extent, the legal archetype of the (almost) limitless power a university had, or at least asserted, over its students. In this era a university was rarely, if ever, subject to a lawsuit. It was a time of *insularity* from legal scrutiny, and like governments, charities and families of that era, the college was considered to be another institution outside the safety rules of the legal system, and in a sense above the law. University law tracked the law of interpersonal family relations, governmental/citizen relations, and charitable organizations regarding liability in civil courts. Disputes were kept and settled quietly within the university, as within a family (or a church). If a matter involved a public university, the matter was considered "governmental" and not subject to private civil lawsuits seeking reparations for injuries.

Then in the 1960s and early 1970s, as Professor Charles A. Wright observed, the Constitution came to campus. This period, detailed in Chapter III, witnessed student challenges to university control and to the idea that college life was insulated from legal scrutiny. Students argued that *in loco parentis* authority had been used on them in extreme and unfair ways by colleges that disciplined and expelled students for participation in the civil rights movement and even for asserting basic Constitutional rights of free speech and association. Beginning with the landmark decision in *Dixon v. Alabama State Board of Education* (discussed in Chapter III), students

---

4. *See* Chapter II for a definition.

succeeded in challenging *in loco parentis* based abuses and won basic Constitutional rights on campus. Students were no longer children, but became *constitutional* adults.

As a result of the rapid fall of *in loco parentis,* student *freedom* ascended over university *authority* and *control.* The University was no longer insulated from legal scrutiny. So much changed in American society in this period in similar ways — rights of women against husbands, children against parents, the disgrace of Nixon and the presidency, lowering of respect for military and police activities, Vietnam etc. — that the profound shift in campus *law* was a footnote in a chapter of social change and upheaval in America. But the shift was a groundbreaking one. With the fall of *in loco parentis,* the American college was no longer insular: it entered a new era of accountability in the courts. The fall of *in loco parentis* and the new role of the legal system on campus facilitated important developments in legal relations between students and administrators (and others) on campus. These developments have had important student safety implications.

In 1987, Ernest L. Boyer, former U.S. Commissioner of Education, published *College: The Undergraduate Experience in America*, in association with the Carnegie Foundation For The Advancement of Teaching. Boyer's book has become widely celebrated as a resource on post-1960s college education in America.[5] The book is a comprehensive survey of college experience including college application issues, academic, curricular, and faculty concerns, campus life, and governance of a university. It is noteworthy that Boyer makes only oblique, indirect, or passing references to university law and the profound *legal* changes which occurred. Commenting upon the gap between academic and social life, Boyer noted:

> [W]e found a *great separation*, sometimes to the point of isolation, between academic and social life on campus. Colleges like to speak of the campus as *community*, and yet what is being learned in most residence halls today has little connection to the classrooms; indeed it may undermine the educational purposes of the college. The idea that a college stands in for parents, *in loco parentis*, is today a faded memory. But on many campuses there is great uncertainty about what should replace it.[6]

Admittedly, Boyer was focused more on policy and academic administration than college law and the effects of change(s) in college law.

---

5. *See* Ernest L. Boyer, College: The Undergraduate Experience in America (1987).

6. *Id.* at 5. (Some emphasis added).

Nevertheless, from his lens, Boyer observed the central perplexing problems that university law has faced and helped to create since the fall of university insularity began in the 1960s. Boyer commented upon the *distance* created between faculty and administration on the one hand and student life on the other. He also recognized the inherent need to make the connection between educational goals and non-academic student life.[7]

Importantly, Boyer stated the principal question presented in modern American university law and policy regarding student safety: "How should tension between student freedom and institutional authority be resolved?"[8] Abruptly altering the *legal* understanding of the university and its relationship(s) to its students ended a long standing system of relations. What would replace *in loco parentis*?

In place of a community ordered by surrogate parental authority, students and colleges began to grow increasingly distant. The profound and sudden shift from an authoritarian and legally insularized university model to a student rights/freedom model where students had basic Constitutional rights soon ushered in a new period in the courts reflecting this distancing. It was the birth of what we refer to as the "bystander" era. In the 1970s and early to mid 1980s (again, somewhat arbitrarily), American courts began hearing lawsuits involving student physical injuries arising from the risks of campus life, not just student Constitutional rights style cases. These cases—detailed, described and critiqued in Chapter IV—were different. The focus in the student civil rights cases was on positive aspects of student freedom from autocratic university control. The new cases were oriented to the negative side of student freedom. Namely, if students were free from autocratic control, what, if any, *duties* were owed to them regarding their safety? Specifically, who now assumed the risks of student life? A prominent group of decided cases (but relatively few in number, and mostly in less prominent jurisdictions) defined a brief, but critical, post-*in loco parentis* period in university law. Several courts of this period reacted to newly won student Constitutional rights by rejecting student injury claims. These courts created a new form of insularity for colleges. The new legal protections were not due to a college

---

7. As Boyer wrote:
   We were especially impressed that many faculty and academic administrators distance themselves from student life and appear to be confused about their obligations in non-academic matters. How can life outside the classroom support the educational mission of the college? How should tension between student freedom and institutional authority be resolved?
   Id. at 5.
8. *Id.* at 5.

being family-like, charity-like or government-like. The logic of the new "by-stander"[9] cases was that new student Constitutional rights and freedoms had created a caste of *uncontrollable* students (legally and socially).

The conclusions of the bystander era cases were harsh and reminiscent of the worker's rights cases of the late 19th century—cases which left workers with little protection at work from injuries arising from work.[10] Some leading university cases stated that students injured in the course of higher education now were in an environment of student freedom and that the university owed them little or no responsibility to protect them from harm. The courts implied that the attainment of Constitutional rights on campus made students adults for all purposes and beyond the control of the university. It was an important leap of logic, particularly because the kinds of Constitutional freedoms and rights students sought to vindicate in the 1960s were very different from the "freedoms" that courts of the bystander era believed students possessed.

Many of the bystander era courts used highly technical tools of legal reasoning (most of the legalese was over the heads of parents and media, and often even confused administrators). Invariably, these courts made reference to a technical legal concept in denying university responsibility for student safety—"duty." These courts said *no* "duty" was owed to students because, as "free" and "uncontrollable" beings, students owed "duties" to protect themselves.

"Duty" thus became the central focus of university law. It was the principal legal rule of the bystander era and the replacement legal archetype for *in loco parentis*: out with legal insularity based on *in loco parentis*, charitable immunity and governmental immunity—in with "duty." For most people, the word "duty" has a straightforward meaning. It is a commonly used word with common usages in English. Lawyers and courts at

---

9. A bystander university is like a stranger who has no power or responsibility to step in to "assist" the endangered students. As with a bystander to a serious injury or crime, there is a disquieting sense of forcing someone legally to assist: and an equally disquieting sense of the immorality of those who would just stand by. By casting a university into this image, the university gained the advantages and disadvantages of this morally and legally ambiguous archetype. The major advantage was insulation from financial responsibility for much student injury. The major disadvantage was a burgeoning sense of hypocrisy or failure; universities were supposed to be places of moral development, yet they opted for the low road or tacitly admitted their inability to meet goals set for and even by them.

10. In the late 19th Century, workers were perceived to have freedom of contract, *inter alia*. Courts often reasoned that a typical worker who had not bargained for specific safety protection with her employer basically assumed all risks at work. Most workers who were maimed at work did not so bargain and were—along with their families—left destitute. In the early 20th Century, the progressive era saw a shift in favor of worker's compensation, now embodied almost universally in America.

times use this word in ways that are similar to common usages and, at other times, in highly technical ways. Not only is the legal concept of "duty" complex, but its meaning has been rapidly changing in recent times. Making sense of legal "duty" is a special task of Chapter V. And making "duty" work for universities who want to facilitate safety and education is the basic theme of Chapter VI. No one interested in or affected by university law can fail to deal with "duty."

Thus, university law went from the clear and firm foundations of *in loco parentis* to more precarious, sometimes obtuse, footing on the new concept of "duty." "Duty" has crystalized as the central legal concept of all the periods post *in loco parentis*, so it is no wonder that even late into the 1990s, highly informed observers like Gary Pavela, editor of a leading law and policy periodical in law and higher education, wrote: "Colleges and universities are in the midst of profound change. There's a sense of rapid acceleration toward an uncertain future."[11] The uncertainty generated is by no means merely legal or theoretical. College administrators and officials need day-to-day practical answers to questions which run the gamut from admissions to graduation and even beyond. Shall we admit this student with a history of violence? If this person is denied the opportunity to graduate, what are the ramifications? How shall I write this letter of recommendation—can I omit reference to disciplinary records? What do I do with this student who has harassed women on campus? American courts, by electing to reconceptualize the relationships between universities and students, have ushered in—perhaps without so intending—a new era of *uncertainty* in university law. A major goal of this book is to speak simultaneously to the legal *and* university community to overcome what has become a crisis in practical university affairs *and* archetypal legal vision. Uncertainty breeds at least two problems: it is disempowering for college administrators, and it undermines safety initiatives by working against the sharing of responsibility for campus safety. Legal uncertainty leads to more distancing and to "cover your rear quarters" strategies.

For a brief time following the fall of *in loco parentis*, many "bystander era" courts used critical, if nebulous, "duty" concepts to reach fairly predictable results. These courts often held that *no* "duty" was owed by a university to a student to protect that student from injury. The university thus was in a no-legal liability situation. The university world took on a new order based on a shift in polarity from a university authority to stu-

---

11. GARY PAVELA, THE POWER OF ASSOCIATION: DEFINING OUR RELATIONSHIP WITH STUDENTS IN THE 21ST CENTURY, 7 SYNTHESIS, No. 3, pp. 529-33, 537-40 (Winter 1996). (Endnote omitted). Originally published as a National Association of Student Personnel Administration (NASPA) White Paper. *Id.* at 540 n.1.

dent freedom paradigm. Because of these cases, and for an interval, the university law situation *seemed* clear in consequence if not in theory, a time to which many university attorneys and some courts still cling. In some cases, the university was now a "bystander" to student injury claims and not legally responsible. The message was that it was better not to get too involved or to "assume" duties to students. This message was unappealing to college administrators and campus law enforcement administrators. Both student affairs administrators and campus police officers had embarked on their careers because of their interest in proactive safety initatives, desire to mentor students, and hope of co- creating better college communities. The courts—and university lawyers—sent them powerful admonitions, however, that literally redefined and minimized the roles of student affairs administrators and security officers. The messages were negative and disempowering and served to break down the bonds of shared responsibility for safety on campus. With distance came danger and frustration.

Again, "duty" can be an elusive legal concept. Thus, even in the heyday of what we refer to as the "bystander" university, some cases imposed "duty" *and* legal responsibility on the university. These cases often cast the college in business terms and saw students as consumers/victims. In the university legal community these cases were typically dismissed as wrongheaded, anomalous, minority jurisdiction cases or, by some, as a feared return of *in loco parentis*. Yet, these cross current cases were paradigmatic of the legal shift from *in loco parentis* to duty. Those who thought that "duty" would simplify the law and simply protect university interests were missing the larger picture which duty was casting. It was never possible for a college to be a complete stranger to student safety and to be a total bystander to dangers on campus.

From the mid 1980s or so to the present, courts have continued to use the concept of "duty" in favor of the rejected notion of *in loco parentis*. However, a shift in the legal use of "duty" has been under way in the courts, and the results courts reach are no longer strongly no-duty or no liability oriented. Universities are losing prominent student injury cases more than ever; the language that the courts use is no longer deferential to the university. Indeed, in some instances, courts are highly critical of university conduct and litigation tactics. The brief perceived halcyon period of the bystander decisions is clearly over (if it ever really existed, as we examine in Chapter IV). This recent legal phenomenon—the consolidation of university safety law around the duty concept—has intensified the uncertainty described by Boyer and Pavela. In Chapter V we discuss the most recent phase of the "duty" era in university law.

Courts today are in an implicit search for the Aristotelian mean and middle ground—a fair balance between the need for university supervision, structure, and guidance and students' need for the freedom to grow and express themselves. Courts today are finding this balance through the legal vehicle of "duty." As we discuss in Chapter V, the legal use of "duty" requires expert guidance in the law of torts generally, negligence law, and some contract law. By no means is the legal state of affairs simple to grasp; courts have looked to a variety of technical legal tools to solve university law problems and have looked for answers in places that were once foreign to university affairs. Moreover, American courts today still lack well defined and appropriate overall legal vision of the university in the post-insularity/*in loco parentis era*. Courts need such an image badly. Chapter V illustrates and discusses this complex situation in ways that those with legal training will follow easily and lay persons interested or involved in university affairs can also readily understand. It is well to remember that any time an industry moves out from under the roof of legal protection, the law will likely be confusing and transitory for a period of time.

Current confusion, then, is a product of uncertainty over legal results *and* legal concepts in times of social and political change and transition. In addition, communication between university officials and the legal system leaves much to be desired. Courts send messages, but what is received and how is it communicated? University officials and administrators have strong views on legal rules, but can courts hear them? Courts need guidance from the university community and vice versa. In the end, universities need guidance on how to manage student affairs in the new era of university law just as courts need to clarify their vision of this aspect of higher education law. The narrow issue of student safety on campus raises much broader theoretical and practical social questions.

In Chapter VI we offer the image of the university as *facilitator*—the appropriate legal and cultural balance between university authority/control and student freedom. Indeed, this image is manifest in the recent caselaw; in that sense our work is more like that of craftsmen than artists. The facilitator model is a model of balance and is thus naturally beige, not black and white. Neither *in loco parentis* nor stranger/bystander archetypes are adequate or appropriate for the modern university environment now. In essence, both are extreme images. The one is strongly authoritarian, the other is absurdly and unnecessarily libertarian. Following the lead of American courts, we build upon the elusive concept of "duty" and offer concrete ways to conceptualize the relationships between university and students to find the right balance. We believe that students can enjoy substantial freedoms in an environment that provides structure and emphasizes shared responsibility for safety. The core idea, explained in detail in Chapter VI, is that a university can provide a reasonably safe place to live and learn and can guide and assist its students and channel their activities and energies without exercising draconian control over all aspects of student relations: students *need* to experience some risks to grow and mature and need to have some responsibility for their own safety and growth as well. There is a middle ground. There exists a place of shared, balanced responsibilities among students and their universities. The facilitator university model is a model of an environment of *shared* values, risks and responsibilities. The facilitator does not accept autocracy or abdication.

The facilitator model is also a shared *legal* and *university affairs* vision. We see courts and university officials and students in partnership, not in conflict. There is an important opportunity at hand to craft a truly interdisciplinary vision of modern higher education law. University administrators and campus police should be empowered to do their jobs effectively. They should be able to turn to law for positive reinforcement of their jobs and for tools to be even more effective. Particularly in the bystander era, the law became anti-disciplinary and disempowered campus officials who came to fear that doing their jobs could cost them dearly in courts of law. New legal rules—and images—can re-empower campus officials and promote greater levels of safety.

This book is not merely about a shift in imaginings and paradigms. We offer concrete proposals for ways to rebuild the safety of our universities. Not long ago, Americans had written off their big cities as havens of crime and degeneration, destined to remain this way because of social forces greater than any government and the powers of the police. However, a minor revolution has occurred in police work—roughly speaking the idea of community policing and "fixing broken windows"—which has had dramatic effects in major cities like New York City. The ideas which turned our urban centers around have application to our universities. Chapter VI explains specific proposals to re-empower the university as facilitator. Safe campuses begin with simple steps designed to institute a sense of community of shared values and meaningful responsibility.

We aim for this book to fill four critical needs.

First, there has been a lack of an appropriate and complete description of where the law of university/student relations and physical safety is and where it is heading. The book describes and maps the law in ways that any lawyer or layperson can understand.

Second, American courts and university personnel need a vision of the modern university and university student relations. What can fill the void left by the fall of *in loco parentis*? A potpourri of conflicting images only adds to uncertainty of law and uncertainty of administration. Legal uncertainty is both disempowering and dangerous. Many administrators and campus police who are faced with uncertain images of their respective roles with students are pushed to minimalist, "cover your rear quarters" postures (*or* fear that they will face personal and professional reputational damage if they 'guess' wrong). This dynamic is disempowering and can leave reasonable campus officials acting in good faith but with the wrong incentives. Ultimately, the safety of students on campus and the productivity of an educational environment turns upon the actions of people in the university environment, not lawyers or judges. How many injured students would have been safe if the law more appropriately encouraged university personnel and campus police to do their jobs? How many students have been injured because common sense gave way to disengagement brought on by legal uncertainty? We need clarification not just in legal rules for lawyers but in expressed *vision*. We need a shared legal and university perspective of student/university relationships with concrete implications.

Thus, third, and related closely, there has been little guidance *from* the courts to the university community and *to* the courts from university lawyers and their constituents. We have relational and relationship problems. University law is a classic context in which to experience the dissonance and confusion of legal rule, result, and real world action. It is also a wonderful place to build bridge(s) between law and university life. We offer a new, shared, interdisciplinary vision of university life. Given the rapid changes in university life and in the law, bridging these gaps is an urgent task.

Fourth, university law is not just the province of university officials, students and the courts. The greater community needs to be apprized of and engaged in the consequences of the legal decisions affecting the parameters of university law. Parents often pay a large part of college tuition: they send their sons and daughters off to institutions whose promotional brochures and catalogs depict serene and positive places. Buildings that look like cathedrals, pictures of happy and diligent students in laboratories, lecture halls, libraries, and on tennis courts or intramural fields, descriptions of exciting academic and co-curricular programs etc., help to lure the family and prospective student into a sense—false *and* inappropriate— that we send our best and brightest off to super-safe sanctuaries. Those of us who read the cases and patrol the campuses, or know students who have been the victim of serious harm, know better. Universities are not the trenches of World War I, but neither are they risk-free utopias. The way courts decide cases and imagine university student relations has a profound impact on student safety *and* education. A productive learning environment is a reasonably safe learning environment. Education and safety are unavoidably interrelated. At a higher level, as Gary Pavela observes, how we imagine our universities is important for all of society. In these times of peace and prosperity, college—not the army, the workplace, or the family—is the place where large numbers of our post-adolescent youth transition into the first stages of adulthood. College is also the place where record numbers of so-called "non-traditional" students seek to improve themselves, retool, and prosper. The strength of students' overall higher education—intellectual, moral, physical, experiential, and spiritual—will determine the collective future. Thus, society at large has a large stake in university law.

We advance a view of the university as a facilitator of student education and development and of students and universities as legally empowered and mutually responsible. This vision is connected to the new university legal category "duty" in ways that are both legally and educationally sound. The proper legal relationship between the university and its students is a product of a *balancing* of rights and responsibilities. For university life to be reasonably safe, there must be mutual, shared responsibility. The university is an environment, like others, which must collectively take charge of its own. The law swung from legal insularity and *in loco parentis* to bystander and partial abdication, but as always there has been a search in the courts for the middle ground. In teaching our students to balance freedom and responsibility, we do best by seeking legal standards for university/student relations that are set by balance, not extremes. Facilitation—a middle point between autocratic control and extreme libertarianism—is such a balance. The facilitator university can restore order and promote free and responsible relationships that last beyond graduation.

II

The Era of *In Loco Parentis* and Legal Insularity

American courts typically say that prior to 1960 the university stood *in loco parentis* to its students. This period—especially as it reached its nadir in the 1950s—featured powerful paradigms of university authority and rights to discipline students. Contrary to popular and some judicial belief, *in loco parentis* era case law put little to no emphasis on protecting college student safety as such. In fact, as legal doctrine, *in loco parentis* was just one feature of a period of university insularity from legal scrutiny. Students enjoyed no specific legal rights to a safe campus.

As the major operative *legal doctrine* in university law prior to 1960, *in loco parentis* performed an important if counter-intuitive function: in this era, university student relations were far less "legal" than today because that doctrine, along with others of the period, made law less important in college/student relations. Some legal doctrines—and this was one of them—facilitate relationships which are relatively immune from private lawsuits. In its heyday, *in loco parentis* located power in the university—not in courts of law, or in students. *In loco parentis* promoted the image of the parental university and insured that most problems were handled within the university, by the university, and often quietly.[1] The most im-

---

1. Resistance to law runs deep in the imagination of the university. Overemphasis on the negative aspects of law—enhanced by anti-lawyer cultural movements in society at large—have stunted opportunities to reconceive the legal image of university/student relations and to envision the *positive* aspects of law and its potential to promote responsible modern university life. *In loco parentis* ingrained an expectation (that will not be fulfilled) that courts and law *should* stay out of university business. This is the primary legacy of that period today. According to most courts and commentators *in loco parentis* died hard and fast in the 1960s and 1970s. Yet it was such a powerful paradigm that even in death it has been spotted vestigially (or chimerically like Elvis). Some commentators incorrectly point to the feared return of *in loco parentis* in cases which today impose duties upon universities to use care for student safety. Protecting student safety was not a feature of *in loco parentis* doctrines as applied to universities. But the culture of insularity—'let's work it out internally'—was a key feature of the *in loco parentis* period. Even today there is a

portant feature of *in loco parentis* was to place a blanket of security and insularity around university culture such that disputes were not justiciable and university life was not predominately juridical. Under the blanket, a university was free to exercise disciplinary power—or not—with wide discretion and little concern for litigation.

Today it is difficult to imagine a period when serious social disputes were not perceived to have *legal* ramifications. Americans litigate almost every issue arising out of interpersonal relations. Yet, not long ago (just 50 years or less), university life enjoyed—like other major social institutions such as government, family, churches and charitable organizations, professional sports etc.—a certain insularity from the courts and law itself.[2] The legal world, in essence, carved out space for university culture to exist without legal scrutiny, at least in most instances. When rare cases did appear as lawsuits, courts typically affirmed the power of the university to exercise authority and discipline over students and thereby reinforced this state of affairs. Only as universities felt the need to establish stronger control over student relations in the 1960s did the case law begin to evolve. A central paradox of the period in which *in loco parentis* flourished is how little case law there is (and was) and how that doctrine fades quickly back in time to uncertain origins. To get the feel for *in loco parentis*, one must appreciate the Zen-like subtlety of what *in loco parentis* did not say and what it did not do. In today's era when interpersonal relations are generally justiciable and juridical, it is tempting to impute to the *in loco parentis* era a level of "legalism" it did not have.

Because the study of university law is a study of the mostly gradual evolution of the application of legal norms (particularly "duty") to university affairs, it should be no surprise that it is hard to determine just where *in loco parentis*—the first legal image of and doctrine regarding American universities—began.

---

tendency among university officials to prefer internal over external or legal solutions. The case law is full of instances where attempts to insulate university affairs have backfired. There is almost a *dread* of legal responsibility and legal rules regulating and facilitating university/student concerns. Law is regarded skeptically and as an 'other' to university culture. The negative attitude towards law in university culture is a major throwback to an era when the law deliberately insulated university life from judicial/legal scrutiny in most instances.

2. Modern university law—no longer legally infatuated with *in loco parentis*—features some attempts to recreate the era of *insularity* into an era of "no-duty" or other *immunity* from civil reparation for personal injury. Universities, once insulated from most legal responsibility to students, now ask courts in the duty era to *immunize* them (provide special protections from responsibilities otherwise imposed by law) from liability with special "no duty" rules. Universities had some success in the 1970s in finding such shelter, but these attempts have largely failed since then.

American law looks to pre-revolutionary war English law for its distant origins. When we look far back in time, we find some references to the power of parents over their children, but many scholars have found the first reference to *in loco parentis,* in connection with teaching, in commentaries on English law by Sir William Blackstone.

Just a few years before the revolutionary war, Blackstone commented on English law to the effect that: the father "may also delegate part of his parental authority, during his life to the tutor or schoolmaster of his child; who is then *in loco parentis,* and has such a portion of the power of the parent committed to his charge, *viz.* that of restraint and correction, as may be necessary to answer the purposes for which he is employed."[3] Although this has become recognized by scholars and courts as *the* seminal statement of *in loco parentis* doctrine, it is remarkable that Blackstone cited no English (or American) case authority for his assertion. Presumably Blackstone had most, if not all, reported cases available to him. Yet several English legal scholars have been unable to find any cases at all using *in loco parentis* in relation to any type of schooling.[4] This is not to say that Blackstone just made up *in loco parentis,* for he may have become aware of this rule through observations of the law or may have anticipated this position as a sensible extension of prevailing principles. Whatever the case, Blackstone is considered to be one of the greatest historical English legal commentators ever (an Oliver Wendell Holmes type), so what he said has stuck.

It is also noteworthy that Blackstone (1) equated the rights of the parent as the *father's* right (no mention of mother here), (2) saw the right as one to be 'delegated' (as one might delegate a power or prerogative to another, *and* (3) conceived the right as one to discipline and to correct the child. *In loco parentis* was thus, in sum, the *delegation* of a *father's* right to *discipline.* This was all very English and pre-modern.

Under English family law—which became the law of America (and changed very little until after World War II)—the father was the head of the family and held power over his wife and children. Wife (and mother) were basically considered "one" with husband/father and the one was the husband/father. The father had almost limitless authority over the children of the household. Wife/mother and children were subject to discipline, deliberate corporal punishment, and even harms caused by gross negligence without much legal recourse. If father/husband overturned the cart while drinking and seriously injured the children, the children had no right to sue him nor did mother. The legal system viewed the parental,

---

3. 1 BLACKSTONE, COMMENTARIES 441 (Oxford: Clarendon Press 1765).

4. *See* John C. Hogan & Mortimer Schwartz, *In Loco Parentis in the United States 1765-1985,* 8 J. LEGAL HIST. 260, 271 n.4. (1987).

particularly the *paternal*, role as virtually immune from legal scrutiny and liability. Families (particularly fathers' rights) were places courts and law mostly stayed out of (unless one family hurt another family). It were as if a man/husband/father held a kind of *sovereignty* over his family affairs. The image was so strong that even today it is common for American courts to refer to the sovereign power of a state in terms of *parens patriae*, an analogy to family law. The idea that a man was king of his own castle was more than just metaphor.

And, so it goes, the father could *delegate* his power over the children. A "delegation" is typically a feature of what we call contract or agency law today and/or a feature of law regarding governmental powers.[5] By delegation, the father paid you to educate his child (mostly male children who were pre-fathers) and you, the schoolmaster, agreed to educate the child. To make this arrangement work, the father must give the schoolmaster much of the nearly limitless paternal power over the child. Otherwise, if the schoolmaster damages the student, the father can sue. Thus, to enable the schoolmaster to do his job without looking over his shoulder at every whipping, the father *delegated* his power. Children were objects of the deal and were almost always subject to some sovereign father or his delegate.

And *in loco parentis* power was paternal, male, often stern, disciplinary power. What the father delegated was the *power* to restrain, correct, even beat. As such, the delegation was not to coddle, protect, or nurture, and there was certainly no *right* of a schoolmaster to do so as such. There was a duty—a contractual duty to the father in which the child had no direct legal interest—to educate. But the very images of the day did not consider it very important to delegate traditional maternal rights, as if education had less to do with nurturing etc. Not blankets and bears but corporal punishment made Johnny right and proper. This is not to say that English schooling of that period was all discipline but no nurturing and protection; it is just that the *legal* paradigm of Blackstone's era put its foremost emphasis on *discipline*. This set the tone for over two centuries of school law—including higher education law. The modern mind, which tends to equate *'parent'* with the balancing of masculine and feminine energies, also tends to impute things to the Blackstone era, which had a very different mindset.

To get some idea of how serious English law was about the absolute power of the father and his delegates, we can look to cases that actually got to court. In one case of the mid 1800s, a schoolmaster felt that he had an obstinate student who needed discipline. The schoolmaster wrote to

---

5. For example, courts today are sometimes confronted with the question of whether a sovereign power has been properly 'delegated' to an agency.

the father asking permission to beat the youngster harshly. The father said yes. One night thereafter the schoolmaster beat the boy for about two and one-half hours with a heavy stick. He literally beat the boy to death. You can only imagine what would happen today legally and politically in this scenario.

Not so back then. The schoolmaster was tried for *manslaughter* (not murder; a prosecutor felt that a murder conviction would not hold). The schoolmaster asserted a defense based on *in loco parentis*: in other words, he seriously contended the legal right to beat a child severely for hours, with substantial risk of death. Only then did the English court disagree and impose a "reasonable and moderate" standard for beatings. The schoolmaster was convicted but sentenced to only four years of penal servitude.[6] In America, people were hung for stealing horses in this period.

It is also well to remember that Blackstone wrote when there was basically no public schooling or even a concept of it. And Blackstone was talking in his Commentaries about school-aged children not college aged pupils, as such. It would take a few more years before the idea of *in loco parentis* came to college life. In fact, because the first discussions of *in loco parentis* in higher education in English law occur well after the revolutionary war, it is not entirely unfair to say that the United States had no particular legal doctrine whatsoever for higher education rights and responsibilities at the time it was born. This may seem unbelievable today, but recall that this was a time when education was typically considered to be a family prerogative—delegated or not—and thus not the subject of much, if any, legal interest.

There was a general belief that the "system" Blackstone referred to just a few years before the Revolution did become the law of America. In a prominent treatise on American law published in the 1820s, a famous American legal commentator, Chancellor James Kent, asserted that *in loco parentis* was the law of the schoolmaster.[7] After the publication(s) of Kent's treatise, American courts began to use *in loco parentis* in cases involving school children. Like the English rules, American rules were oriented first and foremost to the rights to discipline students. The legal questions continued to be basically ones involving the right to employ corporal punishment and otherwise discipline students.

By the mid 1800s in America, the idea that Blackstone's whip could be used on college students entered American decisional law, if at first obliquely. In the 1866 case of *Pratt v. Wheaton College*,[8] the college for-

---

6. *See* Regina v. Hopley, 2 F & F 202, 175 Eng. Rep. 1024 (1860).

7. *See* J. Kent, COMMENTARIES ON AMERICAN LAW 203, 205 (2nd ed. 1832). Hogan & Schwartz indicated that they did not find any cases in America prior to the publication of that treatise. *See* 8 J. LEGAL HISTORY at 271 n.9.

8. 40 Ill. 186 (1866).

bade its students from joining secret societies. The students challenged the authority to make such rules. The Court said the college had such authority under the charter from the state. The power given was paternal, *in loco parentis*-like. The college could "regulate the discipline of [the college] in such manner as [the college] deem[s] proper; and, so long as their rules violate neither divine nor human law, [the courts] have no more authority to interfere than [they] have to control the domestic discipline of a father in his family,"[9] said the court. The notion was that the university— not the law—was sovereign in this domain. This was not the only reference to an *in loco parentis* type rule for college law in the mid 1800s.[10]

Truly, though, it was the turn of the 20th Century before college and university law started to reflect *in loco parentis* law more clearly. There were several cases at the turn of the century which stated the same basic ideas of the paternal power of universities,[11] but two stand out and have become the most well known cases—*Gott v. Berea College* and *Stetson University v. Hunt*.[12] *Gott*, a 1913 case which relied upon the *Wheaton* college case for authority, involved a college rule that prohibited students from going to certain off campus locations. *Gott* made reference to the powers explicit and implicit in a state charter. But importantly, *Gott* specifically stated these powers in terms of *in loco parentis*: colleges "stand *in loco parentis* concerning the physical and moral welfare and mental training of the pupils, and...to that end [may make] *any rule* or *regulation* for the government or betterment of their pupils that a parent could for the same purpose" unless *unlawful* or contrary to public policy.[13] *Gott* made it explicitly clear that as long as a university did not transgress into the prerogatives of other sovereign powers, it was free to do pretty much as it pleased with its students. Dean Wormer would be free to enforce "double secret probation" and play host to honor council proceedings that were less than fair. Only when student problems spilled off campus and into the streets might outside authorities step in to protect the community.

The *Hunt* case similarly held that *in loco parentis* granted wide power to a university to do with its students as it saw fit. In that case a student

---

9. *Id.*

10. *See* Hill v. McCauley, 3 Pa. C. 77 (Pa. County Ct. 1887), which heard, but did not accept, a particular *in loco parentis* argument.

11. *See* Woods v. Simpson, 126 A. 882, 883 (Md. 1924) (college administrators "must, of necessity, be left untrammeled in handling the problems which arise, as their judgment and discretion may dictate"); Booker v. Grand Rapids Medical College, 120 N.W. 589 (Mich. 1909); Barker v. Bryn Mawr College, 122 A. 220 (Pa. 1923).

12. 161 S.W. 204 (Ky. 1913); 102 So. 637 (Fla. 1924).

13. 161 S.W. at 206 (emphasis added).

was suspended for "offensive behavior intruding on the comfort of others retarding the pupil's work." The offense: the student had participated in disruptive behavior in the dormitory to wit "hazing the normals, ringing cow bells and parading in the halls ... at forbidden hours."[14] The court noted that some witnesses viewed this behavior as "bordering on insurrection,"[15] and given the climate of the day, they were not speaking metaphorically. The court noted that the power *in loco parentis* was a typical delegation of power (contract-style) from state and trustees to university officials, and in light of this delegation *judicial review was not proper*. The university rules were vague; there were little to no procedural safeguards for students, and there was the potential for hidden malice. Yet university discretion was wide.[16] The court did not wish to be involved—at all—unless rules became *patently* unreasonable. It was understood that this meant almost never.

There were three indelible features of the *Gott/Hunt in loco parentis* model. First, the power *in loco parentis* was one to discipline, control and regulate. Second, the power was paternal—by analogy to the family and directly as a function of the delegation of *parens patriae* (the paternal power of the state.) Third, the power was a *contractual delegation* of authority among state, trustees, and officials: students were not contracting parties but were subjected to, and governed by, the contract.

Except insofar as to justify indirectly the rules sought to be enforced against students, courts made no mention of responsibility for student injury and safety. In its inception, *in loco parentis* was not about university *duties* towards students but about university rights and *powers* over students. In fact, two features of the *in loco parentis* era are particularly notable in addition to its proclivity to empower a university. First, prior to 1960, universities themselves were rarely held liable to a student for injuries, no matter how the student was injured. Second, university law of the *in loco parentis* era, which raised questions of what duties were owed to students to protect their safety when they were injured, conspicuously ignored and made no reference to *in loco parentis*. In other words the law generally did not hold universities accountable for student safety, and no

14. 102 So. at 639.

15. *Id.*

16. Many law schools practice blind grading where a student is given an exam number to which a professor assigns a grade. If a racist professor gave a paper a "B" grade but upon matchup found the student was of a racial group he "hated", the professor could discover a "math error" and assign a lower or even a failing grade. If the Dean and faculty did not intervene, the student could be dismissed. Under *Hunt*, the student had *no* legal recourse. The law was willing to permit a university to exercise such 'sovereignty' in the era of *in loco parentis*.

one thought that *in loco parentis* required them to be accountable. Indeed, no one thought that *in loco parentis* was even germane to such (generally unsuccessful) assertions of liability. *In loco parentis* was a sword for universities but not for the students who were injured.

There were very few cases in the period of *in loco parentis* where students even attempted to sue universities—or where the issues were ever discussed—for negligently caused physical injuries unrelated to discipline and correction. The lack of case law reflects (1) the generally non-justiciable nature of student/university relations, (2) special immunity rules of the time, (3) lesser developed notions of tort duty and liability, and (4) to some extent, the safer environment of the pre-modern university campus. Fact patterns typically involved laboratory accidents, dormitory injuries, and medical treatment. Even though the injuries were sometimes hideous—and negligence was palpable—students rarely won these cases (which no doubt served to chill many other unreported cases from even being pursued). During the period of *in loco parentis*, students typically were not winning cases establishing duties to protect their physical safety.

Hamburger v. Cornell University[17] is a classic example of a university escaping responsibility to use due care even in an on-campus curriculum-related activity. *Hamburger* is *the* laboratory incident case of its era. In that case, under supervision of an instructor, a college student mixed chemicals and heated them as directed. It was a bad mix and it exploded. The student was severely injured and lost an eye. The student sued the university (Cornell) and at trial succeeded in obtaining $25,000 against the university (a whopping award in 1920s dollars); but the award was reversed on appeal. The appellate courts held that the private university was immune from suit because it was a "charitable organization".

Today, it is rare to see much of what used to be called "charitable immunity." In other words, in most states today, most charitable organizations for most purposes do not receive special protection in tort law but can be sued for their negligence as any other "business" organization. Recently, Congress chose to give some protection from tort law for volunteers of charitable organizations for some torts but it is now unfashionable to openly acknowledge a general "charitable immunity."

Not so just a few decades ago. Until the 1970s (give or take), most courts would say that a charitable organization was generally *immune* from a private civil lawsuit. This meant that one could not sue a charity *even* if the charity were clearly negligent: this immunity was a public policy exception to general rules of responsibility based on ideas that charities—given the special nature of their work—deserved special legal pro-

---

17. 148 N.E. 539 (N.Y. 1925).

tection. There were, however, numerous exceptions to the charitable immunity rules, and if you fit into an "exception" you could sue a charity. There was a great deal of litigation then over two type(s) of issues. First, what is a "charity" (and are you a "charity" or not)? Second, is there an applicable exception to immunity that would permit a lawsuit to proceed? In most cases the private college or university would win on both issues: most often, the college was a charity and no exception applied.

Although the university came close to paying a large award to a student injured in an on-campus curricular activity, *Hamburger* ruled that the university was not subject to lawsuit by a "beneficiary" (the student) of the "charitable organization." After some discussion, the university was determined to be just such a "charitable" institution. It is particularly noteworthy that when liability was seriously considered at the lower levels of the court system, responsibility was purportedly based on ordinary rules of "duty," not *in loco parentis*. Moreover, when the higher court provided immunity to the university, that court did not say that it was based upon, or in spite of, *in loco parentis*. *In loco parentis* was not mentioned.

Similarly, in a case at Northwestern University a student lost an eye, allegedly as a result of the negligence of a dentistry professor in a laboratory. The student sued but lost on the grounds of charitable immunity.[18] No mention was made of *in loco parentis*. A federal court of this period also protected an institution of higher learning when a student operated a laboratory machine—with the protective guard twisted and removed—as ordered by the instructor.[19]

If an institution were not private, it was a public university. In these cases the courts typically found another way to keep universities safe from legal liability—*governmental* immunity.

It surprises a number of people that only recently have American governments been responsible to citizens for wrongdoing in civil actions. Prior to World War II, it was good to be a sovereign political entity in America, as there were only limited avenues of relief open for citizens in the courts. This changed after World War II, at first with regard to the federal government and then more gradually with states. During the heyday of *in loco parentis*, governmental immunity was alive and well in America. Governmental immunity only gradually receded in the 1940s, 1950s and 1960s. As will become relevant in the following chapters, governmental immunity was falling fastest just around the time of the fall of *in loco parentis* in the 1960s.

---

18. *See* Parks v. Northwestern Univ. 75 N.E. 991 (Ill. 1905).
19. *See* Higgons v. Pratt Institute, 45 F.2d 698 (1930).

Typically, because of governmental immunity, a person injured because of the negligence of a governmental agency would be constrained to seek reparation for his injuries in the legislature. In an early Montana case, an injured student pursued such a legislative "claims bill," and received some money this way—a typical procedure in those days—even after there was a constitutional challenge by a taxpayer.[20] The student had fallen down an elevator shaft in a negligently maintained dormitory. Without such special legislative approval, the student had no legal right to sue for basic dormitory safety; the student's sole recourse for civil reparation for personal injuries caused by a public agency's negligence was a bill seeking a special legislative appropriation. This legislative procedure could provide relief, but only in the discretion of the legislature. Otherwise, a student would bear the expense of her own injury.

Even though governmental immunity has been abated in large part, some public universities still attempt to assert governmental immunity as a defense to liability for student injury caused by university negligence. Today, however, governmental immunity arguments regarding routine functions of the university such as premises and dormitory maintenance, are rejected by courts. At one time, being a King allowed you to be a slumlord; not so now (more on this later).

During the heyday of governmental immunity, even university sponsored activities which resulted in medical negligence were immune. In a 1920s scenario, a student at the University of California went to the infirmary for a tonsillectomy. During this operation—by negligence of the physician—the student was seriously and permanently injured. The student had to pay for additional hospital charges to fix the injuries caused by the negligence of the first doctor (the additional charges were not covered by the general infirmary fee). Nonetheless, the university was held immune as a governmental entity.[21] Law in other states immunized such hospitals as *both* governmental *and* charitable entities[22]—the double whammy on students.

It is worth mentioning that the negligent physician was held personally liable.[23] In practice this result—an *individual* being liable—was exceedingly rare, *particularly* outside the medical context. As a leading treatise of the era explained: "[t]he natural person individually responsible for the wrong is always liable for his own tort. It is because such persons are often financially irresponsible, leaving the injured person without relief

---

20. *See* Mills v. Stewart, 247 P. 332 (Mont. 1926).

21. *See* Davie v. Board of Regents, 227 P. 243 (Col. Dist. Ct. App. 1924).

22. *See* Robinson v. Washtenaw Circuit Judge, 119 N.W. 618 (Mich. 1924).

23. *See* Davie v. Board of Regents, 227 P. 247 (Cal. Dist. Ct. App. 1924).

even though he wins a judgment, that the question of the liability of the institution arises."[24] The treatise overstated the legal liability of individuals somewhat, given that some immunities and defenses for certain individuals would have been recognized, but the practical point is well taken.

Thus, although rare, some cases proceeded (or at least could have proceeded) against persons in the university, not the institution itself. For example, if a dormitory fire forced a student to jump from an upper story window because the university neglected to provide legally required fire escapes, the university could successfully avoid liability on grounds of charitable immunity, but the individual trustees might be responsible.[25]

Prior to 1960, and despite overwhelming case law to the contrary, there were some intimations by courts that a student could sue a university for duties breached and not face insurmountable immunity problems. For example, in one case in 1921 that did not involve a university defendant but another charity, a New York court stated that a college or university could be liable to a student for negligently caused injuries received at the hands of an employee of the university.[26] There was no mention of a connection to *in loco parentis*, and the court's statements were made in the context of a case which did not raise questions of university liability as such. Moreover, New York historically was known to provide significantly less charitable immunity to colleges and universities than other states of the period.[27] So the "dicta" (what lawyers call court language that talks about an issue not directly presented in a case) in that case was not surprising given the legal culture of New York at that time.

In a rare, pre-modern example of university liability, a federal appellate court *upheld* a determination of liability against Brigham Young University in 1941 (the decision is somewhat ironic because since then Utah has become a proponent of extreme no-duty rules). A student was injured in a laboratory explosion which occurred while the teacher was out of the room. The court focused in upon ideas of duty (discussed in Chapters IV and V) and determined that a university must adequately and reasonably supervise and instruct students in dangerous laboratory experiments. The court ruled that an appropriate baseline for consideration would be what other universities have done under like or similar circum-

---

24. Edward Elliot & M.M. Chambers, The Colleges and the Courts 431 (1936).

25. *See* Abston v. Waldon Academy, 102 S.W. 351, 355 (Tenn. 1907).

26. *See* Barr v. Brooklyn Children's Aid Soc'y, 190 N.Y.S. 296, 297 (N.Y. Special Term 1921).

27. Elliott & Chambers, *supra* note 24, at 425 & n.15. *See, e.g.,* Green v. Cornell Univ., 184 N.Y.S. 924, *aff'd,* 135 N.E. 900 (N.Y. 1922) (university liable when vehicle negligently driven by university employee.)

stances.[28] Speaking in classic negligence law language, the court did not consider *in loco parentis* as the liability creating rule of its decision. Instead, the court thought of university duty as a special duty germane to universities toward students and appropriate for instructional settings that involve risk of physical injury to students.

. . . .

Some academic observers today are of the opinion that *in loco parentis* was a technical legal rule that placed legal *responsibility* on universities regarding student safety. A few courts, particularly those in what we refer to as the "bystander" era (basically the 1970s, see Chapter IV), seem to have believed this as well. Some language in a few of the seminal *in loco parentis* cases also *seemed* to suggest this (especially to a modern reader, if taken out of context).

Gott v. Berea College, supra, in determining that a school had plenary disciplinary power over students, stated: "college authorities stand *in loco parentis* concerning the physical and moral welfare and mental training of the pupils...."[29] In a similar situation, the *Wheaton College* case, *supra,* stated that a "father"-like university may direct "children" students to do and not do as in a family: in the *Hunt* case, another discipline case, the court linked *in loco parentis* to the "physical welfare" of students.[30]

Two recent leading commentators on *in loco parentis* and university law, Annette Gibbs and James Szablewicz, have concluded that "[a]long with parental authority came an obligation to protect."[31] They have interpreted *Gott* and other cases to impose a duty to protect students on a theory of *in loco parentis,* and thus view certain recent cases holding universities liable for negligence (see Chapter IV) as a *return* to *in loco parentis.* This sentiment has been common, especially among university attorneys, particularly regarding certain recent cases.[32]

This belief that *in loco parentis* was a basis of tort *duty* to students to provide their safety—as opposed to merely the basis of a *right to discipline* them for misconduct—was reinforced by certain cases in what we call the bystander era (the subject of Chapter IV): cases which actually rejected university liability for student injury. Those cases linked no-duty/no liability *results* to the rejection of *in loco parentis.* They reasoned that as

---

28. Brigham Young Univ. v. LillyWhite, 118 F.2d 836 (10th Cir. 1941).

29. *Gott,* 161 S.W. at 206.

30. *See* Pratt v. Wheaton College, 40 Ill. 186, 187 (1866); Stetson Univ. v. Hunt, 102 So. 637, 640.

31. *See* James Szablewicz and Annette Gibbs, *Colleges' Increasing Exposure to Liability: The New In Loco Parentis,* 16 J.L. & EDUC. 453, 455 (1987).

32. *See* George Shur, *A Response to Professors Bickel & Lake,* 7 SYNTHESIS 543 (1996).

in loco parentis fell so too did responsibility for student injury. The premise of these bystander era cases—asserted but unsupported by historical case law—was that *in loco parentis* was a doctrine imposing *duties* on universities to protect students and that these duties were enforceable in private tort actions. *Bradshaw v. Rawlings*, one of the most important cases of this period, observed that "[a]t one time, exercising their rights *and duties in loco parentis*, colleges were able to impose strict regulations."[33]

Given the broad statements of some of the earliest cases and the developments of *in loco parentis* as applied to school age children (in K-12 education today *in loco parentis* is the basis for imposing duties of care), it was easy for commentators and courts to fall into a subtle but important trap regarding notions of *in loco parentis*. As a technical legal doctrine, *in loco parentis was not—ever—a liability/responsibility/duty creating norm in higher education law. In loco parentis was only a legal tool of immunity for universities when they deliberately chose to discipline students.* There is often a tendency to impute, to periods where there is little legal history, legal rules which *would* have been explanatory. And in this sense, *in loco parentis* became larger in retrospect than it ever was in the reality of the time. Thus, the era of *in loco parentis* is somewhat inaptly named. As Theodore Stamatakos wrote in a well-reasoned law review article on this subject:

> The conspicuous absence of appellate court discussion of the doctrine of *in loco parentis* fully supports the conclusion that the doctrine of *in loco parentis* was never operational in the context of personal injury suits in the first place.... [T]he duty to protect students' physical well-being always has been grounded in the realm of traditional tort categories.[34]

When the dominant legal rule governing university relations with students was *in loco parentis*, the era was one of *insularity*. *In loco parentis* was a manifestation of a deeper legal sentiment: universities should generally be free from legal scrutiny. University affairs were generally *university* business and best settled there. *In loco parentis* was the specific tool to protect, to *immunize*, university conduct from legal review when *deliberate* or *intentional* actions were taken to *discipline* and *regulate* students. The courts used other tools to *immunize* universities when students claimed damages for physical harm caused by *accidental* or *negligent* conduct or omissions. The tools used to immunize the university in those circumstances were governmental or charitable tort immunities. The respon-

---

33. Bradshaw v. Rawlings, 612 F.2d 135, 139-40 (3d Cir. 1979) (emphasis added).

34. Theodore Stamatakos, *The Doctrine of In Loco Parentis, Tort Liability and the Student-College Relationship*, 65 IND. L.J. 471, 484 (1990).

sibilities immunized against were responsibilities grounded in traditional tort responsibility (to exercise reasonable care for student safety). It would have been utterly incoherent to ground this responsibility in some imagined family law because courts of the historical period knew of no such legal parental responsibilities. Indeed, if *in loco parentis* had been applied it would have been a no-duty rule because *in loco parentis* was a historical device to protect ordinary family sovereignty. Only lately, as *in loco parentis* mutated in K-12 education law, did the notion that it created legal responsibility for minors/students arise.

It is also important to observe that the era of *in loco parentis* arose in a time when wide areas of human activity existed free from legal scrutiny. As developed further in Chapter IV, it was not long ago that families, charities, governments, most business activity, and certain spheres of private inaction (like failing to rescue a stranger) were subject to actual or *de facto* tort immunities. Prior to the 1950s, many social institutions took on their own kind of insularity from legal norms. You did not sue your parents for neglect; or sue a church for sexual abuse; or sue a government if it wounded you with friendly fire in combat. Defective products reached consumers with very little chance for legal redress if injury were to occur, and courts hesitated to require anyone to respond to "strangers" in distress. American courts of this period thus saw universities simply as institutional candidates for insularity as well. In an *era of insularities,* universities became yet another jurisdictional island.

It would be much easier in some ways today to understand the university/student relationship if courts had specifically stated that, in addition to traditional text book legal immunities, a *university immunity* existed. They did not say so, but in practice they did effectively create such an immunity. Courts did this by viewing the university as neither fish nor fowl *but as an amalgam of functions that separately and in combination deserved immunity. University was part family, charity, and/or government. But different.*

Thus, in its *disciplinary* role, the university was like a family—a father—to its students. It gave them guidance and set rules and enforceable boundaries. In the family, a father had powerful rights to exercise discipline and only the most egregious examples of parental abuse (sometimes) made it to court. Historical courts recognized virtually no family *responsibility* at all to care for a child, however. Care and feeding and abuse and neglect were not justiciable. Unlike today, the historical legal system stayed out of family life for the most part (even where gross parental negligence directly caused injury to the child). Indeed, the father's *de facto* legal right to discipline and even abuse and neglect a child was one of the broadest immunities from tort responsibility that the common law ever carved out of tort law.

Because parental immunity was vast, it is not surprising then that when a university neglected to use care for student safety — as opposed to when it exercised discipline and authority deliberately — the courts were not willing to say that a university was *family* for *all purposes*. *In loco parentis* could have easily been the rule for insularity itself: instead courts opted for other rules, in conjunction with in *loco parentis,* to create a unique legal insularity just for the university. It was too much to give a university the role of father/parent in all respects. Perhaps a father could beat a child, but the college could not neglect the care of student welfare and hide behind the putative rule of a parent. The parental delegation had been to discipline, not to neglect, the student.

The university, for example, also operated like a business, albeit a special one. Businesses were typically subject to rules of contract and tort law. Some businesses were special in that they were not for profit and/or were charitable in nature. Although not exactly like more traditional charitable organizations, many private universities certainly had strong similarities to them. Similar to family, similar to charity, but not exactly the same.

And some universities were set up as public universities. These institutions behaved in some ways as businesses, but also like small governmental entities. Their missions were set by the people and for the people, and strong public financial support was a key feature. However, public universities were not cities or towns *per se* and, given their family-like relations to students and the business-like aspects of their private counterparts, public universities were *sui generis* governmental entities. Similar to governments, but not exactly the same.

Therefore, when a court looked at a university it saw a unique hybrid legal entity entitled to significant insularity from judicial scrutiny. In some ways a university was like a family, in others like a charity, in other cases like a government or some combination thereof. Legal insularity thus was expressed through a tailoring of these patches of legal thinking.

For example, while generally immune from lawsuit, charities were rarely immune from suit regarding deliberate intentional torts and also generally had to honor contracts they entered into. Charities had no special rights to discipline and thus charitable immunity rules were not useful to protect universities who disciplined and regulated students. Family immunities, however, were perfect for this. A public university could assert governmental immunity protections which were quite broad; however, the Achilles heel of governmental immunities, even in the historical era, were *process based* claims. Failure to provide adequate process to a citizen could land any governmental entity in a heap of trouble. And that was precisely the issue in many of the *in loco parentis* cases. For that type of issue — *e.g.* summary dismissal of a student — a family/parent/father immunity was much better to insulate a public university. The father did not have to give the son notice, discovery, hearing, etc. to apply the horsewhip to the rear end. There was no right to due process in a family.

Nonetheless, when a student was injured through accidental or negligent means there was something inappropriate about providing a father's *de facto* right to neglect. After all, these were institutions with tuition paid (contracts) and that served public and/or private missions for the benefit of the public at large. The university was like family and like father, but it was not family or father. Similarity was not identity. And in cases involving K-12 students, it eventually became clearer and clearer that public and private school children were entitled to some care from school teachers. In short, the kind of powerful immunity granted to the father was not exactly appropriate for university/student relationships. Immunities of other kinds were considered to provide the appropriate level of insularity from lawsuits. Charitable or governmental immunities were considered more appropriate when the question was negligent failure to use reasonable care to prevent student injury. In short, the cases as a whole pointed unmistakably to the idea that most negligently caused injuries were immune to lawsuit; but there were some cases imposing liability. The courts acted (intervened) just enough to send the message that they were watching and would not allow too much latitude in terms of neglect of safety — certainly not the way they would almost completely defer to parents. A balance — detente — was struck nonetheless. The balance favored the university very, very heavily and the college won in almost every instance where it acted in good faith (even if negligently).

An underlying message was that university life in the era of *in loco parentis* — truly the *insularity* era — was subject to some very marginal scrutiny in the courts, particularly regarding physical safety of students that could be protected by good faith and reasonable care. When negligence caused physical injuries to students, as Stamatakos correctly observed, courts applied traditional tort rules — especially duty analysis — and, when appropriate, immunities relating to *charities* and *governments*. The technical legal immunity afforded by *in loco parentis* was a defense to disciplinary claims. *In loco parentis*, in this sense, was neither an *immunity* to lawsuits alleging neglect or unreasonable omissions to care for student safety, *nor* a source of any responsibility or *duty* to care for student safety. A few courts later in the bystander era suggested otherwise in dicta, but they were wrong in reading too much into an earlier period.

In loco parentis was the most prominent feature of the law in this period of university legal insularity, and hence the era deserves to be remembered as the era of *in loco parentis*. However, the legal rules of *in loco parentis* were just a *feature* of an overall system protecting colleges. The era in which *in loco parentis* dominated was a period where the law sought to define appropriate levels of university *insularity* from legal responsibility. The law did this by drawing upon—selectively—a variety of legal paradigms from other recognized areas of insularity.[35] Universities were viewed variously as part family, part charity, part government, part public, part private. Underneath it all, the notion of duty—destined to become central—was immanent and growing. The greatest paradox of the *in loco parentis* era was that a seed was planted within it—duty— that would eventually grow to cover over, and even obscure, the true history of *in loco parentis*. As universities moved more and more into the public eye (recall that in *Animal House,* the final battle for the soul of Faber University spills into the streets of the town), the notions of insularity came under attack. First, as we shall see in the next chapter, the attacks came upon civil rights grounds and were directed at *in loco parentis* universities. That aspect of insularity was removed first. Later came attacks upon insularity from negligence based tort responsibility. At first substantially rebuked in the bystander era, as we discuss in Chapter IV, these attacks on that aspect of insularity also eroded university immunities and insularity (See Chapters IV and V).

The fall of insularity happened rather quickly in legal terms. Again, many have viewed the rise of university legal responsibility as the return of *in loco parentis*. But as powerful as this misperception is—it remains the legal vision in a few remaining cases—it is historically and conceptually misguided. *The story of in loco parentis is one of the rise and decline of insularity from legal responsibility and the rise of justiciability of university life.* Universities, like many other social institutions (including government and charities), have increasingly been asked to come to the legal system and explain and defend their conduct. In this sense, the fall of insularity is, for better or for worse, a key feature of modern university tort law and an understandable consequence of the fall of the patchwork of immunities that once protected the university.

The legal system, like life in general, is not beyond living out some imagined realities that never were. The pull to Avalon or the retreat to Valhalla are signals of a society in transition, uncertain of its roots and future. So it is with *in loco parentis*. The dread of a feared return to *in loco parentis* reflects concerns over where college law is headed but is not an accurate reflection of where it has been.

---

35. The law also had other protective doctrines, like rules of proximate causation and affirmative defenses, that augmented university insularity. We discuss these doctrines particularly in Chapter IV and V.

III

Revolutions on University Campuses—The 1960s Civil Rights Movements (and Beyond) and the Death of *In Loco Parentis*

The roots of the era in which *in loco parentis* flourished—truly, the era of university legal insularity—were the collection of legal immunities which largely kept university affairs out of the courts. The law had used a combination of various protections afforded to families, charities and governmental entities to insulate university life from justiciability. Yet, in the 1960s and afterward, American law made major changes in the very legal rules which had previously insulated families, charities, and governments from significant legal responsibility for negligently and deliberately caused injuries. Major social initiatives forced changes in women's and children's rights, and charitable institutions were no longer conceived to be above the law, particularly as abuses and scandals rocked the sense of sanctity of charities and modern insurance became more available. Perhaps most importantly, in the 1960s large numbers of Americans began to challenge the government itself over fundamental issues like civil rights, the rights to make war and draft citizens to fight wars, the role of police in society, and even the nature of the Presidency itself. American society and law underwent change in precisely those areas that had once protected university affairs. The fall of *in loco parentis* came swiftly and in that context.

The demise of *in loco parentis* was hastened by the fact that university life in the 1960s (and 1970s) became a focal point of the major social issues of the time. "Baby boom" students increasingly became members of cultures of social revolution. The targets of reformers in college were the improper (and sometimes racially motivated) denial of civil rights, denial

35

of procedural due process, unequal treatment of women, and abuses of authoritarian governmental power, etc. Students picketed, rioted, sat in, organized, marched, and *litigated*. Students asked the courts to intervene in university life. Essentially for the first time with respect to certain problems, the courts accepted the invitation. The era of insularity was over: university life would be increasingly justiciable.

From a practicing lawyers' perspective, the alleged harms that a student might suffer in college life fall into one of two very basic categories. First, students can be harmed in economic ways (like being expelled and losing tuition and future jobs) or in intangible ways (such as being denied civil rights or having their privacy invaded). Or, second, a student can be harmed physically, either in person (killed, injured, etc.) or by damage to their tangible physical property (damaged car, etc.) Although there is a great deal of legal esoterica to go along with this, it is usually safe to assume that the first type of harm became a *contract* claim or a civil rights lawsuit (or some highly specialized tort law remedy, but this has very little to do with the main theme here). The latter type of harm became tort, typically negligence, lawsuits—the stuff of personal injury lawyers and tort reform. The law divides harms up into certain somewhat arbitrary camps and then provides certain ways to remedy those harms. Economic intangible-type harms go most often to contract civil rights style cases; personal injury and property damage go to tort claims.

An illustration. You buy a vacuum cleaner. It does not work. You return it. The seller refuses to take it back. You sue for breach of contract or warranty. The vacuum cleaner did not live up to the promises of the bargain struck. You made a bad economic deal. Now, if the vacuum cleaner explodes and injures you, or damages your house, it is another matter. Those problems would be remedied in *tort* actions. The day after Christmas is contract day: the fifth of July is tort day.

These distinctions have become important in university law and essential to understanding how *in loco parentis* and university insularity died. This is because the 1960s civil rights movement raised questions of basic civil rights and the bargains struck between universities and students. Students who were expelled or disciplined needed to vindicate *economic* or *intangible* rights. To do these things, students sued universities in civil rights and/or breach of contract lawsuits. *In loco parentis* had been the insulating doctrine that the university used to defend those types of lawsuits. In the 1960s, the defensive power of *in loco parentis* came to a halt. Only later (for the most part), as we discuss in Chapters IV and V, did students begin to successfully challenge the other aspects of insularity— insularity from tort lawsuits alleging personal injury. The fall of *in loco parentis* in the 1960s correlated exactly with the rise of student economic power and the rise of student civil rights. The fall of *in loco parentis* was not immediately correlated, however, with a change in student rights to physical security.

The first cases were cases by students at *public* universities (hence *quasi*-governmental entities) raising demands for basic constitutional rights. In 1969, Professor Charles A. Wright wrote that the constitution had come to American campuses and transformed them.[1] That idea would have been novel just ten years earlier.

Most university law commentators view the landmark 1961 decision of the United States Court of Appeals (Fifth Circuit) in *Dixon v. Alabama State Board of Education*[2] as the watershed decision in this era of university law. *Dixon* ultimately set the stage for the radical revision of student rights which the Supreme Court engineered in the wake of the Kent State massacre in the case of *Scheuer v. Rhodes*.[3]

In *Dixon,* six black students were essentially expelled for participating in civil rights demonstrations seeking the desegregation of lunch counters and other places of public accommodation.[4] The students received notice of their expulsion via letter from the President of Alabama State College. They were not told what specific misconduct got them expelled. The letter was a paragon of vagueness. Reference was made to "this general problem of Alabama State College" and to several general school regulations, one of which was capitalized in the expulsion letter (and thus apparently was the rule violated). That highlighted rule empowered the college to expel for "Conduct Prejudicial to the School," "Conduct Unbecoming a Student or Future Teacher in Schools in Alabama," "Insubordination and Insurrection," or "Inciting Other Pupils to Like Conduct".[5] Like Dean Wormer's "double secret probation," such rules could mean just about anything. In this case, if you were a black student in Alabama in 1960, you had better not protest Alabama's then blatantly racist public policy, even off campus.

The *Dixon* court reviewed the information the Alabama State Board of Education considered before ordering expulsion. The students, along with some other black students, had entered a lunch grill and were refused service. The police were brought in to order them to leave. Over the next few days, a series of demonstrations occurred in which some of these six

---

1. *See* Charles A. Wright, *The Constitution on the Campus*, 22 VAND. L. REV. 1027 (1969).

2. 294 F. 2d 150 (5th Cir. 1961), *cert. denied,* 368 U.S. 930 (1961).

3. 416 U.S. 232 (1974).

4. *See* JUAN WILLIAMS, EYES ON THE PRIZE, AMERICA'S CIVIL RIGHTS YEARS, 1954-1965, (1987); DAVID HALBERSTAM, THE CHILDREN (1998).

5. *Dixon,* 294 F.2d at 152.

plaintiff students participated. In concert with the Governor, the President of the College and the Board expelled the students.[6]

The legal issue was whether the students had a right to any hearing *or* notice before expulsion. In other words, a public university sought to summarily expel students without prior notification, without a hearing the students could even attend, and by way of vague rules, summary assertion, and perfunctory letter. *Dixon* is a prime example of what many believed *in loco parentis* meant in that period. Immunity had become impunity.[7] The idea of *in loco parentis* had taken such deep root that even the lower federal court in *Dixon* agreed with the college.

The Fifth Circuit disagreed and overturned longstanding protections against judicial review of university action that deprived students of their right to attend the university. Students at public universities—the court held—were entitled to at least fundamental due process. Notice and some opportunity for a hearing were essential minimums before permanent expulsion. The court reasoned that education is so basic and vital in modern society that a public, tax supported university cannot expel a student for alleged misconduct without meeting minimum constitutional due process requirements.

There was no mention of *in loco parentis* as such as a defense to the college's actions. In fact, the college reworded the *in loco parentis* doctrine into a new contract/voluntary association argument. The Board of Education regulations read, in part:

> Attendance at any college is on the basis of a mutual decision of the student's *parents* and of the *college*. Attendance [**15] at a particular college is voluntary and is different from attendance at a public school where the pupil may be required to attend a particular school which is located in the neighborhood or district in which the pupil's family may live. Just as a student may choose to withdraw from a particular college at any time for any personally-determined reason, the college may also at any time decline to continue to accept responsibility for the supervision and service to any student with whom the relationship becomes unpleasant and difficult.[8]

---

6. *Dixon, supra*, 294 F.2d at 152.

7. The asserted power of the college in *Dixon* was even greater. The college president admitted that typically other students did receive notice and some opportunity to be heard before expulsion. Thus in *Dixon,* the university actually asserted the right to arbitrarily give some students process and deny it to others. The college in *Dixon* pushed *in loco parentis* doctrine to ridiculous limits. There were very few cases prior to *Dixon* which challenged procedural safeguards at colleges, and admittedly the cases had upheld whatever process was provided to the students. *See id.* at 157-158. But, as the *Dixon* court observed, although some of the cases suggested otherwise, no case had flatly said that a university could provide *no* notice and process at all. *See id.*

8. *Dixon*, 294 F.2d at 156 (emphasis added).

The college argued that this regulation constituted—as if by contract—a waiver of any right to notice and hearing prior to expulsion. The argument was very much in line with a key feature of historical *in loco parentis* reasoning: the parent delegates by contract the power to discipline to the college, and the contract controls. Although there was no right to due process before dad beat you with a whip, colleges were in fact beginning to use more and more process in the management of student discipline. The provision of some process was becoming customary by the 1960s. Hence, the college felt the need to fall back to a Dean Wormer ideal: "we have been giving you students basic rights but we retain the right to take them away."

Constitutionalizing the question, *Dixon* rejected this argument and killed *in loco parentis* at its root. *Dixon* established that a state entity—a public college—cannot condition the privilege of an education (*Dixon* did not establish a right to public post-secondary education, just a right to be treated fairly if one were attending public college) upon a waiver or renunciation of basic rights of fair play and due process. This was *critical* to the death of *in loco parentis*. *Dixon* established—and other courts soon followed—that whatever *contractual* relations existed in a public university, they were subject to an irreducible minimum of *constitutional* rights inhering to the *student*. Such rights were not ever granted in the family.

Dixon also subtly shifted *in loco parentis*. As the regulation suggested, education had been a primary function of the contract between *parent* and college. The court in *Dixon*, however, specifically shifted the focus to *student*: "[w]e do not read [this regulation] to clearly indicate an intent on the part of the *student* to waive notice and a hearing before expulsion."[9] To the extent that university law was contractual, the student became the party in interest. The shift was subtle but changed the nature of the contract from one involving delegation of parental prerogative to one with a kinship to consumer/service contracts at large. *Dixon* set the stage for the student consumerism of the following decades. *Dixon* signaled a shift in the basic paradigm of post-secondary education: college was a student/university relationship primarily, not primarily the delegation of family relationship prerogatives.

Dixon did not specify exactly what procedures must be followed to protect students rights but did provide famous guidelines for public universities to follow:

> For the guidance of the parties in the event of further proceedings, we state our views on the nature of the notice and hearing required by due

---

9. *Dixon*, 294 F.2d at 156 (emphasis added).

process prior to expulsion from a state college or university. They should, we think, comply with the following standards. The notice should contain a statement of the specific charges and grounds which, if proven, would justify expulsion under the regulations of the Board of Education. The nature of the hearing should vary depending upon the circumstances of the particular case. The case before us requires something more than an informal interview with an administrative authority of the college. By its nature, a charge of misconduct, as opposed to a failure to meet the scholastic standards of the college, depends upon a collection of the facts concerning the charged misconduct, easily colored by the point of view of the witnesses. In such circumstances, a hearing which gives the Board or the administrative authorities of the college an opportunity to hear both sides in considerable detail is best suited to protect the rights of all involved. This is not to imply that a full-dress judicial hearing, with the right to cross-examine witnesses, is required. Such a hearing, with the attending publicity and disturbance of college activities, might be detrimental to the college's educational atmosphere and impractical to carry out. Nevertheless, the rudiments of an adversary proceeding may be preserved without encroaching upon the interests of the college. In the instant case, the student should be given the names of the witnesses against him and an oral or written report on the facts to which each witness testifies. He should also be given the opportunity to present to the Board, or at least to an administrative official of the college, his own defense against the charges and to produce either oral testimony or written affidavits of witnesses in his behalf. If the hearing is not before the Board directly, the results and findings of the hearing should be presented in a report to the student's inspection. If these rudimentary elements of fair play are followed in a case of misconduct of this particular type, we felt that the requirements of due process of law will have been fulfilled.[10]

The watch-word for these guidelines was *flexibility*. *Dixon* did not foresee that universities would be burdened with creating miniature court systems or arbitration boards. However, *some* process was essential.[11] If anything is remarkable about *Dixon* it is how little process would be required. Even when dealing with a blatantly arbitrary college administration, *Dixon* still showed significant deference to college administrators.

Dixon signaled the beginning of more than just dismissal/expulsion process rights for students, although acceptance of those rights continued

---

10. *Dixon*, 294 F.2d at 158-9.

11. It is worth noting that the right to some process was extended to *secondary* education. *See, e.g.* Goss v. Lopez, 419 U.S. 565 (1975) (Interim suspension of high school student requires some minimal process). At that time *in loco parentis* doctrine in K-12 required duties to supervise and discipline. Nevertheless, the Supreme Court acknowledged that some constitutional rights were protected in this environment.

to solidify in the courts.[12] A new era of constitutional protection for a variety of student rights was under way.

Among others, students won the following basic rights:[13]

- The right to engage in political speech and to publish political messages free from censorship;
- The right to participate in, work for and establish student organizations;
- Equal access to college funds for organizations, despite the unpopularity of religious and political viewpoints put forth by those organizations;
- The right to be protected against unreasonable searches and seizures;
- Some rights to process even in academic performance evaluations.

---

12. For example, *see, e.g.,* Greenhill v. Bailey, 519 F. 2d 5 (8th Cir. 1975), where a student was entitled to a hearing after dismissal from medical school for alleged insufficient intellectual ability.

13. *See* Robert D. Bickel & Peter F. Lake, *Reconceptualizing the University's Duty to Provide a Safe Learning Environment: A Criticism of the Doctrine of In Loco Parentis and the Restatement (Second) of Torts,* 20 J.C. & U.L. 261, 268-69, n.32 (1994). *See especially,* Tinker v. Des Moines Indep. Community Sch. Dist., 393 U.S. 503 (1969) (even secondary school students have a right to engage in passive speech, including the wearing of black arm bands protesting United States political actions, so long as students do not overtly disrupt the orderly conduct of classes or related school programs or interfere with the rights of other students in the learning environment); Healy v. James, 408 U.S. 169 (1972) (A public univ. may not deny recognition to a student organization solely on the basis of its disagreement with the political views of the organization, or its undifferentiated fear that recognition of the organization will lead to disruption); Papish v. Board of Curators of the Univ. of Mo., 410 U.S. 667 (1973) (A state university may not censor the editorial content of a student newspaper solely on the basis of its view that the editorial is "offensive" to the university's constituencies). *See also,* New Times, Inc. v. Arizona Bd. of Regents, 519 P.2d 169 (Ariz. 1974) (*en banc*); Joyner v. Whiting, 477 F.2d 456 (4th Cir. 1973); Stanley v. Magrath, 719 F.2d 279 (8th Cir. 1983) (Restricting the university's right to censor the content of student publications); Gay Students Org. of the Univ. of N.H. v. Bonner, 509 F. 2d 652 (1st Cir. 1974); Gay Alliance of Students v. Matthews, 544 F.2d 162 (4th Cir. 1976); Gay Lib v. University of Mo., 558 F.2d 848 (8th Cir. 1977); Gay Activists Alliance v. Board of Regents of Univ. of Okla., 638 P.2d 1116 (Okla. 1981); Gay Student Serv. v. Texas A&M Univ., 737 F.2d 1317 (5th Cir. 1984) (A public university may not deny recognition to a student organization solely on the basis of its disagreement with the content of the organization's speech); Carroll v. Blinken, 957 F.2d 991 (2d Cir. 1992) (equal access to student activity fees); Soglin v. Kauffman, 418 F.2d 163 (7th Cir. 1969) ("misconduct" as standard for disciplinary action is unconstitutionally vague); Piazzola v. Watkins, 422 F.2d 284 (5th Cir. 1971) (As regards intrusion by law enforcement officials, students at a public university are entitled to Fourth Amendment protections).

These rights were not absolute but were subject to balancing against the university's responsibility to provide for the orderly conduct of classes and other programs and to protect the rights of other students, particularly to a safe learning environment.[14]

Dixon and its progeny established that unfettered powers to discipline, regulate and expel students were no longer constitutionally permissible at a public university. Indeed, the entire parental rights paradigm was dead. Courts now viewed the party in interest as the student and the rights asserted as the contractual/constitutional rights of students. Public universities looked less like parents and were now legally reconfigured to be more like governmental entities—more like cities and towns than like mom and dad. *In loco parentis* died, then, in two ways. First, it was no longer a viable legal defense against students who challenged improper discipline; the question had been constitutionalized—and students now had constitutional rights. Second, *in loco parentis* died as the *image* of student/university relations. Students were now *constitutional* "adults" (better, nonminors) and sought protection from government-entity universities with whom they, the students, had a "contractual" relationship. Students became citizen-consumers (not wards); universities became "the man"—commercial/governmental entities. The second shift—the shift in image—was immensely powerful and would impact *private* college students' rights and also the future of student physical safety on campus.

To preview the latter point, a crucial observation is in order. Exactly at the time that students succeeded in changing their imagined student/university relationship to governmental/commercial paradigms, the law of governmental and commercial responsibility for citizen/consumer safety was in a formative stage. Governments still had few *duties* to protect citizens from harm; commercial entities were increasingly required to protect consumers, but as of Spring, 1965, these responsibilities were still slender. For example, strict product liability did not solidify in the courts until the late 1960s and 1970s. Tenant's rights were still forming, and women enjoyed little legal protection from stalkers. Cases like the Agent Orange litigation were still in the future. In short, there was a hidden side-effect to student civil rights victories. Students won new rights and championed a new legal image of their status and relationship to the university. However, that image had a major weakness in that it imagined the university in roles as government and business at a time when duties to provide for physical security of citizens, and consumers were only just beginning to take shape. This was a time when the police could legally ignore cries for help from endangered citizens, and businesses and landowners

---

14. *See Tinker, supra* note 12.

had little responsibility to keep dangerous people away from customers and tenants. These legal rules would change, but the timing was such that students had won a paradoxical victory for a time. Constitutional rights now won would beget a period in which universities could, like governments and businesses, stand by and not prevent grave danger. The bystander era, detailed in Chapter IV, would be part backlash, but also it was the almost inevitable consequence of the precise timing of the shift in image. Had *in loco parentis* fallen in the late 1980s, university law would have looked very different. By the late 1980s, citizen/consumer rights were much better established.

Now, major shifts had occurred in public universities, but what would happen in *private* universities to *in loco parentis* defenses? After all, *constitutional* protections were almost entirely the province of governmental litigation. Would *in loco parentis* survive for private colleges? The answer would be "no," although the civil rights cases were not directly applicable to private colleges. The demise of *in loco parentis*—brought on by constitutional rights cases against public universities—was a feature of the much larger momentum away from university legal insularity, and this movement would capture private colleges as well. When students began to assert similar rights at private colleges—process, privacy, and speech rights for example—the courts began to recognize validity to those claims as well, even if somewhat more slowly.[15]

When such issues arose at private schools, the courts typically fell back upon the "well-settled rule that the relations between a student and a private university are a matter of contract."[16] The contract theory—armed to protect economic and intangible rights—had been of little help to students in the *in loco parentis* era. For one thing, they were not typically the contracting party. For another, these contracts were subject to university-favorable rules regarding interpretation and enforcement. Historically, the most notorious way to read these contracts favorably to university power would be to determine that parent/student had somehow waived rights or

---

15. *Compare Slaughter v. Brigham Young University,* 514 F.2d 622 (10th Cir. 1975), where the court used constitutional due process as a benchmark for determining whether a private university's process for dismissal was fair or arbitrary, with *Albert v. Carovano,* 851 F.2d 561 (2nd Cir. 1988), showing deference to statutorily mandated disciplinary roles, but refusing to review student claims that the college failed to follow rules. And see *Militana v. University of Miami,* 236 So. 2d 162 (Fla. Dist. Ct. App. 1970), holding that notice and opportunity to be heard might be required in discipline cases, but not in cases of purely academic dismissal. *See also* H.L. Silets, *Of Students' Rights and Honor: The Application of Fourteenth Amendment's Due Process Strictures to Honor Code Proceedings At Private Colleges and Universities,* 64 DENVER U. L. REV. 47 (1987).

16. *Dixon,* 294 F.2d at 157.

had never been given them in the first place. Thus, it was not uncommon for a court to rule that rights to notice and hearing were waived—that there in essence were no rights to be heard or notified prior to expulsion, even at expensive private colleges.[17]

Fundamental rights to fair process were not waivable in the public university context, as *Dixon* held, and that idea soon had its impact in the *private* college context. In the 1960s and 1970s courts shifted to a more pro-consumer contract law stance, and retreated from the older style of contract law cases. As *Dixon* stated in regard to private college case law, "the right to notice and hearing is so fundamental to the conduct of our society that the waiver must be clear and explicit."[18] Private colleges might limit students' process rights, but only upon clearer and more explicit terms.

Over time, the contract between the student and a private college has begun to look less and less like an ordinary contract of any typical variety. There have been three critical variables at work. First, college education, even when available at private schools, is eminently connected to major features of public interest. Private colleges have always been key functionaries in the public domain in America and how they perform and what they teach have affected all of society. Where would the United States be today without Harvard, MIT, Stanford etc. and their Nobel prize winners and Supreme Court Justices? Second, the college contract itself was an odd collection of printed form catalogues, applications, rules, etc. that were offered on a "take it or leave it" basis. It would seem odd for a student/applicant to write a major college and demand "renegotiation" of the contract. It would also take a non-intuitive perspective to see the college admission/acceptance process like the purchase of a car. For most students and parents, education is not a "transaction" first and foremost, even if today a private college education does cost the equivalent of a house. College law is rooted in contract in a very unusual way. Third, it seems odd that college students who typically pay less to go to state schools should receive more than private college students. College is college after all; what would be the social justification for differentiating between public and private students in this way? Moreover, what would justify devoting so much social resource to educate people without even minimal guarantees of fair play in their education? What types of people would such a system produce?

In line with the first variable, students have continued to push the line between public and private higher education. Modern universities increas-

---

17. *See, e.g.,* Anthony v. Syracuse Univ., 231 N.Y.S. 435 (N.Y. App. Div. 1928); Barker v. Bryn Mawr, 122 A. 220 (Pa. 1923).

18. *Dixon,* 294 F. 2d at 157.

ingly intertwine themselves with government programs, and students have attacked along that front. Students have argued that large private schools are sometimes like cities in that they provide the services of small municipalities—sewer, water, police, health care, street maintenance, etc. Students have likewise argued that education serves such a fundamental function in society that it is sufficiently similar to an activity of government. Students have lost these cases, often to the consternation of commentators who have offered competing, non-contract models of university student relations, such as quasi-corporate fiduciary models.[19]

---

19. As Brian Jackson wrote in a recent law review article:

Dixon v. Alabama often is hailed as a pivotal rejection of the *in loco parentis* doctrine. But despite the *Dixon* decision, thousands of students at private universities remain outside the scope of constitutional protection. Since the *Dartmouth College* case recognized the independent nature of private education in the United States, the courts have been nearly unanimous in holding that private colleges and universities are not instruments of the state. As a result, actions by these schools cannot be attributed to the state for constitutional purposes. The *Dixon* decision thus left untouched thousands of students attending private colleges and universities. These students have no substantive or procedural constitutional safeguards.

A number of writers have questioned this bright-line distinction between the public and private contexts. They have advanced several justifications for recognizing certain universities as instruments of the state. The courts, however, have been unwilling to extend constitutional protections to students attending these private universities. In *Blackburn v. Fisk University,* for example, a student argued that the university should be treated as an arm of the state since it exhibited many of the characteristics of a municipality. The student noted that the university provided municipal services, including health and sanitation services, a police force, roads, and public housing. The Sixth Circuit, however, followed other courts in finding these governmental functions to be insufficient to qualify as state action. Likewise, courts have been unsympathetic to claims that the inherent importance of the educational enterprise constitutes a sufficient "public function" to satisfy the state action doctrine.

The courts' reluctance to extend constitutional protections to university students is unfortunate. Contrary to the *Fisk* ruling, many multiuniversities are in fact small cities. The university police may be the only law enforcement officers students encounter. Courts should give serious consideration to the practical effects of the modern university's size and complexity. While it may not be possible to apply constitutional limitations to private universities without seriously undermining the state action doctrine, the idea should be considered carefully.

Brian Jackson, *The Lingering Legacy of In Loco Parentis: An Historical Survey and Proposal for Reform,* 44 VAND. L. REV. 1135, 1153-55 (1991) (footnotes omitted). For writers challenging the posture of the courts see Robert B. McKay, *The Student as Private Citizen,* 45 DEN. L.J. 558, 560 (1968); William Cohen, *The Private-Public Legal Aspects*

But the attacks on the public/private distinction has had its effects, most notably in the arena of contract law. Increasingly courts began to review the college contract with what amounts to suspicion. As a recent commentator observed:

> The contractual method, however, is also seriously flawed. Several critics of the contractual approach are quick to point out the failure of the analogy: Students and colleges do not engage in an "arm's length" agreement. Without such bargaining, quasi-contracts, unconscionable contracts, and contracts of adhesion all emerge as impairments to contractual analysis. Not all potential students are free to attend the college of their choice, nor are students able to negotiate the terms contained in a college bulletin.[20]

This logic has influenced the development of student rights litigation in the courts and the custom and practices of private colleges.

The 1984 decision of the 8th Circuit Federal Court of Appeals in *Corso v. Creighton University*[21] provides a good example. In that case a medical student was expelled from a private university medical program. The student was given process but claimed that the process given was not the correct process specified by contract with the school. In considering the student's claim, the *Corso* court agreed that a student claim of this sort (economic and intangible interest) is a contract claim stating that "[t]he relationship between a university and student is contractual in nature."[22] (The court looked principally to the student handbook, but was constrained to consider various other forms and bulletins etc., provided to the student).

Critically, the *Corso* court viewed the "deal" as a printed form "adhesion" contract. With an adhesion contract all ambiguities and inconsistencies are read in favor of the student. And the court decides what is "clear" and "ambiguous." This type of logic gives the contract aspects of public policy and operates to protect student interests. In *Corso* it did just that.

Although *Corso* had received what would have been "due process" minimums under *Dixon*, the "contract" as interpreted by the court actually afforded *more* than minimum due process to the student. In essence, a private university student received greater protection than minimum constitutional standards through special rules of contract interpretation.

---

of Institutions of Higher Education, 45 DEN. L.J. 643, 646-47 (1968); Alvin L. Goldman, *The University and the Liberty of its Students-A Fiduciary Theory,* 54 KY. L.J. 643, 650 (1966); Comment, *Common Law Rights for Private University Students: Beyond the State Action Principle,* 84 YALE L.J. 120, 122-23 (1974).

20. Theodore C. Stamatakos, *The Doctrine of In Loco Parentis, Tort Liability and the Student-College Relationship,* 65 IND. L.J. 471, 477 (footnote omitted.)

21. 731 F.2d 529 (8th Cir. 1984).

22. *Id.* at 531.

Many writers on the law of contracts have noted that contract law has often mutated into forms of reasoning that do not mirror the ancient concept of a contract as an arms length bargain between equal parties. It looks like contract law, but in reality it is a hybrid (tort like?) view. *Corso* is just such an example: the student won the case and was entitled to extra-constitutional protection because of "contract."

The shift in contract analysis brought about corresponding customs and practices in the private university "industry" itself. The "industry" has arrived at a point today where it appears that private university students are entitled—through some theory or another—to proceedings which are "fundamentally fair." Even private universities are in the habit of providing significant process today, particularly in professional schools.[23] Universities collectively have taken the position that students should be provided orderly and fair procedures.[24] Thus, the original legal paradox that private schools would provide *less* than public schools has resolved itself practically (incidentally, public institutions also typically provide more than minimal process today).

This area of the law has evolved to the point where one major commentator, Victoria Dodd, has pronounced that contract is no longer the true (or appropriate) basis for analyzing the legal relationship of private university relations with students:

> [L]aws of contract are not in fact being applied in student-university cases. Nor should they be. Instead, theories of tort law should be applied more frequently to issues concerning the student-university relationship, as the basic conceptual premises of contract law are not truly reflective of that relationship and thus are not appropriate analytical tools in the education law area.[25]

Indeed 'contract' analysis had taken on an air of unreality as the results in private college cases have closely tracked those in public university contexts. Contract law in the university context had become quasi-constitutional. And, as Victoria Dodd has noted, the law of torts has been increasingly applied in the private university context. One feature of treating

---

23. *For example, see Boehm v. Univ. of Pennsylvania*, 553 A. 2d 575 (Pa. 1990) in which extensive procedures—nearly mimicking trial—were provided.

24. The Joint Statement on Rights and Freedom of Students, (1992), published annually by a joint committee of AAUP (American Association of University Professors) and other key organizations specifically stated that students should enjoy protection from arbitrary and prejudiced procedures. Prominent scholars in higher education law, like William Kaplin and Barbara Lee would agree. *See* William A. Kaplin & Barbara A. Lee, The Law of Higher Education, 3d Edition (Jossey-Bass, Inc. 1995).

25. Victoria J. Dodd, *The Non-Contractual Nature of the Student-University Contractual Relationship*, 33 U. Kan. L. Rev. 701, 702 (1985).

students as consumers/customers is that the development of "business" torts would influence private and ultimately public post-secondary education (more on this in Chapter V). In redefining the student/university contract relationship, courts, almost as if sleepwalking, wandered into forms of analysis that would set the stage for still further inroads into the insularity of university life.

By the end of the 1960s and the early 1970s the era of *in loco parentis* was dead—constitutionally and contractually, publically and privately— on modern American campuses. Economic and intangible rights (civil rights, privacy, speech rights etc.) were vindicated in new models of student/university relations that stressed student (citizen/consumer) freedom and rights over university (government/business) power and authority. More significantly, a major feature of university insularity had ended. For the purposes of these rights, university life was now legally non-immunized public activity and/or commercial activity; it was no longer protected governmental activity or nonjusticiable family or charitable activity. University conduct was becoming subject to judicial review and to legal, not simply institutional, norms.

But victories in the arena of such economic and intangible rights did not settle—one way or the other—the very difficult questions of apportioning risks and responsibilities regarding student physical safety on campus. The citadel of *in loco parentis* fell so quickly that it seemed that Rome was sacked on the first try. But Rome did not fall in one blow, and the civil rights cases (broadly speaking) seemed to throw a system of law, once in balance, into a substantial imbalance. The reaction of the courts to this newly empowered student freedom model of university relations would be mixed initially with regard to student safety. This is the study of the next chapter, the "bystander era", in which university law explored how the student freedoms won in the economic and intangible dimensions would translate into rights and duties regarding physical safety. The law was immature in these areas and would reflect the newness, variety, and even kneejerkiness of such a nascent and transitional period.

IV

The Rise of the "Bystander" University in the 1970s and 1980s— The "Duty"/"No Duty" Era

Like European politics after the fall of the Berlin wall and the Soviet Union, American universities of the 1960's were in a major political/legal transitional state. A crisis of identity was born at the time a new and very large group of mostly young people formed and went to the university— baby boom "tweenagers",[1] people no longer under parental control but in between that control and mature adulthood. As the numbers and types of students rose, American university campuses became more potentially dangerous and divisive places. American courts were now faced with a new wave of lawsuits by injured students against their schools. In the period ranging roughly from 1970 to the mid-1980s, American courts stopped relying upon the fallen parental legal model and began an approach to lawsuits using the legal analytical/doctrinal tools of "duty" and "no duty."

Certain well known court decisions in this period cast the university in the legal and cultural role of helpless "bystander" to student life and danger. In the role of bystanders, colleges had no legal duties to students and hence were not legally responsible for harm. Universities typically saw certain key cases in this period as providing (appropriate) protection from students' lawsuits in light of the reshuffling of student rights and university responsibilities.[2] However, this was a period of crosscurrents

---

1. We borrow this term from our friend and colleague Professor Emeritus Norman Oler, University of Pennsylvania, although we acknowledge that we may not always use it in precisely the way he intends.

2. As the 1980's progressed, and then into the 1990's, the thinking was that pro-university, no-liability case law was part of a larger anti-tort, anti-victim, pro-business, pro-individual responsibility movement in the law of torts. University lawyers often see tort reform as an ally and allied development. As we explain in this and following chapters, several tort law developments no doubt aided universities in defending some lawsuits.

49

and mixed messages in university law. There were also cases which imposed new legal duties on colleges. Ultimately, universities avoided legal responsibility in some student caused injury cases, particularly those involving alcohol use by minors; in other areas, legal responsibility began to move onto campus. The "duty" era was in a formative stage. For reasons we explore in this chapter, it appeared to some that new "no duty" rules would come to dominate. It would not be so.

There are four "famous" cases (other similar cases could be used) which are emblematic of the no-duty, bystander university period—*Bradshaw v. Rawlings,* a decision of a federal appellate court in 1979; *Baldwin v. Zoradi,* a decision of a lower California appellate court in 1981; *Beach v. University of Utah,* a decision of the Utah Supreme Court in 1986; and, *Rabel v. Illinois Wesleyan University,* an intermediate Illinois appellate court decision in 1987.[3] These courts all used duty/no duty concepts to limit the liability of a university for student injury. No duty rules functioned to an extent like the historical trilogy of immunities, but now on a very different basis in theory. The image these decisions conveyed was that of a newly disabled university (no longer able to exercise parental discipline and control), helplessly watching hordes of "free" students (often) suffused with alcohol (or drugs), hormones, and poor judgment. There is a striking similarity in the rhetoric of these decisions to the rhetoric used by many sociologists and criminologists of this period regarding crime in our cities. Campus disorder and danger, like urban crime, were believed to be beyond the control of universities.

The facts of these four cases show prototypical modern campus problems—repackage these cases slightly and you have all too typical student injury scenarios. *Bradshaw,* a case involving off-campus parties (and the most famous case of the four), went like this. On April 13, 1975 an eighteen year old college sophomore was seriously injured in an automobile

---

However, the connections between tort reform and the demise of *in loco parentis* can be overplayed and misjudged. Empirical data bears this out. In a very recent article, Perry Zirkel has evaluated university litigation statistics and determined "explosion" is an apt metaphor regarding university litigation. Predication that conservative tort reform movements might plateau litigation rates have not been accurate. Zirkel's prediction that "the current" [i.e. 1980's] plateau effect is likely to continue during the next decade based on the "conservative" trend in our society, particularly in the dramatically shifted composition of the federal judiciary "is defined by [the data] for the 1990s." Perry Zirkel, *The Volume of Higher Education Litigation: An Update,* 126 ED. LAW. REP. 21 (1998).

3. Bradshaw v. Rawlings, 612 F. 2d 135 (3d Cir. 1979); Baldwin v. Zoradi, 176 Cal. Rptr. 809 (Cal. Ct. App. 1981); Beach v. University of Utah, 726 P.2d 413 (Utah 1986); Rabel v. Illinois Wesleyan Univ., 514 N.E. 2d 552 (Ill. App. Ct. 1987).

accident. He was riding as a passenger in the backseat of a vehicle driven by an intoxicated fellow student. They had just come from an off-campus sophomore class picnic. The drinking age was twenty-one in Pennsylvania: this was a *sophomore* class event where most individuals were underage.

The "picnic" was actually little more than an off-campus drinking fest. The driver, for example, drank for several hours to the point where he blacked out and was unable to recall anything from the time he left the picnic until after the accident. The picnic, an annual event, was planned with a faculty advisor, who co-signed the check that was later used to buy beer. The case report does not indicate that the faculty advisor or any other responsible faculty member attended the picnic. Copies of flyers for the event were made on college equipment and tacked up all over campus. The unmistakable message conveyed by the prominently featured beer symbolism on the flyers was that it was a "wet" event. The sophomore class president (underage) succeeded in purchasing six or seven half kegs of beer from a local distributor (who got in big legal trouble as a result of the sale). And the city of Doylestown, Pennsylvania became a defendant because the accident resulted when the drunken student lost control of the vehicle after encountering a road hazard.

The *Bradshaw* facts portray a "system" of alcohol use broken or besieged at almost every conceivable point. Underage students were led to irresponsible, unlawful drinking and the inevitable drive home from the off-campus party; and vendors of liquor selling to underage drinkers. A university allowed itself to facilitate a student function yet seemed incapable of exercising even minimal responsibility for its own actions or the potential consequences to its students. There was the student preference for an off-campus event—limiting college drinking problems on college premises perhaps, but to what end? In addition, *Bradshaw* portrays a society that has a taste for recreation in cars and the use of alcohol. There was also a city government struggling with questions of infrastructure. And there was no sense whatsoever among the several actors and parties of shared responsibility to reduce danger and increase safety: everyone acted independently and unsafely.

Beach (Spring, 1979), also a liquor related case, involves not partying and picnics, but the difficult problems associated with student curricular activities which carry on off campus. Of all four cases, *Beach* is the least defensible and most likely to be discredited by a majority of future courts. In *Beach*, an underage freshman biology student at the University of Utah was rendered quadriplegic during a required field trip in the Deep Creek mountains of Utah. The field trip—a weekend camp out/expedition at a remote location—was a required part of the course in which she was enrolled. The trip was supervised by a professor who told the students that they were to follow instructions during "class time" (whatever boundary that was) but afterwards could "do their own thing." During the trip, the student fell from a cliff into a rocky crevice in an area where she laid suffering for several hours until she was discovered and rescued.[4]

Field trips, particularly remote location camping/hiking/repelling trips, involve risks (there is no mention of consent/release forms in the *Beach* opinion, or even a legitimate discussion of such risks) and students can get hurt. Danger, even obvious danger, is a fact of life, and thus relevant to the planning of academically sanctioned field trips for students. In this context, the *Beach* record discloses some facts which should concern university administrators and parents. On a prior trip, the same underage student had, in the risk minimizing words of *Beach's* Justice Zimmerman, "experienced only one minor problem."[5] During the earlier trip (under the same professor's control), the student drank wine and fell asleep in some bushes near camp. She was found by other students and returned to safety. As if that were enough, the student told the professor "that the incident was unusual."[6] Yet, when an underage student drinks unlawfully and/or in violation of university regulations, *loses consciousness,* and requires assistance from others, we know that this is an indication of greater problems and often a predictor of future similar behavior. This is not a minor incident: we now know that little things count in large amounts (*e.g.* fixing broken locks can stop intruders). Although the court in *Beach* treated the incidents as if they were functionally unrelated, there was a striking similarity in events.

The second time, the results were serious. On the fateful Sunday, the students were taken to a lamb roast hosted by a local rancher. This was a *freshman* biology course in a state with a twenty-one year old drinking age; nonetheless, the professor himself stated "that he assumed most

---

4. *See Beach v. University of Utah, supra,* 726 P. 2d 413, 414-15.

5. *Id.* at 414. An important feature of judge-made case law is that judges in courts of last resort have tremendous control over what "facts" are reported and how they are characterized. Usually fact finding is left for a jury—a basic constitutional right—but when judges use "duty"—as we shall see—the judge circumvents the jury and takes control not just of law but of fact and image as well. Judges are understandably reluctant to exercise these powers, but activist (so called) *conservative* judges (or judges deciding cases conservatively) have taken to "duty" as a way to create a kind of judicial tort reform which can limit a plaintiff's access to a trial by jury. The power to control or limit what goes to a jury is one of the most powerful political tools in American government and for practical purposes is heavily vested in the hands of judges.

6. *Beach, id.* at 414.

people at the lamb roast were drinking alcohol and that he had several beers."[7] The liquor was apparently flowing quite freely because the student consumed a mixed drink plus three or four home brewed (higher alcohol?) beers at the roast (enough liquor to intoxicate an average 20 year old female in a short period of time). *And*, the professor (who had been drinking) *drove* the student and others in a van back to the campsite. Fortunately, there was no vehicular mishap; but this van was an "alcohol wagon." While in the back of the van, the students drank whiskey from some unidentified source.[8] Yet according to the testimony as reported by the court, when the van reached the campsite, "[the student] did not act inebriated or in any way impaired, but appeared to be well-oriented and alert."[9] Common sense (and subsequent events) suggests that either she was wrong in her reported self-assessment (also common if you are drinking), or that she was a person who had used (and abused?) alcohol in ways that raised her apparent tolerance for alcohol. The professor had also been drinking, which typically impairs one's judgment and particularly one's ability to assess the impairment of others. Something was certainly amiss with the student because in attempting to reach her tent—just one hundred and twenty five feet from the van—she got lost. She called for assistance, but no one helped her. The next morning she was finally found.[10] *Beach* is to field trips what *Bradshaw* is to off-campus parties, and worse.

Beach presents a sad scenario, which in multi-form could easily be repeated at any college. Modern universities now conduct more field trips, externships and study abroad as an integral part of courses, summer programs, etc. In many cases the very educational mission of the off-campus curriculum event relates to danger—to study huckleberries in field biology you must go where the bears and the briars are. And like *Bradshaw*, *Beach* involves the deliberate use and abuse of alcohol, as well as the difficulties of monitoring and facilitating "tweenager" alcohol use by university officials and instructors. *Beach* is also like *Bradshaw* in that it shocks and surprises most parents who learn about it. Parents may anticipate that their college age children will encounter and even possibly misuse alcohol. But they do not expect universities to facilitate dangerous underage drinking on an *academic* field trip planned and conducted by a professor and to ignore tell-tale signs of abuse and danger. Colleges should not enhance or facilitate underage drinking risks in any context.

---

7. *Id.* at 415.
8. *See id.*
9. *See id.*
10. *See id.*

Baldwin v. Zoradi involved injuries sustained off campus stemming from on-campus drinking.[11] Because the case was dismissed on the pleadings — a technical procedural way to end litigation before facts are fully discovered or proven — the "facts" of *Baldwin* must arise by way of presumptions from allegations made in the pleadings.[12] The victim in *Baldwin* was a student at a California state university. She was injured in a car wreck that was the product of a speeding contest, itself the by-product of (underage) drinking at a university dorm. Students involved were underaged, yet had consumed alcohol on campus in violation of university rules prohibiting their alcohol use and in violation of California law.[13]

The salient feature of *Baldwin* was the assertion (treated as fact) that not only did the university fail to enforce anti-drinking rules in *this* instance — where "mass quantities were consumed" — but that in *general*, the university "looked the other way" regarding on-campus drinking. The culture was one where rules and catalogs conveyed the image of regulated liquor consumption, but reality was exactly the opposite. The court itself related one aspect of the plaintiff's claim (again, treated as if the facts were true):

> The Trustees and dormitory advisors permitted a dangerous condition to exist at the residence hall in that consumption of alcohol by minors occurred regularly, and the said defendants knew or should have known of such occurrence and taken appropriate steps to stop the activity. By knowingly acquiescing in the consumption of alcohol by minors on campus over an extended period of time, the Trustees, and their employees, created an unsafe condition, to wit, a safe haven or enclave where large groups of minors could, would and did gather and consume alcoholic beverages, to an excess, with complete impunity from any laws or rules and regulations.[14]

---

11. *See* Baldwin v. Zoradi, 176 Cal. Rptr. 806 (Cal. Ct. App. 1981).

12. In this case, the court presumed that all of the allegations of the complaint were true. *See id.* at 811. In essence, the court decides the question: "even if everything you say is true, are you entitled to a legal remedy?" This type of inquiry *procedurally* focuses litigation upon *legal* questions, particularly legal questions of *duty*. In this way a court — not a jury — can decide to end a case, even before all facts are discovered or demonstrated. The result of this way of managing the legal questions presented is that the cases are more like epitaphs than biographies: they tend to be pithy, aphoristic distillations, or contain just snippets of information. There is no pretense that the "truth" has been elicited. However unlikely (because there are limits on what can be stated in a complaint), it is possible that the "facts" stated in a complaint are largely erroneous, incomplete or exaggerated.

13. *See Baldwin,* 176 Cal. Rptr. at 809-13. *See also,* Rabel v. Illinois Wesleyan Univ., 514 N.E.2d 552, 560 (Ill. App. Ct. 1987).

14. *Baldwin,* 176 Cal. Rptr. at 812.

The student victim claimed not just that university culture was dangerous. She claimed it was a sham.

Baldwin is a classic example of risks which expand into the community from inside the university culture. A culture of underage drinking and students with automobiles away from home is a dangerous mixture. Moreover, *Baldwin* illustrates a fundamental hypocrisy that can occur in "tweenager" drinking regulation on campus. Official rules prohibit underage and unsupervised drinking, but the college culture can actually facilitate drinking and its deadly combination with vehicles. What better way to sell your parents on the idea of giving you a car at college than to pursue the path of a "science nerd" to a school with "tough" regulations on drinking? Schizophrenia on how best to work with large groups of young people entering a culture suffused with alcohol, drugs, sex, and automobiles has led to almost Kafka-esque situations, such as those described at California Polytech State University. *Baldwin* is to on-campus drinking what *Bradshaw* is to off-campus drinking—the results can be the same—serious injury.

Rabel,[15] another case dismissed on the pleadings, is the consummate fraternity "prank/hazing" case. One afternoon in 1982, a young female college student was called upon to meet a visitor in the dormitory lobby. The visitor was a male student who was involved with a fraternity. He had just come from a fraternity sponsored liquor-friendly party with a mission (*cf.* Jake and Elwood Blues). This however was no "mission from God." The visitor had been instructed by members of the fraternity to abduct a female student and then run a gauntlet of fraternity brothers who would strike him as he passed by (apparently a traditional activity). The good frat soldier did just that: he forcibly grabbed the female student, threw her over his shoulder, and ran towards his task. But he was not up to the task; as he ran with her he fell and, among other things, crushed her skull in the fall.[16] She suffered permanent, life-altering head injuries. In any other location and circumstances but on a college campus, this could be kidnaping and home invasion, battery, assault, and/or assorted other crimes, torts, and wrongs.

The fraternity member and the fraternity settled out (for relatively small sums), leaving the university faced with assertions—treated as fact—that were strikingly similar to those made in *Baldwin*:

> [The university] holds itself out to the public, prospective students and others as a University that does not allow alcoholic beverages on its

---

15. Rabel v. Illinois Wesleyan Univ., 514 N.E.2d 552 (Ill. App. Ct. 1987).
16. *See id.* at 554-55.

campus or in its fraternity houses, and as a University whose agents stated primary concern is the general student welfare.

[The university] by and through its agents and employees stated to [plaintiff and plaintiff's family], the public and prospective students by direct statement and otherwise that the University strictly controlled the activities of its students, including a ban on alcohol consumption and further, it represented and held itself out as having a strong religious background with a tradition of strong supervision and control of student activities and a premium price was charged to students as tuition to this private University in reliance upon those statements and others.

. . .

At all times described herein, [the university] was aware of the excessive drinking occurring at the Fiji Fraternity and was aware of the lengthy and boisterous parties and activities, including the activities at Pfeiffer Hall described herein on May 1, 1982.

[The university], not regarding its duty to the Plaintiff personally and as a student at Illinois Wesleyan University, and its duty to others arising out of its specific representations to [plaintiff and plaintiff's family] the public and prospective students, its stated policies, its customs and practices, its high tuition, and the special relationship between [the university] and its students, failed to take any effective action on April 30, 1982 or May 1, 1982 to discourage the excessive drinking of its students and others, or to discourage the lengthy and boisterous party and activities associated with that party, or to supervise and control said party or to provide adequate protection to the University community at large and to [plaintiff] in particular.[17]

This time a non-partying student was victimized by intoxicated students on campus. The "look the other way" culture in this case involved a particularly well-known risk-related association—the college fraternity. In addition to prohibiting alcohol generally, many universities have sanctioned, facilitated, and encouraged certain associational living arrangements. Safety rules abound regarding fraternities, etc., but in *Rabel*, as in other cases, these rules were honored in the breach.

Bradshaw, Baldwin, Beach and *Rabel* are variations of a common and sometimes deadly theme—alcohol, college students, and activities like driving, field trips, and dormitory and fraternity parties threaten student safety. Implicitly, these courts sensed the common theme and reacted to it in light of a common perception of the new relational reality on campus. The dominant image in these cases was that of newly empowered students who were beyond the control of the modern university. To the

---

17. *Rabel*, 514 N.E.2d at 556-57 *citing Bradshaw*, 612 F.2d 135.

courts, the university was a helpless "bystander" to such student misconduct; no "duty" was owed to these "adults." Nor *should* a duty be owed given the "new" role of colleges.

In each of these cases—in spite of, nay *because of,* the facts—the courts determined that *as a matter of law* (translated: no jury evaluation of the university's conduct in the matter) the university was held *not* responsible for the student's injuries. These courts looked with some dismay upon a college-aged generation with whom they had lost touch or over whom they were losing control. The torch had been passed to a new generation, suffused with alcohol and committed to the notion that they should no longer ask what their university could do to protect them.

These courts chose particular images and particular legal tools to create a new legal climate on university campuses. The image was that of the helpless bystander university brought about as a direct result of student freedom won in the civil rights movements. The legal tool was "duty," which was used to limit liability and to keep juries out of the university legal process.

Bradshaw, the frequently cited and seminal case (although it was, ironically, a federal court decision guessing at what the law of Pennsylvania would become),[18] portrayed the following extended image. Consider *Bradshaw's* own often quoted words:

> Our beginning point is a recognition that the modern American college is not an insurer of the safety of its students. Whatever may have been its responsibility in an earlier era, the authoritarian role of today's college administrations has been notably diluted in recent decades. Trustees, administrators, and faculties have been required to yield to the expanding rights and privileges of their students. By constitutional amendment, written and unwritten law, and through the evolution of new customs,

---

18. *Bradshaw, supra.* In some instances, federal courts are invested with the special jurisdictional opportunity to hear what are, in essence, cases involving *state law* only. If the right mix of parties or issues is present, a single automobile accident could end up in federal court. When a federal court decides such a case, it is bound to follow state law; it is to act, at least substantially, as if it were a court in that state bound by the precedents of the state supreme court. Sometimes, as in *Bradshaw,* the state courts have not answered the questions raised in the federal case. Yet, in such an instance, the federal court is to make a *guess* (an educated guess, called by lawyers an *Erie* guess, so named after a U.S. Supreme Court case which ratified this process). It is law; but it is a guess and lacks the weight of a decision of the state supreme court itself. Yet it often takes years— even decades—for a state court to reach the precise issues of the federal case. In the mean time, that case stands. In the case of *Bradshaw,* it took on a life of its own. *See Bradshaw,* 612 F. 2d at 136-37, 141-43. When the state does reach the issue, it is also faced with numerous other decisions affecting the federal court ruling. All things equal—and they never are—it is not uncommon for a state to ratify what a federal court has done.

rights formerly possessed by college administrations have been trans-
ferred to students. College students today are no longer minors; they are
now regarded as adults in almost every phase of community life. For
example except for purposes of purchasing alcoholic beverages, eighteen
year old persons are considered adults by the Commonwealth of Pennsylvania. They may vote, marry, make a will, qualify as a personal representative, serve as a guardian of the estate of a minor, wager at race-
tracks, register as a public accountant, practice veterinary medicine,
qualify as a practical nurse, drive trucks, ambulances and other official
fire vehicles, perform general fire-fighting duties, and qualify as a private
detective. Pennsylvania has set eighteen as the age at which criminal acts
are no longer treated as those of a juvenile, and eighteen year old students may waive their testimonial privilege protecting confidential statements to school personnel. Moreover, a person may join the Pennsylvania militia at an even younger age than eighteen and may hunt without
adult supervision at age sixteen. As a result of these and other similar
developments in our society, eighteen year old students are now identified with an expansive bundle of individual and social interests and possess discrete rights not held by college students from decades past. There
was a time when college administrators and faculties assumed a role *in
loco parentis*. Students were committed to their charge because the students were considered minors. A special relationship was created between
college and student that imposed a duty on the college to exercise control over student conduct and, reciprocally, gave the students certain
rights of protection by the college. The campus revolutions of the late
sixties and early seventies were a direct attack by the students on rigid controls by the colleges and were an all-pervasive affirmative demand for
more student rights. In general, the students succeeded, peaceably and
otherwise, in acquiring a new status at colleges throughout the country.
These movements, taking place almost simultaneously with legislation
and case law lowering the age of majority, produced fundamental changes
in our society. A dramatic reapportionment of responsibilities and social
interest of general security took place. Regulation by the college of student life on and off campus has become limited. Adult students now
demand and receive expanded rights of privacy in their college life including, for example, liberal, if not unlimited, partial visiting hours. College
administrators no longer control the broad arena of general morals. At
one time, exercising their rights and duties *in loco parentis,* colleges were
able to impose strict regulations. But today students vigorously claim
the right to define and regulate their own lives. Especially have they
demanded and received satisfaction of their interest in self-assertion in both
physical and mental activities, and have vindicated what may be called
the interest in freedom of the individual will. In 1972 Justice Douglas
summarized the change:

> Students—who, by reason of the Twenty-sixth Amendment, be-
> come eligible to vote when 18 years of age—are adults who are

members of the college or university community. Their interest and concerns are often quite different from those of the faculty. They often have values, views, and ideologies that are at war with the ones which the college has traditionally espoused or indoctrinated.

Healy v. James, 408 U.S. 169, 197, 92 S. Ct. 2338, 2354, 33 L.Ed.2d 266 (1972) (Douglas, J., concurring).

Thus, for purposes of examining fundamental relationships that underlie tort liability, the competing interests of the student and of the institution of higher learning are much different today than they were in the past. At the risk of oversimplification, the change has occurred because society considers the modern college student an adult, not a child of tender years.[19]

Bradshaw—the sophomore drinking party case—saw that students had become emancipated from "minor" status and, by gaining so many freedoms, had become "adults."[20] In one magic moment, students went from being "children" to fully functioning adults, with no in-between time. Students had won freedom—the triumph of the individual—while responsibility as a college virtue had waned (as had the authoritarian model of student/university relations). The shift was abrupt, dramatic, and polar.

Bradshaw was cited and quoted extensively in *Beach, Baldwin,* and *Rabel.* Indeed, *Bradshaw* became the judicially self-serving declaration of student independence and the announcement of the birth of the new "adult" student body. *Bradshaw* birthed the bystander (helpless) university. The other three decisions amplified *Bradshaw* and added their own touches to the new post *in loco parentis* legal archetype.

Baldwin—the dormitory drinking/drag race case—imagined that drinking on university campuses was uncontrollable. Almost unthinkably, *Baldwin* also believed that not enforcing policies and rules prohibiting underaged drinking was actually in the best interest of society. In *Baldwin's* own words with respect to controlling college drinking:

> Nor is it in the best interests of society to do so. The transfer of prerogatives and rights from college administrators to the students is salubrious when seen in the context of a proper goal of postsecondary education—the maturation of the students. Only by giving them responsibilities can students grow into responsible adulthood. Although the alleged lack of supervision had a disastrous result to this plaintiff, the overall policy of stimulating student growth is in the public interest....

---

19. *Bradshaw*, 612 F.2d at 138-41 (emphasis added; footnotes and citations omitted).

20. The students were not merely "constitutional" adults; they were adults to whom the university owed no duty of supervision or protection or obligation to be actively involved in risk minimization.

> In respect to the burden to the defendant and the consequences to the community of imposing a duty to exercise care with resulting liability for breach, it would be difficult to so police a modern university campus as to eradicate alcoholic ingestion.[21]

College anti-drinking rules were now to have a nudge-nudge-*wink-wink* quality:

> Since the turbulent '60's California colleges and universities have been in the forefront of extension of student rights with a concomitant withering of faculty and administrative omnipotence. Drug use has proliferated. Although the consumption of alcoholic beverages by persons under 21 years of age is proscribed by law (Bus. & Prof. Code, § 25658), the use of alcohol by college students is not so unusual or heinous by contemporary standards as to require special efforts by college administrators to stamp it out. Although the university reserved to itself the right to take disciplinary action for drinking on campus, this merely follows state law. (Bus. & Prof. Code, § 25608.) The same may be said of the provisions of the license agreement prohibiting alcoholic beverages. We do not believe they created a mandatory duty. As stated in *Bradshaw v. Rawlings, supra, 612 F.2d at page 141:* "[Plaintiff] has concentrated on the school regulation, imposing sanctions on the use of alcohol by students.... We are not impressed that this regulation, in and of itself, is sufficient to place the college in a custodial relationship with its students for purposes of imposing a duty of protection in this case.... A college regulation that essentially tracks a state law and prohibits conduct that to students under twenty-one is already prohibited by state law does not, in our view, indicate that the college voluntarily assumed a custodial relationship with its students so as to (impose a duty of protection.)[22]

Baldwin believed that abusive college age drinking did not require any unusual collegiate response and that the fact that there were anti-drinking rules and regulations did not mean that the college actually had to enforce them. Again, *Baldwin* tied this to the 1960's student "revolution." *Baldwin* took a final step as well in concluding that somehow this state of affairs was best for student maturation. The *Baldwin* court seemed to lack any vision that the freedom of which it spoke operated in an environment that should include/provide some structure directed toward the progression from adolescence to adulthood. Rather, the Baldwin court seemed to say that students must be left free to drink themselves to death — free to be unreasonably unsafe.

Beach, also quoting *Baldwin*, emphasized "realism", and focused upon how, in its view, a university could not and should not exercise

---

21. *Baldwin,* 176 Cal. Rptr. at 818.
22. *Id.* at 817.

control over its students. The image is one of a Hobson's choice of university "helplessness," and an alternative of fascist-like control:

> We also must consider the nature of the institution. Elementary and high schools certainly can be characterized as a mixture of custodial and educational institutions, largely because those who attend them are juveniles. However, colleges and universities are educational institutions, not custodial. *Accord Baldwin v. Zoradi,* 123 Cal. App. 3d at 281-82, 176 Cal. Rptr. at 813. Their purpose is to educate in a manner which will assist the graduate to perform well in the civic, community, family, and professional positions he or she may undertake in the future. It would be unrealistic to impose upon an institution of higher education the additional role of custodian over its adult students and to charge it with responsibility for preventing students from illegally consuming alcohol and, should they do so, with responsibility for assuring their safety and the safety of others. *Accord Bradshaw v. Rawlings,* 612 F.2d at 138; *Baldwin v. Zoradi,* 123 Cal.App.3d at 290-91, 176 Cal.Rptr. at 818. Fulfilling this charge would require the institution to babysit each student, a task beyond the resources of any school. But more importantly, such measures would be inconsistent with the nature of the relationship between the student and the institution, for it would produce a repressive and inhospitable environment, largely inconsistent with the objectives of a modern college education.[23]

Beach envisioned a draconian choice between custodial control (like a sanitarium or jail) and merely performing *educational* functions. For *Beach,* safety and responsible regulation were in zero sum relationships with education: drive up the rules, drive out the students. There is also a trace of the belief that *Animal House* culture is impossible to control. The university could try to wipe out drinking but it would ultimately fail and cause backlash. (Do not try to teach the pig to sing: it annoys the pig and does not succeed because pigs do not sing).

Beach also hammered at the status of the student as an *adult. Beach,* like *Bradshaw* and *Baldwin,* saw a tough choice — "babysit" students as "children" in a "custodial" setting (treating them like "wards"), *or* treat them like "adults" and stand by and let them injure themselves. Standing by was practical *and* just, said *Beach,* because the students had demanded, and won, adulthood status. *Beach* turned "Constitutional" adulthood into a much larger image of students as adults.

Beach chose particularly strong language and analogies to convey this "overnight shift" into adulthood:

> The students whose relationship to the University we are asked to characterize as "custodial" are not juveniles. Beach was twenty years of

---

23. *Beach,* 726 P.2d at 419 (emphasis added; footnote omitted).

age at the time of the accident. She may have been denied the right to drink by Utah law, but in virtually all other respects she was entitled to be treated as an adult. She had a constitutional right to vote, U.S. Const. amend. XXVI, § 1, she was to be chargeable on her contracts, U.C.A., 1953, §§ 15-2-1 and 2 (1986 ed.) and if she had committed a crime, she would be tried and sentenced as an adult. U.C.A., 1953 §§78-3a-2 and 16 (1977 ed., Supp. 1986). Had she not been a college student, but an employee in industry, she could not argue realistically that her employer would be responsible for compensating her for injuries incurred by her voluntary intoxication if she violated state liquor laws during her off-hours while traveling on company business. We do not believe that Beach should be viewed as fragile and in need of protection simply because she had the luxury of attending an institution of higher education.

Not only are students such as Beach adults, but law and society have increasingly come to recognize their status as such in the past decade or two. Nowhere is this more true than in the relations between students and institutions of higher education.[24]

Beach chose to compare a student in college to a worker (and assumed the result in a factually similar worker/employee case). There is an undercurrent that unlike hard working people in business and those who chose (or were drafted into) military service, the life of the college student is a rights dripping, luxuriating experience, a position from which one is ill suited to ask for duties from a university.

Beach took this even further by determining that these adults were still subject to university authority but had lost the right to ask for correlative duties from the university. In a famous footnote (many of the most important nuggets of jurisprudence occur in footnotes), the *Beach* Court stated that:

> This is not to say that an institution might not choose to require of students certain standards of behavior in their personal lives and subject them to discipline for failing to meet those standards. However, the fact that a student might accept those conditions on attendance at the institution would not change the character of their relationship; the student would still be an adult and responsible for his or her behavior. Neither attendance at college *nor agreement to submit to certain behavior standards* makes the student less an autonomous adult or the institution more a caretaker.[25]

You can almost see the "you wanted it this way—you got it" attitude in the *Beach* decision. Students won civil rights, but had left a bitter taste in the mouths of some courts. There was no hint of any possibility of shared responsibility (or meaningful intermediate definitions of the stu-

---

24. *Beach,* 726 P.2d at 418. (footnote omitted).
25. *Beach,* 726 P.2d at 419 n.5 (emphasis added).

dent-university relationship) outside the classroom. Students, *Beach* observed, had demanded "total" freedom as to their conduct on campus and in society, and this demand was seen as one for freedom without structure.[26]

Rabel, also quoting *Beach* extensively, seized upon the notion that higher education does not create a "custodial" relationship but rather a merely "educational" relationship. *Rabel*, like *Beach*, feared that if the university were to have any affirmative duty regarding student conduct that threatened safety, it would become an "insurer" of student safety (blameless, but financially responsible). And, *Rabel* focused upon how "unrealistic" it would be to ask a university to protect students and prevent such events as fraternity drinking and pranks.[27] *Rabel* reads like a pre-mayor Guiliani New Yorker's testament to how it is impossible to stop graffiti, clean up 42nd Street, and reduce crime in Manhattan. The image is of a university community run awash in a sea of freedom and license, with the only alternative being custodial care or backbreaking insurance (strict liability). The causes of campus related student injuries — particularly drinking injuries — seemed to be beyond the control of a university. The modern university was seemingly powerless.

In sum, *Bradshaw, Baldwin, Beach* and *Rabel* painted the following images of the new, post *in loco parentis* era on campus:

- Students are "adults." They went from being "children", in most instances *directly* into this role;
- Students are no longer in "custody" or under "university" control; Universities cannot and should not "babysit" students;
- A student's loss of a right to protection from harm is directly related to student freedoms/individual rights won in the turbulent '60's and early '70's. Baby boom, baby bust;
- Universities are not, cannot be, and should not be insurers or underwriters of dangerous behavior on campus;
- Universities cannot "realistically" enforce campus regulations, especially those involving alcohol use and campus activities (including fraternities);
- Universities can promulgate all sorts of rules regarding the same, and even if they do and can enforce them, they are not responsible to do so or to do so responsibly;

---

26. The observations were wrong in fact and law. A person who asks that another have some responsibility for his safety is not automatically asking for a legal custodial relationship. Moreover, the *Beach* court itself recognized that a college has a duty to *prepare* students for adulthood and that responsibility extends beyond the classroom.

27. *See Rabel*, 514 N.E.2d at 561-62.

- Students are to bear the consequences of their "adult" choices (although in some instances fraternities and alcohol vendors will share in the responsibility);
- College is a luxury and a luxurious lifestyle in terms of personal freedom;
- Campus police and policing are disempowered in much the way the police were disempowered in major cities; crime/injury will rise on campus due to social factors beyond the control of the university and their police;
- College students will resist university control regarding their physical safety: the campus drinking culture is like drug resistant bacteria for which there is no cure;
- Society is better off letting some students drink, crash, and burn because the overall population of students will then get what they want from college and will be better citizens because of lessons learned;
- The university is the crucible for major social problems, but is helpless to do much except "educate" students in academic subjects in the classrooms;
- The university's role is educational, primarily, in the limited sense of providing courses, exams etc. The campus is now a *limited* purpose community—the purpose is education only;
- Safety and education are fundamentally inversely related variables. A safer learning environment is a babysitting, custodial environment at odds with what modern students expect;
- It is just and fair to exact a price from students who want freedom. Students forfeit rights to demand safe learning environments, reasonable alcohol use on campus, and even dormitory safety in return for other freedom; (*e.g.,* constitutional freedoms);
- College drinking, by minors especially, is an inevitable fact of campus life, with unavoidable bad consequences. As *Bradshaw* admitted: "What we know as men and women we must not forget as judges, and this panel of judges is able to bear witness to the fact that beer drinking by college students is a common experience. That this is true is not to suggest that reality always comports with state law and college rules. It does not";[28]
- Courts need to protect universities from injury claims, especially those involving alcohol;

---

28. *Bradshaw*, 612 F.2d at 142.

- Most defendants must act reasonably, but universities are unique defendants;Universities are best when they act as bystanders to non-educational student pursuits.

In each of those famous[29] cases, the courts concluded that the university was not legally responsible for harm caused because there was no legal duty. The image of the disempowered bystander, non-custodial university was cemented by the legal tool of duty. The legal question in these types of cases became: "does this type of university/student relationship create legal duty?" By crafting the question of law in terms of duty, these courts linked American university law to a confusing, changing and sometimes obtuse set of legal rules. The practical, bottom-line effect was to temporarily limit claims against universities at the outset of litigation and to keep cases from discovery, litigation, and jury trial.[30]

The political effect of using a "no duty" benchmark was to create what was in essence a new *de facto* university *immunity*. By referring to legal rules of such complexity, only experts would find their way through them. These types of legal rules make it difficult to see what is going on and why and make it easy to make facile, simplistic, or contestable arguments succeed. *In loco parentis* was so legally easy; the new "duty" era was (and remains) highly complex. Problematically, complex and murky legal rules can be very disempowering for non-lawyers who must administer activities under these rules. The duty era has been criticized by university foot soldiers and lieutenants because it is not easy for non-lawyers to understand what the law requires. Thus, even in the heyday of the perceived Halcyon period of the bystander cases — a period which ostensibly should have made administration happy — campus police, deans of students, etc. were perplexed and disempowered.

The duty era has been so doctrinally complex that it has been easy to overlook the paradoxes of this formative era in the caselaw. Consider the *crosscurrent* cases. Although *Bradshaw, Baldwin, Beach* and *Rabel* received most of the notoriety, there were cases decided at about the same time which did not insulate university conduct from legal scrutiny. The bystander era was thus an ambiguous time; some case law flew in the face of the more dominant images of the no-liability cases. But before looking at such cases — cases which seem to contradict *Bradshaw, Baldwin, Beach and Rabel* — a long look at duty and tort responsibility

---

29. These cases became famous even though they were nothing more than two intermediate appellate court decisions, a decision of a federal court making an "Erie" guess, and a Utah Supreme Court decision (a small jurisdiction, not noted for setting or stating legal trends).

30. The practical legal effect of this "no-duty" view was to keep a court or jury from evaluating the reasonableness of university conduct.

is in order so as to understand what these four key cases did and did not say, and what they might have said.

. . .

In general, if someone has been injured physically by some university misconduct or omission, that person looks to the law of torts for a potential remedy. A contractual relationship may form a predicate, but it is tort law which solves the problem. There are three basic theories on which to proceed: in other words, tort law forces someone to put their claim in a box that *tort* law understands. The three basic ways to sue in tort—the boxes—are negligence, intentional torts, and strict liability. For practical purposes, a university is rarely responsible under an intentional tort or true strict liability theory.[31] (For example, a university rarely intentionally injures a student physically and does not usually sell dangerous products, or engage in highly dangerous activities which call out for "strict" liability). Negligence law—one box of tort rules—is *the* major vehicle by which people sue universities. The claims of negligence are various: negligent maintenance of premises, negligent security, negligent representations, negligent failure to give reasonable warnings, negligent failure to control or protect against dangerous persons, negligent supervision of a field trip, or lab experiment, and the list go on.

Although the ways in which people can be negligent are as numerous as sunsets, the law of negligence regulates the basic *form* that almost every negligence case must take. King size sheets are a standard size, but can come in a number of colors. Negligence law is like that. To standardize cases, the law of negligence forces injury victims to fit their claims into a standard formula.

It works like this. If a person feels wronged by a negligence-based tort—a victim of negligence—that plaintiff must assert and prove four "elements." The elements are the basic building blocks of a claim. They are:

(1) Duty
(2) Breach of duty
(3) Causation ("in fact" and "proximate"), and
(4) Damage

With some limited exceptions, this formula is virtually universal in the United States. If a plaintiff succeeds in asserting and proving all four of these things, the plaintiff has established a "prima facie case" of negli-

---

31. Universities can be liable for the torts of certain employees under what is known as vicarious liability. In some ways, some vicarious liability functions enough like some strict liability that it may seem to be so. It is not. Most often, someone(s) in the university was at least negligent when a vicarious liability theory succeeds.

gence. What this means is that the plaintiff wins the lawsuit *unless* the defendant can provide a valid "affirmative defense" (more on this in a bit).

These four elements—duty, breach of duty, causation, damage—are legal ways of identifying essential aspects of a claim of negligence against any party, not just a university or its officials and administrators. University law is then, simply, the not so unusual application of general legal rules of negligence to the special circumstances of university culture. The elements also serve to apportion responsibility among the various actors in a litigation. The plaintiff—the injured party—must come forward, assert, and prove these elements. (There is no Ed McMahon who appears on the doorstep with the negligence prize—a plaintiff must claim it.)

Some elements (or more precisely, aspects thereof) are ones which a court—a judge—must rule on, while others are for juries to decide. Generally, questions of whether a duty is owed, or whether a certain *type* of damage is to be allowed, are questions for a judge to decide—no jury. Questions of breach of duty and causation and questions of whether a legally permissible type of damage actually occurred are usually left to a jury. Because litigation, particularly a jury trial, is expensive and time consuming—and somewhat unpredictable—defendants (including universities) often seek to end litigation by asserting that the judge-decided issues are not in favor of the plaintiff/claimant. Duty is one such question. This is principally why *Bradshaw, Baldwin, Beach* and *Rabel* are duty cases and also why the modern law of university liability is so focused on duty questions. It is tactically sound for lawyers representing universities to raise and attack duty questions. No duty, no jury, no liability.

But what are these elements—duty, breach, causation and damage—and what roles do they serve? Duty, the first element, is foremost. In American law, in order to be responsible for any consequences of negligence, you must first owe someone a duty. The concept is simple, yet also elusively complex at times and constantly changes as society does. Thus, I might be remiss in allowing the bannister on my stairwell to become loose or the light to burn out, but that does not mean that I owe a duty to a stranger on the street to fix them. I am negligent, but I do not owe *that* person a duty to be responsible for my stairwell. Someone I *invite* over to my house presents a different issue—they might fall on the stairwell. *Duty is about setting limits on responsibilities owed to others.* Duty acknowledges responsibility; no duty, or the absence of duty, creates a free space—a legally safe place to chew with your mouth open or drive a dirty car. Although nowhere in the Bill of Rights as such, legal duty is very much about freedom and responsibility, so it is natural for people to become as concerned over tort duties as many constitutional rights issues. A great deal of the heated debate about tort reform is fueled by the fundamental questions raised by tort law.

At the risk of being overly simplistic, a person interested in university law could see that duty, as a first element in a *prima facie* case, comes in three flavors—no duty, ordinary duty, and special duty. In some cases, people have no duty at all—American courts often say that there is no legal duty to come to the aid of a stranger (there are reasons to doubt whether this is or will remain true, but that is another matter). Again, if there is no duty, there is no liability, and the case is over. Judges know how important, how terminating, a no-duty rule is, so they do not say "no-duty" very often.

More often than not in negligence cases (so much so you could do pretty well just knowing this), courts say there is a duty. What is the typical, ordinary duty? When one has an ordinary duty, one must exercise some care for others' safety. To identify the appropriate level of care, courts postulate a *standard of care* which, if matched or exceeded, satisfies the duty owed (because there is such similarity between *duty* and *standard of care* courts and lawyers often use these terms interchangeably).[32] In most instances, the standard of care that is owed is the level of care that an ordinary and prudent person would exercise in like or similar circumstances. Would someone in your shoes—being reasonable and prudent—have looked both ways when entering the intersection? Etc. It does not seem like much to ask people to act like reasonable and prudent individuals in their conduct which could injure others, so courts have historically been willing to allow this standard of care to apply in a very large range of circumstances. Owing an ordinary duty is very common. It is perhaps the most common legal rule in America, and because it is so common it is almost invisible.

In a few situations, one owes a duty because of special circumstances (where otherwise no duty is owed) or owes a special duty. For instance, American courts often say that ordinarily no duty is owed to assist a stranger, but special circumstances can change this rule. For example, there is a duty to aid a stranger if your conduct or instrumentality (example, a car or truck) caused the need for aid (even if you were innocent—that is, even though you caused the peril accidentally and non-negligently).[33] No duty, because of special circumstances, transmutes into a duty owed with an ordinary standard of care. Or sometimes a duty is owed, but the duty is special because it has a special standard of care associated with it. Notable examples of this in many jurisdictions are duties owed to people who enter onto private land or properties and are injured by conditions on the property. In most states for example, a

---

32. In particular, if you have no duty, you need exercise no care at all for another's safety.

33. *See* RESTATEMENT (SECOND) OF TORTS §§ 314, 322 (1965).

trespasser is owed a small level of care (a special, lower than reasonable care, duty) and other entrants are owed higher levels of care than that owed to trespassers. Or professionals like doctors, lawyers, and accountants owe special professional levels of care—special professional duties. They must use a different level of care than an ordinary person due to their special expertise—special duty, special standard of care. Learning about duty under special circumstances and special duty is an important task of law students (and lawyers) and can be complex and confusing even to experienced judges. Nonetheless, the complexity is overshadowed in practical affairs by rules of ordinary duty which are both simple and more significant in most cases. There is a definite and still progressing legal trend to continue to simplify duty law to a single ordinary standard of care—that is, a duty to exercise reasonable care under the circumstances. Such a general rule would simply say that a person is expected to do what the reasonable person would have done in the same situation.[34]

Two final words on duty are in order.

First, the term "duty" technically refers to the first element in a *prima facie* case of negligence. As such, it is the foremost consideration in a negligence case because without duty there is nothing more to discuss—the case is over. Because duty is in that sense necessary for negligence, there has been a somewhat confusing tendency to use the term "duty" (perhaps another term would be better) to also mean "legal liability." Thus, sometimes courts will say or suggest that imposing a duty means imposing liability, or will say that a certain person has a duty in the sense that they are liable to another party. In fact, the existence of a legal duty is not *sufficient* for legal liability (it is a *necessary* condition) because the other aspects of the *prima facie* case must be met. The immediate post-*in loco parentis* cases had a tendency to use duty in this confusing and oversimplified "duty = liability" sense: courts often spoke as if recognizing a legal duty would be tantamount to making universities always liable and hence insurers of student safety. These courts were obviously speaking loosely, even metaphorically. Technically, to say that duty mandates liability is false because an injured student must prove breach of duty (negligent conduct in a particular set of facts), causation (that the university's failure to exercise reasonable care caused the injury), and damage (and then fend off affirmative defenses if any—such as the allegation that plaintiff/student was comparatively negligent). As we shall see, these are some substantial obstacles for a plaintiff and are often the

---

34. Thus negligence is failing to do what the reasonable person would have done in the situation or doing something that the reasonable person would not have done in the same situation.

real issues in university cases. For example, a university may have done everything with reasonable care (no breach), may not be the source of injury (no causation), or face a highly irresponsible student (recovery diminished or defeated under rules of comparative fault).

Second, because duty is so fundamental—so important in balancing rights and responsibilities—courts today typically make the duty element of a *prima facie* case the place in litigation at which they consider most of the social policy issues that a given case raises. Courts like *Baldwin* have openly acknowledged that student injury cases are "on the cutting edge of tort law."[35] Policy/factor analysis and the weighing of competing factors is particularly necessary in university case law. Tort law is fundamentally common law, which courts have the responsibility to assess and reevaluate as social circumstances change. You hear a great deal about "judicial activism" these days, but in most states a judge who refuses to consider major social changes would fail to meet common law and, in some cases, constitutional duties.

Although there are no legal limitations on the policies and factors which courts may consider (except those imposed by a legislature, Congress, or Constitutions—but this is not typical), American courts deciding college student injury cases have settled on some fairly consistent factors and policies to balance and weigh out in determining duty. The factors and policies most often used are those that were articulated in the famous *Tarasoff*[36] case, which imposed liability upon a university when it failed to protect an off-campus non-student from a dangerous person on campus. Functionally restated, these factors/policies are (we will see these factors in a similar form again in Chapter VI):[37]

(1) the foreseeability of harm/danger;
(2) the seriousness of the harm;
(3) the closeness between the defendant's conduct and the injury produced;
(4) the moral blameworthiness of the defendants' conduct;
(5) the policy of preventing future harm;

---

35. *Baldwin, supra*, 176 Cal. Rptr. at 821.

36. *See* Tarasoff v. Regents of the Univ. of Cal., 551 P.2d 334 (Cal. 1976); Peter F. Lake, *Common Law Duty in Negligence Law: The Recent Consolidation of a Consensus on the Expansion of the Analyses of Duty and the New Conservative Liability Use of Policy Considerations,* 34 SAN DIEGO L. REV. 1503 (1997); *Baldwin, supra* 176 Cal. Rptr. at 816 (stating nearly identical factors).

37. *See Tarasoff*, 551 P.2d at 342.

(6) the burden on and consequences to the defendant and the community should a duty be imposed;

(7) the cost, availability, and prevalence of insurance, if any.

No single policy or factor (or set thereof) is dispositive of duty. All the factors are to be weighed and balanced, if relevant. Most courts agree, however, that when imposing duty, foreseeability is the most important factor. Generally, if the type of harm is foreseeable when a defendant misbehaves (fails to do what the reasonable person would have done), there should be a duty owed to the victim to use reasonable care to prevent that type of harm; but if the type of harm is unforeseeable, strange, or bizarre, a presumption against duty would be appropriate.

The list of social policies and factors is so important and pervasive that courts often speak as if these concerns are dispositive not just of duty but of liability as well. As *Bradshaw* put it:

> The statement that there is or is not a duty begs the essential question, which is whether the plaintiff's interests are entitled to legal protection against the defendant's conduct. "[D]uty' is not sacrosanct in itself, but only an expression of the sum total of those considerations of policy which lead the law to say that a particular plaintiff is entitled to protection.[38]

Although the entire negligence case is permeated with these concerns, one or more of the identified factors and policies have often been used in recent times to justify conservative, liability limiting results by limiting the scope of duty. Tort lawyers and law professors have watched and noted the developments of the law of tort duty, which has evolved in the last fifty or so years (particularly the last 25 years) in the use of policy/factor analyses.[39] This evolution has been particularly prominent in university law cases. Courts are increasingly willing to reexamine rules of decision in light of shifting social concerns. In areas of rapid social evolution — like university culture — the law is apt to change rapidly as well. Thus, university law and negligence/duty law in the university context have changed and should be expected to change. Of course, this is difficult for university officials because to do their jobs they must find ways to anticipate and work with legal change and indeterminacy. Without a sense of the animating policies and principles governing the

---

38. *Bradshaw*, 612 F.2d at 138, *quoting* W. PROSSER, LAW OF TORTS (3d ed. 1964).

39. *See, e.g.*, John M. Adler, *Relying Upon the Reasonableness of Strangers: Some Observations About the Current State of Common Law Affirmative Duties to Aid or Protect Others*, 1991 WIS. L. REV. 867 (1991); Gary T. Schwartz, *The Beginning and the Possible End of the Rise of Modern American Tort Law*, 26 GA. L. REV. 601 (1992).

law, officials can find it hard to navigate. Fear of being "wrong" can be disempowering (but as we discuss in Chapter VI, there are some surprisingly simple ways to work with this legal climate.) The first step for administrators is to recognize the dynamic nature of duty and its underlying concerns. The law of duty works well with images of a facilitator university as it encourages a balanced model of shared responsibility for campus safety.

The second element—breach of duty—is typically a question of fact for a jury or factfinder (a judge may intercede if reasonable jurors cannot differ over a question of fact, such as breach of duty, but this type of judicial intervention is not terribly common and is procedurally discouraged). The central question is this: you have a duty and an applicable standard of care (if you did not, we would not be here)—did you use the amount of care minimally necessary to comply with that duty and standard? For example, we all have a duty to use reasonable care when we drive down the street. Usually we exercise the amount of care that is reasonable under the circumstances—we drive within the speed limit, we keep a lookout, we obey traffic signals, we keep our car in a serviceable and safe condition, etc. Sometimes, however, we do not—for example, when we fail to come to a complete stop at a stop sign. Observe the connection between duty and negligence: just because you have a duty does not mean that you *breached* it. Indeed, most of us, most often, do our duty. Universities often have duties these days, and most often, in our experience at least, universities do what is reasonable and more. It is worth remembering that when someone is hurt, it almost always seems—in retrospect—that more could have been done to prevent the injury, but that is not the question in a negligence case. *Breach* of duty asks the more limited question, "Did you do what was reasonable here?" The law rarely imposes a responsibility to do everything possible to avoid injury. The burden on a defendant to do so would ordinarily be too great (see factor 6). That standard of care would be more like a strict liability standard, and we know of no case which has ever applied true strict liability standards in a situation of student injury.

The third element, causation, is actually two elements in one. Lawyers and judges divide causation questions into two parts—*factual* causation and legal or *proximate* causation. The basic idea behind both types of causation is to link a defendant to a given injury. In some cases the link is painfully obvious (many automobile accidents for example). In other cases it is not at all clear (some environmental pollution injuries to humans, electro-magnetic field radiation cases, for example).

To link someone to an injury, there are two causal steps to take. First, did the breach of duty *actually*, *in fact*, cause the harm? Assume you are exceeding the speed limit in your car (negligent conduct in the sense that a duty is owed to other motorists and pedestrians, and is breached); assume further that a pedestrian crosses against the crosswalk light five blocks away and is struck by another car. She would have been struck even had you been within the speed limit. There is no link, no *actual* causation. But if there is actual causation—say I drop a match at a campsite causing a fire which burns down a house three miles away—we need a second step in causal analysis. We need a relief valve to protect some defendants from some consequences of their conduct. This step is a policy laden analysis called proximate causation.

Lack of proximate causation is what you, the defendant, hope to escape with if you have breached a duty and, in fact, have caused legally compensable damage. It is easy to imagine a system that has no such safety value; after all, if by your fault someone is injured, you should pay, right? In fact, most plaintiffs can successfully show proximate causation in most cases, and defendants are usually out of luck on this liability avoiding element. However, there are occasions when a jury is permitted to exonerate a defendant from liability *even* when that defendant is at fault and in fact caused harm.

A classic example of this is famous (to lawyers) "intervening" cause analysis. Lets say you stop at the Fast-Mart to get gas. You are in a hurry and overfill your tank, spilling gasoline all over the concrete. You are negligent in the sense that you have a duty to fill your tank as a reasonable person would, and a reasonable person who is aware of the various problems with gasoline will take care not to spill large quantities of gasoline on the ground (duty, breach). Now say that another person is having an argument with someone right next to your car. This bad person sees the gasoline trail and chooses a disastrous action—he throws a match into the gasoline with the purpose to cause a fire that will burn the person he is angry with. Now, your negligent conduct has in fact caused an injury. Had you not spilled gas, this dangerous (malicious) fool would not have been able to burn someone this way. But you may be able to avoid liability. You are allowed to argue that the bad person's deliberate action (a civil battery—trust us) is *so* bad that it acts as an intervening cause, cutting off your liability. You argue that it is not foreseeable to you that someone would turn your mistake into an inhumane crime and it is not fair that you should pay for this injury. In this sense, an ordinary person might say that you did not cause the injury. At one time, you won this argument outright because of technical legal rules; today you still have an excellent shot at winning, but you will likely have to do so in front of a jury. Notice how the question would shift if you negligently spilled poison around young school children, and one young child ingested poison thinking it was 'food.' You might try to argue that the child caused his own injury. Best of luck.

Proximate cause is about saying "yes, my carelessness is 'connected to' this injury, but it's not fair to make me pay for this injury." (Brothers and sisters who babysit for younger siblings know this argument well and deploy it when something gets broken if parents are away). These questions are highly fact intensive making it difficult for the law to be fair and consistent, just as it is difficult for parents to decide whom to punish. Courts and juries hearing tort cases are thrust into this very real situation. Fancy legal rules aside, proximate cause is fairly basic yet difficult and intuitive stuff. Indeed Judge Richard Posner, one of the country's leading jurists and most brilliant writers on the subject of tort law, observes that juries are often required to be intuitive when deciding negligence issues.

Rabel, for example, would have presented a different analytic perspective if the judges had allowed the case to go to a jury on the issue of negligence (if the court would have recognized some duty.) Assume (like most courts today would) that a resident student is owed a duty of reasonable protection in her dormitory from dangerous persons and that a university does have the power to modify and even control some fraternity behavior. Nonetheless, the victim in *Rabel* was abducted and assaulted by a fraternity member who used his student status as a way to perpetrate the attack. A jury could find—or might not find—that this type of deliberate intentional attack was so unforeseeable and unstoppable that it would be unfair to hold a university liable for the female student's injuries, particularly in light of how little can be done to stop such a deliberate attack by a "friend." It would almost be like asking a landlord to stop all domestic abuse, which courts are reluctant to do. These are all contentious points of fact/policy, but they are the types of question often reserved for a jury of our peers in American tort litigation. *Rabel* effectively decided a proximate cause issue but did so under duty rules preempting a jury's evaluation of the university's management of its dormitories and its fraternities.

The fourth element—damage—is easiest here because we have been dealing with questions of physical security and safety on campus. American courts typically recognize that physical injury to a student creates some standard legally compensable types of damages. This element is rarely at issue in university tort litigation when a student has been physically injured. Punitive damages—which get the attention of the media—are similarly rarely at issue because a plaintiff must show a very bad state of mind (for example, malicious conduct) on the part of the university to gain such damages. Most often, the claim is that a university was simply negligent, and punitive damages are not appropriate.

Now that we have considered all the essential elements of negligence above, assume that a plaintiff has made out a "prima facie case" — meaning that the plaintiff has pled and proven duty, breach, causation (both types), and damage. Does the plaintiff win?[40] The answer depends upon the remaining aspects of the overall case, the *affirmative defenses.* A defendant (university) faced with a valid *prima facie* case of negligence can defend (and avoid liability or reduce the plaintiff's damages) by pleading and proving so-called affirmative defenses. The most popular of these defenses come in two basic flavors—that plaintiffs did not use reasonable care for their own safety ("contributory negligence") and/or the plaintiff voluntarily proceeded in the face of a known danger effectively demonstrating that the plaintiff was willing to accept the responsibility for any injury caused by the risk ("assumption of risk"). Each of those defenses seeks an evaluation of the plaintiff's (student's) own conduct to the extent that it may have contributed to the plaintiff's (student's) injury. These defenses are based on notions of shared responsibility—that is, that the student has a responsibility to exercise reasonable care for her/his own safety under the circumstances, even where the university has been negligent.

Most states once treated these defenses as virtually absolute defenses (one major reason why there was not much tort litigation years ago was because so few plaintiffs are blameless in situations where they are injured). This meant that if you sued someone but, for example, were yourself derelict in taking care for your own safety in the incident in question, you recovered nothing because you were not blameless. These harsh, all or nothing (mostly nothing), rules have changed.

Today, American courts follow rules of "comparative fault." These rules vary a bit from state to state but usually permit a faulty plaintiff to weigh in against a faulty defendant in front of a jury. The jury is asked to decide whether, for example, a plaintiff is 20% at fault and a defendant 80% at fault. In the old days that plaintiff got nothing: any plaintiff fault barred recovery completely. Today that plaintiff recovers 80% of the total injury claim. What is compared is, in essence, the strength of the *prima facie* case versus the strength of the affirmative defenses. Although this is an oversimplified account, this is in fact what happens in most actual cases. The most technical and controversial questions are left for law school classrooms, unusually situated litigants, and the media. But, most of the time, comparative fault is easy to administer, at least in terms of what the law requires.[41]

---

40. The question of whether a plaintiff who wins gets paid (and by whom) is a more complex problem. In university law, however, where universities are usually defendants with insurance, the answers are easier because plaintiffs generally recover their damage awards.

41. Consider how *Beach* might have gone differently. In *Beach*, the biology field trip case, assume that the professor/university had a duty to use reasonable care in the plan-

Almost all of this *prima facie*/affirmative defense/comparative fault complexity can be avoided if a court simply says "no duty is owed." No duty means no liability. Otherwise, to establish liability a plaintiff must prove a *prima facie* case and avoid affirmative defenses. Pseudo- formulaically, negligence law looks something like this:

Prima Facie Case

$$L \ = \ D \ + \ B \ + \ C \ + \ D \ + \ \overline{AD}$$

| (Liability for loss) | (Duty) | (Breach) | (Causation) | (Damage) | (No Affirmative Defenses or offset for affirmative defenses in comparative fault) |

Duty is the trump card in the liability equation, and it is easy to see why courts can fall into the trap of equating "duty" with "liability." A determination of duty does not entail liability *per se*, but it almost certainly invites further litigation and often gives a case a "settlement-value." As a practical matter, a plaintiff who establishes duty typically has a case with what we call "settlement value": a defendant knows that some further litigation will occur and that there is always at least a statistical chance that the plaintiff will recover. There is also the nuisance value of further litigation. So a duty determination does have, practically, some monetary implications. It is against this legal backdrop that *Bradshaw, Baldwin, Beach,* and *Rabel* cast the new images of the modern university. No-duty rules protect against litigation and reduce monetary settlements with injured students.

The bystander courts chose not to see the university as a place of ordinary duty—ordinary risks and responsibility—but rather as unusual places where no duty or only special duty (or duty under special circumstances), if any, was owed. This decision to treat the university as nonordinary was fraught with technical/conceptual legal problems which these courts typically avoided by not adverting to them. The lay university community and the public were, in general, in no position to assess the technical legal problems with these cases. These cases came to stand for the more understandable idea that a university had no affirmative duty to protect its students from student-created injuries (particularly

---

ning and general supervision of the field trips and that the professor breached this duty when he openly allowed the students to drink with him in the van and when he operated the van after he had been drinking. The injured student could recover, but her recovery would be significantly reduced to the extent that her own conduct was careless (a shared responsibility for careless conduct by both parties).

those involving alcohol). Colloquial understandings of case law are particularly powerful when case law is highly technical.

To find a way to protect universities from liability and litigation, these cases were very creative. These four famous cases linked their no duty results to one of the last vestiges of no-duty rules in America[42] — no duty to rescue a stranger rules. On its face, this is a rather odd and technical choice of images. In the area of rescue law, American courts continue to say that there is typically no general non-statutory duty to rescue or to protect someone, unless you have a "special" relationship with that person.[43] That is, absent a special relationship, a person cannot be liable for his failure to act (the law calls this "nonfeasance") but only for his affirmative conduct/acts that place another person in a position of peril. For the most part, strangers are those people who are not legally special. Yet even some people with whom we are intimate are not legally special. Special relationships are defined in the law and are quite limited.

Practically speaking, you do have what amounts to a special relationship, however, if in your affirmative conduct you injure someone or if you significantly start to rescue someone and botch it. In these situations you owe basically the ordinary duty (to exercise reasonable care whenever you act affirmatively and your act will present unreasonable risk to another person if you fail to exercise due care.) So what the law appears to say is that you can watch someone else's child drown with legal im-

---

42. At one time, many years ago, no-duty rules were very evident in the common law. In fact they were so common that it was hard to sue anyone in many cases of otherwise negligently caused injury. For example, there was generally no duty to protect a worker at a workplace. For the most part there was no duty to protect a family member, little duty to a guest passenger in a car, no duty to protect the purchaser or victim of a product unless you sold it to them (and even then there were ways to escape liability), and no duty to act affirmatively for the benefit of a stranger. Governments and charities were only occasionally responsible for harm caused. The twentieth century has seen the steady erosion of these rules. *See* Joseph W. Little, *Erosion of No-Duty Negligence Rules in England, the United States, and Common Law Commonwealth Nations,* 20 Hous. L. Rev. 959 (1983). In fact, there has been an overwhelming trend to simplify the law of torts around the ordinary duty concept. *See* Gary T. Schwartz, *The Beginning and the Possible End of the Rise of Modern American Tort Law,* 26 Ga. L. Rev. 601, 701 (1992). *See also* Peter F. Lake, *Revisiting Tarasoff,* 58 Alb. L. Rev. 97 (1994).

However, one particular strain of no-duty rules has remained resistant to modern trends — no duty to rescue rules. *See* Peter F. Lake, *Recognizing the Importance to the Duty to Rescue,* 46 DePaul L. Rev. 315, 316 & n.1 (1997) (see citations in note 1). There is considerable reason to believe that what courts say about rescue law is based upon faulty historical reasoning, bootstrapping of caselaw, and academic politics, but that is another matter. *See id.*

43. *See* Lake, *supra,* 46 DePaul L. Rev. at 316.

punity unless you throw the child in the pool, or start to help but quit, or have some special relationship with that child (or the child's parent for the protection of the child).[44] Don't cause harm, don't get involved, don't worry, be a bystander (unless there is a special relationship)—these are the messages of many bystander cases, a last bastion of no-duty rules. University cases went to this last holdout of a bygone legal era, an era in which duty was unusual.

Bradshaw, Baldwin, Beach and *Rabel* saw the university as just such a non-acting bystander who would have a duty to students *only* if a special relationship existed. Each court saw special relations as being only accepted by the slowly developing common law—examples today are (1) employer/employee, (2) parent/child, (3) custodians (as in a sanitarium or jail) or (4) those who have charge and control of a dangerous person, with respect to those endangered by the dangerous person, and (5) some landowners/some entrants on land. The courts recognize other relationships, but there is little consistency and the cases are still few in number. The only potentially applicable special relationship according to the bystander courts was (3), custodial control.

Indeed, *Bradshaw, Baldwin, Beach* and *Rabel* focused upon the custodial control special relationships. In light of newly won student freedom, however, the deck was stacked against student injury claims. Each of these cases determined that students were beyond university control for purposes of establishing a special relationship because students were not in the *custodial* control of the university. As odd as it might seem, these courts analogized universities to non-acting bystanders and students to strangers in peril—and then held that universities lacked sufficient control to protect students from injury. Students became a class of people who needed rescue, but no one was responsible to save them except themselves or possibly outsiders to the college. Why did this reasoning (policy) prevail?

The answer lies in the fact that duties to rescue are thought of as *affirmative* duties, to which special rules apply (negative duties are duties to refrain from injuring people by your actions, activities, and conduct). The underlying idea is that it is burdensome and difficult to ask someone to affirmatively act for the benefit of others, so limits on duty are necessary. The essence of the immediate post *in loco parentis* cases was that university law was analogous to rescue law. This rather unusual analogy was augmented by assuming that the only way to create duty was by having custodial control over a person, even though there are recognized special relationships that do not require "custody." These courts chose a

---

44. Needless to say, some modern courts have refused to follow this logic and have questioned these kinds of results.

strange image and then took an extreme view of how such rules might create responsibility for a college.

Beach, the near fatal field trip case, for example, set the legal argument up precisely in these terms.

First, *Beach* focused on the essential element of duty: "One essential element of a negligence action is a duty of reasonable care owed to the plaintiff by defendant. Absent a showing of a duty, Beach could not recover."[45]

Second, *Beach* cast the university's role in terms of *affirmative* duty by observing:

> Here, Beach contends that Cuellar [the field trip professor] and the University breached their affirmative duty to supervise and protect her. Ordinarily, a party does not have an affirmative duty to care for another. Absent unusual circumstances which justify imposing such an affirmative responsibility, 'one has no duty to look after the safety of another who has become voluntarily intoxicated and thus limited his ability to protect himself.' The law imposes upon one party an affirmative duty to act only when certain special relationships exist between the parties. These relationships generally arise when one assumes responsibility for another's safety or deprives another of his or her normal opportunities for self-protection. The essence of a special relationship is dependence by one party upon the other or mutual dependence between the parties.[46]

Beach put the question of duty to students in terms of no-duty/special duty.

Third, *Beach* characterized the university/student relationship as *non-custodial*. Students were now "adults" over whom it would be "unrealistic" and improper to assert custodial duties. As the court stated:

> Beach argues that a special relationship, arising out of the state statute prohibiting alcohol consumption by minors and the University's corollary rule, should be deemed to exist for a number of policy reasons. At bottom, however, Beach simply claims that a large, modern university has a custodial relationship with its adult students and that this relationship imposes upon it the duty to prevent students from violating liquor control laws whenever those students are involved directly or indirectly in a University activity. We cannot agree . . . [c]olleges and universities are educational institutions, not custodial.[47]

It were as if to control and protect students, a university would have to imprison them, employ them under strict supervision, treat them like

---

45. *Beach, supra*, 726 P.2d at 415 (citations omitted).
46. *Beach*, 726 P.2d at 415-16 (citations omitted).
47. *Id.* at 417-18, 419.

parents would treat very young children, or treat them like special guests at the Victorian Inn.[48] *Beach* saw no gray area, no middle ground, no subtlety regarding control—students thus became legal strangers on campus. Other social phenomena may have been simultaneously at work but this legal paradigm most certainly contributed directly to the distancing of the student/university relationships of the kind that leading commentators like Ernest Boyer and Gary Pavela have described.

Bradshaw, Baldwin, and *Rabel* echoed nearly identical sentiments. *Bradshaw*, the seminal case, sought to protect the college's "interest in the nature of its relationship with its *adult* students, as well as an interest in avoiding responsibilities that it is incapable of performing."[49] Viewing the university as a (helpless) bystander, *Bradshaw* specifically invoked the no duty to rescue/special duty rules:

> Bradshaw has concentrated on the school regulation imposing sanctions on the use of alcohol by students. The regulation states: "Possession or consumption of alcohol or malt beverages on the property of the College or at any College sponsored or related affair off campus will result in disciplinary action. The same rule will apply to every student regardless of age. App. at 726a-727a. We are not impressed that this regulation, in and of itself, is sufficient to place the college in a *custodial relationship* with its students for purposes of imposing a duty of protection in this case....
>
> A college regulation that essentially tracks a state law and prohibits conduct that to students under twenty-one is already prohibited by state law does not, in our view, indicate that the college voluntarily assumed a *custodial relationship* with its students....
>
> . . .
>
> The centerpiece of Bradshaw's argument is that beer drinking by underage college students, in itself, creates the special relationship on which to predicate liability and, furthermore, that the college has both the opportunity and the means of exercising control over beer drinking by students at an off campus gathering.
>
> . . .
>
> [Given the realities of beer drinking by college students], we think it would be placing an *impossible* burden on the college to impose a duty in this case."[50]

---

48. *See id.* at 415 n.2. The notion that a professor simply has a duty to provide reasonable supervision and guidance for freshman students on a field trip, was ignored. Taken to its extreme, *Beach's* logic would allow a university to send twenty students on a field trip abroad, with no supervision. But of course, the *Beach* court might argue its no duty holding was limited to situations in which students consume alcohol.

49. *Bradshaw, supra,* 612 F.2d at 318 (emphasis added).

50. *Bradshaw,* 612 F.2d at 141, 142.

Bradshaw said that beer drinking by college students was a way of life, (and, implicitly, excessive drinking is a fact of that life), that the university is powerless to stop it, and that there is no legal duty to do anything about it. Under *Bradshaw* there is no special relationship between the university and the student. The college regulates drinking but in effect has no legal responsibility to intervene, even when it knows or should know of likely danger to students. In a bystander universe, a university may literally look the other way or even facilitate conduct that creates risks of injury without creating any liability. *Bradshaw* believed and ruled that the causes of tweenage drinking—and its tacit ratification by government and society—run far too deep for colleges.

Likewise, *Baldwin* specifically determined that university liability raises questions of "nonfeasance rather than misfeasance."[51] This is a technical legal way of saying that the duty question is one of no duty/special duty varieties. *Baldwin* required a special, custodial relationship as a precondition to legal liability for "nonfeasance." Even in the context of alcohol rules and regulated dormitory living arrangements, *Baldwin* said that there was no such relationship between students and the college.

Rabel followed that logic and concluded:

> "[w]e do not believe that the university, by its handbook, regulations, or policies voluntarily assumed or placed itself in a custodial relationship with its students, for purposes of imposing a duty to protect its students from the injury occasioned here. The university's responsibility to its students, as an institution of higher education, is to properly educate them. It would be *unrealistic* to impose upon a university the additional role of custodian over its adult students and to charge it with the responsibility for assuring their safety and the safety of others. Imposing such a duty of protection would place the university in the position of an *insurer* of the safety of the students."[52]

Rabel, like the other three prominent bystander cases, believed that it would be unrealistic to ask the now disempowered university to exercise the control necessary to protect student safety. According to *Rabel*, if a duty were imposed, the university could never meet the standard of care required of it and would always be in breach despite its best lawful efforts. Hence a university would be like an insurer of student safety, rather than a typical reasonable person who would be liable only when conduct in a given situation fell below the minimum level of care expected under the circumstances.

---

51. *Baldwin, supra,* 176 Cal. Rptr. at 812.
52. *Rabel, supra,* 514 N.E.2d 560-61 (emphasis added).

Bradshaw, Baldwin, Beach, and *Rabel* turned the cultural/political image of a helpless university into legal doctrine. These courts determined in effect that universities were not active participants in student life but were passive bystanders/observers. To win cases—to establish university responsibility for conditions causing student harm—students would have to show a special relationship arising from custodial control. For these courts, being a student subject to rules and regulations was not special enough. There was even the suggestion that being in dormitories and participating in school sponsored events (dangerous, even irresponsible events and activities) was not special. The only relationships that would be sufficiently "special" would be those based on *custodial* control. But according to these cases, all control—especially *custodial* control— was lost for legal liability purposes when *in loco parentis* died.

The looming political/cultural questions became these: Now that the university was not legally responsible for the negative consequences of campus life, who or what would fill the void? Would universities benevolently continue with measures designed to protect students? Would parents and students demand safety in the marketplace and create Volvo-universities (and Corvairs)? Would students, like true revolutionaries, create their own regulations and government? How far apart would the law push students and universities? To some extent, the answers to these questions were delayed and the key court decisions featured some obtuse rhetoric. Large numbers of students and parents still anticipated safe, sanctuary-like higher education: we have not seen a single college brochure or promotional document of this era which even alluded to the radical shift in law augured in these four cases.

The four central cases were, in the end, overtly driven by image and policy. But there was another side to these cases and to the bystander era. Both in technical legal terms and in political effect, the cases contained within them flaws, oversimplifications, and problems that began to manifest even during the heyday of the bystander university (the early 1970s to early/mid-1980s). After all, a university was in many respects like other businesses that courts dealt with all the time. Crosscurrents of responsibility appeared in the caselaw at the same time the bystander college was born.

. . .

At the time the fall of insularity was under way, the outside community increasingly began to spill onto campus and *vice versa*. The larger community was sometimes endangered by college activities and sometimes the outside community endangered the college. Courts saw that student "life" claims—when a student was injured or was injured by another student— were fundamentally different from problems among community and students. In addition, as the insular university died, the *business* university began to be born. Courts began to ask: Why should universities be treated unlike other businesses? Rescue law and bystander images had brought new protections into play, but the rise of business safety paradigms in law made colleges seem more like activities on the mainland.

Moreover, the no duty to rescue/special duty approach to university student relations had to confront at least three technical problems in legal doctrine. First, most businesses are in "special" relations at most times with their business customers on business premises. This means, *inter alia,* that most businesses have a duty to protect customers from unreasonable risks, even when customers, acting negligently, contribute to their own injury. (There are some cases where people walk into traffic barriers in parking lots or try to climb on boxes to get something off a top shelf in a store and are injured: courts almost unanimously agree that these people must be assisted when injured, and that reasonable steps must be taken to protect against such injury. The law now regards it as too draconian and immoral—in most cases—to "punish" an injured person who needs assistance.[53] Generally, the law has a strong preference for mitigating reasonably avoidable further damage, regardless of fault.) Universities own property and buildings and invite students (and the public in many cases) to do educational business. The business invitor has a legally special relationship to the business invitee. Did the non-insularized university become like a business now and therefore owe its students reasonable protection as business invitees of the university?

The second legal problem was closely related to the first. Beginning in the 1960's and 1970's, American law radically redefined the relationship between landlord and tenant. Most of the focus early on was on slum lords and slum tenants. Later, the rules spread to most all residential style tenancies. The old common law idea was that the tenant was in a *caveat emptor* (let the buyer/tenant beware) situation: if you lease an apartment with rats, lead paint, and broken pipes, bargain for a better

---

53. Judicial antipathy to college students who drink and are injured was reflected in a recent case in Illinois where a young college drinker landed injured on a train platform and required assistance. The Illinois court treated the student like a trespasser and held that there was no duty to rescue a trespasser who injuries were from off-premise conditions or activities. *See* Rhodes v. Illinois Cent. Gulf R.R., 665 N.E.2d 1260 (Ill. 1996). The rule in that case, although very narrow, is still out of step with what most courts have said. The case is very fact driven. The student had been on a dangerous drinking escapade off campus and then the student did receive some care from trained personnel. Only when the student got to the hospital, did anyone discover the severity of the head injury. By then it was too late. It would have been better to view the case in "no breach" terms.

place to live in on the free market, or put up with it. That longstanding common law attitude died hard in this period, as landlords became legally responsible for the basic habitability of an apartment and became responsible to exercise reasonable care for the safety of tenants and even guests of tenants. In fact, American courts began to recognize that dangerous conditions in a slum house could cause injury to innocent third parties *off* premises. They reacted by imposing duties on landlords to protect against some such harm—gunshots from known tenant/drug dealers killing innocent third parties and such. This was an area where no duty shifted into duty because of a new special relationship, brought on by shifting social policy.

This shift was highly significant. One feature of much of modern university life has been the often common university desire to have at least some students live on campus, near campus, in university housing, or in fraternities. Some community and technical colleges aside, American campuses are not just educational places, they are also living arrangements for most students.[54] The university legally became a *landlord* with a very unusual, and often unusually large, client base. Were universities legally responsible to fix broken locks, make premises reasonably safe, keep dangerous people out, and protect the public from dangerous students? Was the non-insularized university a *landlord* for legal purposes now?

Third, to trigger rescue law—the law of affirmative duty—courts require that the claim be for *non*feasance rather than *mis*feasance. Most tort and negligence cases involve *mis*feasance, and the issue is so obvious that it is never discussed or argued. In a few cases it is an issue. The basic intuitive idea is simple, but the application (which is which?) is often extremely difficult in the unusual cases which raise the issue. Nonfeasance involves the mere failure to act for someone's benefit; *mis*feasance involves an action you take causing harm.

Simple? I'm on vacation at a lakefront resort and a stranger's child falls in the lake. I could help at no risk to myself. My human instincts tell me to help this child, but I do nothing. I make the news as the moral monster who did nothing. I get sued. I win. I win because my failure to act is *non*feasance, and there is generally no duty to others for nonfeasance unless there is a special relationship between them. Just being fellow humans and my being in a position to save a child at no risk to myself is not legally special.

The flip side is this: If I drive my car at 80 miles an hour into you "by accident," my action is *mis*feasance. I *drove* (an action or activity) into you. Action requires that I exercise at least reasonable care for your safety. I have a duty, whether or not I have a special relationship with

---

54. This is the very model of the Jeffersonian university. Many colleges still require students to live on campus as much for economic reasons as educational ones.

you. This duty is owed to everyone (or at least foreseeable anyones). It is easy to see why characterizing someone as a mere bystander is so important; it lowers that person's legal responsibility for harm. Bystanders are innocent until proven special.

Obviously, it is not always this simple. Suppose I am driving along at the speed limit and merely neglect to apply the brakes. *Non*feasance or *mis*feasance? The courts always say misfeasance. They postulate that although you omitted to put on the brakes, you did so in the overall context of the driving activity. Drawing the line between action and inaction can be tricky. Such line drawing has been controversial, and legal scholars admit that when a court in a tough case characterizes the behavior of a defendant as either nonfeasance or misfeasance, the characterization is really just a conclusion—based on underlying policy considerations—that sets up either a no duty or duty result with consequent liability implications. In other words, the distinction begs the question—is a duty owed and why, or why not? Some courts have abandoned that ancient analysis entirely and simply address the policy questions involved in tough cases straightforwardly.

The tricky central argument of the four prominent cases of the immediate post *in loco parentis* era was that, if the university did anything wrong at all, the omission was only nonfeasance—a failure to act, like the failure of a bystander to rescue a stranger's child in distress. However, to other courts, the modern university now carried on activities with impact on and off campus. And, fundamentally, some student injury cases looked (and look now) more and more like the "no foot on the brake pedal" situation. Universities effectively attract and house large groups of people; sponsor events and field trips; often *require* students to live on campus and participate in off-campus activities; and plan, regulate and administer most aspects of student life. Universities literally co-create an environment for students and control almost all of the major strategic questions—how and how many to house, where to house, types of housing, what activities to promote, prohibit, etc. It is not exactly Disney World, where litter never hits the ground and the parade always runs, but neither is the university an entirely accidental or unplanned congregation. Somewhere between sparse rural exurbia and theme park lie universities and small cities. Is university life an *activity*—a *community*? Or is it a *condition*—a passive backdrop to the activities of students? Are there times when a university is a bystander but other times when it is not? Is a university community always an activity or condition but never both, or constantly alternating?

The bystander image raised three fundamental legal problems—is the college a business, a landlord, and/or an activity? These internal legal/doctrinal problems were present even in the heyday of the no duty university and manifested in cases of that period as crosscurrent case law imposing legal responsibility. The insulation of the no-duty rules of the bystander era was thus far less comprehensive than the protections of previous eras in university law.

These legal problems were also associated with a major political/moral issue. American courts may say that a mere bystander has no legal duty to assist a stranger, but it is interesting that these same courts typically say that there is a *moral* duty to help others in distress. Cases finding no liability are therefore pyrrhic victories for any entity with a public reputation. The courts say, you win, but we condemn you. It is quite a highwire act to win the legal no-duty-to-rescue issue *and* win the political/moral issue. (It's like the insanity defense. I am not guilty—but I'm insane). You are struck with either admitting that you *should* (morally) have done more or admitting that you were totally helpless, incompetent, or incapable. A university could argue that in a given case there was nothing reasonable to do or that it was too far away to help, but these are technically breach and causation, not no-duty arguments. When you play the no-duty-to-rescue card, you admit to being wrong and/or you admit, in effect, to *global* helplessness in a situation. *Situational* helpless, far more defensible morally, is not usually a duty argument.

Of course, a modern university does not want to admit to being a moral monster, nor would it be good for business to put messages of incapacity in catalogs and promotional material. Universities know that parents and most students usually expect that the university community will be reasonably or fairly safe, and many parents still believe that they send their children off to an especially safe place. So how did a university find the high road?

The undercurrent of the cases in the moral/political dimension was that college aged drinking (including underage drinking) was not so "unusual or heinous," as *Baldwin* put it, to cry out for some special response from the college. Even if it were, the power to stop it had withered according to the *Bradshaw* and *Baldwin* courts. Even more fundamentally, there was a sense of *quid pro quo*: universities gave the students the rights to do the very things they now wanted the university to protect them from when they got injured. *Bradshaw, Baldwin, Beach* and *Rabel* each very explicitly yielded the moral high ground to the university. Universities were not to blame, *students* were. Universities were not disempowered; they had used their power to grant civil rights. *Baldwin*, for example, went so far as to state that California colleges had been "in the forefront of extension of student rights." Somehow, institutions that resisted the civil rights cases were now to be *praised* for foresight and largesse. Courts found the hard to find high road by blaming students and by reinterpreting the history of student protests for basic and constitutionally fair treatment into some imagined student movement for rights to license and abusive drinking or into an imagined period in which universities graciously provided broad liberties.

Even granting this moral/political high road to the universities did not forestall some burgeoning problems. First, students had won their constitutional rights, but did this mean that the outside community was entitled to less protection? A case arising because a woman is killed by a known dangerous student (*Tarasoff* case) could not be pegged with either rationale. If campuses were incubating libertarian excess and license, the greater community was at risk.

Second, was there an essential zero sum link between the civil rights won by students and rights to safe campuses? The Beastie Boys sing of fighting for your right to party, yet the civil rights cases were about freedom from summary dismissal, freedom of speech, freedom to protest, racial equality, etc. The cases were not about rights to use drugs and alcohol but involved due process and equal protection type issues.[55] There was an unspoken assumption in the principal bystander cases that long-haired hippie freaks who wanted rights also invariably wanted to smoke pot and drink with underage girls, engage in drag races, etc. This type of assumption would come to be tested and found to be inaccurate as too broad brush.

Yet recent developments have shown how powerful images in court decisions can be. In 1998, students literally did riot for the right to party and have underaged drinking fests. Over time, a sense of entitlement has been fostered that has led otherwise bright young people to argue for absurd things and take ridiculous and indefensible positions (some college students literally have written in college newspapers to justify aggressive protests over "beer rights"). Legal images are very influential, and it is vitally important to choose appropriate images, particularly with students who are in formative developmental stages.

---

55. This rationale is an insult to the students who pursued some of the civil rights era's most famous cases. In *Dixon,* students were involved in efforts to desegregate places of public accommodation and demonstrated to protest institutionalized Southern racism. In cases like *Scheuer v. Rhodes,* 416 U.S. 232 (1974), the families of students shot and killed by the Ohio National Guard successfully established in the United States Supreme Court that a state government cannot shoot student protesters whose views are in conflict with views of the state or their university when they present no threat of deadly force to others. *Scheuer v. Rhodes,* defends the very essence of free speech and assembly. The events of May 4, 1970 at Kent State are at the cutting edge of the First Amendment and continue to be remembered as a watershed period of First Amendment law. Cases involving free speech, association, assembly, and press are often brought by those who share views unpopular with mainstream opinion. These cases remind us of John Stuart Mill's urging that we must protect the marketplace of ideas so that "unpopular" ideas may take their place in the path to truth.

Third, there was some serious revisionist history going on in the period. Some universities suddenly became champions of many rights other universities fought so hard to stop. In the civil rights era, abuses of *in loco parentis* authority were so bad that students were forced to litigate or quit their college education.[56] The rights given were often won over the objections of many colleges and were not motivated to create lawless campuses with unsafe levels of disorder.

And fourth, *so what?* Even if students won civil rights and diminished the powers of universities (which they did), does the university have any less of a responsibility to operate a reasonably safe and protective learning environment? Are campus safety and the reduction of student drinking generally related to the academic program? Some schools went so far as to take the reactive message of *Bradshaw, et al.* to mean that they owed no duty to minimize the risk that a female resident student would be attacked in her dorm room by a criminal intruder. No one can seriously contend that increased security—which can prevent criminal intrusion and worse—diminishes the overall academic mission or unduly intrudes upon some rights of a "free" student. To the contrary, it has become more and more obvious that marginal dollars spent on more security and safety improve the overall *educational* mission of a school.

To the extent that there was a "you got what you deserve" attitude by universities after the civil rights cases, new generations hit campuses and asked whether the issue was fairness or the efficiency and effectiveness of the overall program. And they asked why they should be pegged with the perceived belligerence and turbulence of another generation. The current generation of student both parties and is a victim of the party: modern students inherited a system they did not create through revolutionary action. As to that group "turnabout is fair play" has less meaning. Intergenerational dumping and treating post- boomers as lazy, drinking slackers (an image contradicted by most students but enhanced by the riotous few of recent times) has helped to keep the intergenerational problems somewhat at bay. And as attitutes towards modern generations of students change, such arguments will lose force.

The first manifestations of these legal and political/moral questions were seen in cases decided contemporaneously with *Bradshaw, Baldwin, Beach,* and *Rabel.* Certain crosscurrent cases were very much a part of the bystander period, even though they did not become the dominant images of that era. For reasons involving the politics of university law, the four bystander cases (and some other similar cases) became perceived as

---

56. One of the authors has a friend and colleague who was disciplined by his university for suggesting, in the early 1960's, that it admit black students.

majority cases; the other (crosscurrent) cases were viewed as minority, wrong, and anomalous cases.

. . .

A digression on the politics of university caselaw is in order. How could certain cases become the perceived majority in the face of obvious crosscurrents?

Colleges and universities typically spend most of their energy on fairly predicable and repeating legal questions. They usually have their own lawyers, who work in house (and out) principally for the university client. University lawyers have national organizations and several journals and publications just for them. They are a practice group with reliable institutional clients. On the other hand, student cases involving physical injury are usually handled by personal injury attorneys who may see just one university case in a lifetime. Most students never need a lawyer; the few who do are usually one time clients. Perhaps there should be an organized group of student-rights-to-physical-safety lawyers, and perhaps there should be institutional clients (like student (labor) unions?) to argue their rights. But for the most part there are not. Students and their lawyers approach the law usually as individuals and with individuated claims. In contrast, universities and their lawyers often approach the law collectively and institutionally. A given lawsuit may have long term policy implications for a college. How the law is made and then promoted has a great deal to do with this.

A concrete example may be offered using the *Beach case*. At oral argument, legal counsel for the injured student conceded a major point that not all students' lawyers would concede in other cases. The lawyer "conceded that the mere relationship of *student to teacher* was not enough" to establish a "special" relationship for duty.[57] Why would a lawyer concede this? Sometimes lawyers concede arguments at oral argument because they feel that tactically it is in the best interests of that client. If a panel of judges seems unsympathetic to a case, it may be best to abandon certain arguments even if a lawyer thinks the arguments are right. A lawyer is not charged, as such, with making good law or making good arguments for good law; lawyers' primary duties are to their clients. A given student's lawyer must make the argument that will win for her client, even if every student afterwards will lose. A lawyer does not represent student group rights by representing a given student. It is a little unfair, then, for a court to make law for other students through concessions of specific lawyers for non-institutional student clients.

---

57. *See Beach, supra* 726 P.2d at 416.

On the other side, a university lawyer represents an ongoing institution (with very similar interests to other universities). A given case might be one where today's losing argument is tomorrow's winner, or *vice versa*. The university lawyer takes the long look because she must evaluate *all* of her client's interests and all cases a client will be involved in—not just this one case. A university lawyer should be careful not to concede points that might be important in future or other cases (possibly in front of other judges). The university legal counsel's job requires a more long term strategy.

This fact has one very important corollary—the cases which get litigated and reported. University lawyers can look at a number of cases and choose to settle some—or all—of them. Almost invariably, they will settle a bad case with bad facts and any case which can make bad or dangerous precedent. Lawyers representing injured students do not have to settle, but often a settlement offer in hand is better than a jury trial and/or lengthy appeals. The plaintiff's lawyer does not have much incentive in most cases "to make law or precedent": in fact, a plaintiff's lawyer caught using a client and injuring his client's rights in trying to make precedent (perhaps hoping to get other clients) could be disciplined professionally. Again, client interests dominate, and one-time individual clients have different interests than long term institutional clients.

In a perfect world, every appellate decision (and that is principally how we assess what the law of student safety is) would be a university winner. Because of this, hand-selected university winners—the cases to fight and win in final appeal—would be the only reported cases. But university lawyers sometimes have incentives to fight cases they ultimately lose in the appellate process. This is often a result of a deliberate test of where the margin is in the courts: how far can I push for rules protecting my client's interest until the courts back off? Other times there is a bit of miscalculation that occurs.

So when you read caselaw in the university field, you will likely see a highly select group of cases, and most should be university winners. These cases were more likely selected to be the appellate cases for their precedential value by university attorneys rather than by any student attorneys attempting to change a system of law. There are many cases settled that never see much, if any, light of day (some unfavorable appellate decisions are actually erased by terms of settlements, which is an overt manipulation of how the law appears). From the university point of view, a settlement makes the case go away; a lost motion to dismiss can produce judicial rhetoric you will live with for a long time, or have to pay extra to settle.

Once these selective cases are decided, they are then discussed among university lawyers. Their clients can see the cases but need help with judicial rationales and with "what does this mean to me" questions. Here lies the danger of some inbreeding and insularity. University law has the risk of being what university lawyers say it is. We do not suggest that university lawyers purposefully give their clients less then the complete picture of the law. Not at all. But there is a tendency to become so convinced of your client's interests that it can color your perception at the margin.

There is no judicial review of what the clients hear from their attorneys, except for the next case. And because university lawyers are so good at what they do, losing cases are rare and come along very slowly. The cycle builds and can suffer—like stock market corrections—major and unexpected shocks. On the subject of student safety, these shocks came in some of the crosscurrent cases. Over time, the perceived "minority" jurisdiction cases became the dominant trends in college law. The crosscurrents were there all along and were ultimately more representative of the future of higher education student safety law.

. . .

In several crosscurrent cases, decided contemporaneously with the bystander cases, courts held that universities had duties to:

- Protect students (especially resident students) from foreseeable criminal intrusions by dangerous people in the community. Students residing in campus housing were owed the basic rights of tenants to a reasonably secure and safe place to live;
- Treat students and some non-students like business invitees and to use reasonable care in premises construction and maintenance. Universities had duties similar to businessmen towards their customers or business visitors;
- Use reasonable care in planning and executing student activities, like field trips. Reasonable care did not mean all possible care, and students were expected to use care for their own safety and acknowledge and accept certain risks;
- Protect off campus non-students who were foreseeably endangered by dangerous activities/dangerous persons on campus. On the rare occasions when campus danger spilled over into the community at large, the university became responsible to use reasonable care for the safety of foreseeably endangered individuals.

These cases appeared to run counter to the no-duty position of the four famous bystander cases. They were seen as a return to *in loco parentis*.[58] This mistaken perception was fueled by the legal political dynam-

---

58. *See* James J. Szablewicz and Annette Gibbs, *College's Increasing Exposure to Liability: The New In Loco Parentis*, 16 J. L. & EDUC. 453 (1987); Perry Zirkel and Henry

ics of university law. The perception that these cases signaled a return to *in loco parentis* was wrong.[59] All of the cases of the bystander period had more in common than was perceived. American courts had taken their first steps into the world of duty paradigms to describe student/university relations. The bystander era was an era of caution, backlash to student rights, and concerns over the perceived helplessness of modern universities in the face of student alcohol use; it was also an era in which the university shouldered important new legal responsibilities. The paradox of the caselaw was that it reflected a general flow in one new direction towards duty analysis. Even as *Bradshaw, Baldwin, Beach* and *Rabel* were decided, other courts were exploring the problems with their reasoning when applied in other contexts.

The most famous crosscurrent case of the period which acknowledged the rights of students to safe campus housing was the 1983 decision of the Massachusetts Supreme Court in *Mullins v. Pine Manor College,*[60] although it was not the first case to so hold.[61] In *Mullins,* a female student was attacked on campus by a non- student assailant. The college was located in a highly populated area in greater Boston. *Mullins* determined that a resident student, for purposes of living arrangements, is in a sufficient special relationship with the college to create duty under special circumstances. Under *Mullins,* a college must use reasonable care to prevent foreseeable criminal attacks on campus.

Mullins held that a duty to protect the resident students existed because:

- Customarily, the college provides for campus security, especially for resident students;
- Pine Manor college featured a high concentration of young people—especially young women—creating a risk in that this is a favorable target for criminal activity (especially sexually related criminal conduct);
- A college is in a better position to take steps to minimize these risks to students than the students themselves; Students

---

F. Reichner, *Is the In Loco Parentis Doctrine Dead?*, 15 J.L. & EDUC. 271 (1986); Brian Jackson, *The Lingering Legacy of In Loco Parentis: An Historical Survey and Proposal For Reform*, 44 VAND. L. REV. 1135 (1991).

59. *See* Theodore C. Stamatakos, *The Doctrine of In Loco Parentis, Tort Liability and the Student-College Relationship*, 65 IND. L.J. 471, 472 (1990).

60. 449 N.E.2d 331 (Mass. 1983).

61. *See* Duarte v. State, 148 Cal. Rptr. 804 *vacated*, 151 Cal. Rptr. 727 (Cal. Ct. App. 1979) (unofficial published opinion) (1978). After *Mullins,* most courts followed the *Mullins* rule or have had distinguishable facts. *See* Bickel and Lake, *supra* 20 J. C. & U.L. at 281-82 & n.82 (see citations in note 82 in particular).

can only do so much to institute personal security measures in residence halls;

- The college retains the authority to determine most security measures, not students;
- The college undertakes, in return for fees and rent, an array of services. When one provides a service (activity/acting: duty), the service must be performed with reasonable care;
- Students who rely upon the fact that the college provides security are lulled into a sense that security is provided and this may work to their detriment in that they will relax their vigilance.

Mullins, although frequently misunderstood, made two other points perfectly plain. First, this responsibility was *not* parental, derived from or *in loco parentis*. No one says that landlords must act *in loco parentis* for tenants. *Mullins* treated resident students in the same general way as the law treats ordinary tenants. What the college asked for in *Mullins* was a standard of care for tenants' safety that would have been *less* than that owed *by slum lords to slum tenants*. The court gave parity, not parenting.

Second, *Mullins* made it crystal clear that student rights were not won at the expense of student safety. In its own (and famous) words the *Mullins* court said:

> [c]hange in college life, reflected in the general decline of the theory that the college stands *in loco parentis* to its students, arguably cuts against this view. The fact that the college need not police the morals of its resident students ... *does not entitle it to abandon any effort to ensure their physical safety.* Parents, students, and the general community still have a *reasonable* expectation, *fostered in part by the colleges themselves,* that reasonable care will be exercised to protect resident students from foreseeable harm.[62]

The *Mullins* Court correctly observed that college responsibility for safety in student housing did not rise or fall with *in loco parentis*. The rise of landlord/tenant responsibility was more directly related to the fall of governmental and charitable immunities. In particular, a college has a duty to protect students—using *reasonable, not all possible* care—from foreseeable criminal and dangerous conduct which might come into campus from the community. If an attack like the one in *Mullins* were unforeseeable, or could not be prevented with reasonable precautions and security, the university was not liable: there *is* a duty, it just does not extend to unforeseeable problems (risks). Moreover, a duty has not been breached if reasonable care has been used.

---

62. *Mullins, supra,* 449 N.E.2d at 335-36 (emphasis added) (footnote omitted).

In addition to landlord/tenant responsibility, a university would have a duty to students and others who come to campus with legitimate university business or related interests (employees, visitors, etc). This duty was a duty arising from the special relationship considered to exist between these entrants as invitees and the landowner/premises-operator/ university. Even *Bradshaw* and *Beach* acknowledged that a business invitee — one who comes to a landowner's premises for some business or commercial purpose — is entitled to reasonable care because a special relationship exists.

Again, the standard of care owed to such persons, including students, is reasonable care — not all possible care. In addition to fixing broken stairs, etc., this includes using reasonable care to protect against assaults and room invasions, *if and to the extent reasonably possible.* Many attacks will occur that are unforseeble or not reasonably preventable: if an intruder wants to get at a student badly enough, they probably can penetrate even very good security systems. But some simple and reasonable steps can be taken to prevent and protect students. Fixing broken locks, better lighting, and security patrols are common solutions to the problem of preventing criminal intrusion, and the law should encourage them.

Even during the heyday of the bystander era, courts were thus willing to say that a duty existed to keep safe premises (other than just residential premises for resident students and guests), and that a university would have to maintain reasonably safe grounds (like walkways) for students and others coming to campus with business to conduct.[63] These duties were duties owed by any *business* to its customers, etc. Courts were quick to see the analogy between students who pay to attend a college and business invitees in other commercial contexts. As we will see in the next chapter, these cases have multiplied, in spite of some attempts by colleges to avoid business-like responsibility.

During the bystander era, only *Rabel* really challenged the *Mullins* rule in square and precise legal terms on the issues of premises safety. Functionally, the other three major cases were off-premises injury cases. The attack in *Rabel* occurred on premises against a student. *Rabel* rejected a landlord/tenant duty (now, *Rabel* is a clear minority position on this point) but never addressed the (obvious to lawyers) issue of the status of the student as a business invitee. A recent case in Illinois has pointed out this flaw (and it is such an obvious flaw that a person taking the bar exam would be marked off for missing it) in *Rabel*.[64] Technically,

---

63. *See* Isaacson v. Husson College, 332 A.2d 757 (Me. 1975); Shannon v. Washington Univ., 575 S.W.2d 235 (Mo. Ct. App. 1975).

64. *See Leonardi v. Bradley Univ.*, 625 N.E.2d 431, 434 (Ill. App. Ct. 1993). The *Leonardi* court found no premises duty because the sexual assault occurred in a non-

the plaintiff did not argue the point in *Rabel,* but appellate courts are usually free to consider issues not raised by counsel, and in a case of this importance the omission is significant. It is particularly significant given that today most courts *would* consider the issue *and* find a duty, and that many courts of even that period did so. Judicial myopia often indicates an intense focus on something else. In spite of *Rabel,* American courts have generally not provided universities with opportunities to perpetuate sub-standard living or other business facilities. Moreover, courts do not see this parity with business as akin to parental responsibility. Even today parents do not have such tort duties. Businesses do.

In addition to landlord/tenant and business premises liability, issues of liability for student activities arose in the bystander era. *Beach* and *Bradshaw* are student *activity* cases and involve non-residential, off-premises injury. In each instance the university facilitated the activities. *Beach* was a class field trip planned and supervised by a professor; *Bradshaw* was an off-campus class picnic which was aided by college officials signing checks and permitting use of university facilities.

Bradshaw and *Beach* were (and are still) touted by university lawyers as determining that universities do not have custody over students in the vast majority of university sponsored/facilitated events and *therefore* have no duty to protect students from harm at all. Yet, the university in each of these cases was hardly a helpless stranger/bystander. Perhaps the universities did enough (perhaps not), but it is undeniable that they did *some* things. Legally then, *Beach* and *Bradshaw* are a stretch when viewed through a nonfeasance lens. These courts cast the role of the university as that of a non-acting, passive bystander such that the matter was one of no duty or special duty. Yet typically when a defendant acts, or plans an activity, or in some way facilitates a situation by positive actions, the defendant must answer—like a driver who fails to apply the brakes—to a claim of misfeasance which means that a duty is owed to act with reasonable care. To qualify for the limited liability provisions of being a true bystander, one must ordinarily convince a court of his passivity and unconnectedness to the incident and people in question. This is so because no-duty-to-rescue rules are special protections for unusual circumstances and are usually reserved for true strangers.

Viewed in a traditional light, the most disturbing legal/doctrinal aspect of *Bradshaw* and *Beach* was that both cases assumed away obvious problems with viewing universities as passive strangers to students. In so

---

university owned premises—a fraternity house. The court intimated strongly that the result would have been different if the attack were in a dormitory or on a walkway owned by the university. The Court also pointed out that the weight of out-of-state authority now went in favor of premises duties to students.

doing, these courts made a subtle but very profound legal mistake. *Beach* and *Bradshaw* assumed that students were beyond all university control—at least with respect to drinking—and therefore felt there was no duty. *Beach* and *Bradshaw* held that duty requires a finding of custody, and that since there was no custody, there was therefore no duty. Superficially, that makes sense, but if you make that argument on almost any bar exam, you will fail because it is dead wrong, even if subtly so. Duty is also owed when someone acts, carries on an action, etc. This is misfeasance, and only *nonfeasance* qualifies for no duty, subject to custodial, power, and control exceptions. Misfeasance does not raise legal issues of "control": only some nonfeasance issues raise problems of control and only a subset of cases require *custodial* control. Moreover, if there is no way to exercise duty reasonably—if there is nothing to do that will work, no way to control if so required—you have a legal duty but you are not legally *liable* because you did not *breach* a duty. Courts require you to exercise only that level of control that you actually have (if they emphasize control at all). There are legally significant forms of control that count for duty that are far short of custodial control. These types of control are ones that universities often do exercise, such as control over field trips and residence security.[65]

Were the judges in *Bradshaw* and *Beach* unaware that custodial control is only rarely necessary for affirmative duty? Probably not. The rationale they chose generated results they favored. No duty means no jury, no hearings, no further litigation—other rationales might require more hearings, discovery, and even jury trials. These courts adopted a no-duty rationale as a way to circumvent litigation, a path typically encouraged by defendants/universities/university attorneys who desire to obtain judgement quickly, efficiently, inexpensively, and without a jury evaluation of the university's conduct. However, the fall of traditional tort immunities forced these courts into this tortured logic in order to protect the college or university from tort exposure. It may be surprising and disturbing to laypersons, but even in university cases the rules of tort law do sometimes bend—like light around strong gravitational fields—when university concerns are imagined by a court to be unique and relevant to the issue of liability. Obviously, these two courts in particular (and *Rabel* for a different reason) felt very strongly that there should be no legal liability as a matter of law. They felt that universities should still enjoy a type of *immunity* from lawsuits, at least when injury occurred to

---

65. *Bradshaw* and *Beach* also suggest that "duty" is strict liability and used "insurer/babysitter" images to reinforce that idea. But that is also flatly false and a basic bar exam point. No case has ever seriously contended that universities owed more than reasonable care regarding student safety.

a student who had become voluntarily intoxicated or had been harmed because of another student's intoxication. The results may or may not have been proper in those cases, but the rationales were demonstrably flawed.

At the same time, however, that these courts (mis) characterized university facilitated activities as *student* activities to which the university was a passive bystander, other courts began to view university facilitated student activities/student injury litigation through more accurate (if still complex) lenses. The wrong legal/doctrinal answers of *Bradshaw* and *Beach* were nonetheless relatively easy to state and had a superficial intuitive appeal. The correct legal way to handle legal responsibility for university facilitated student activities is more legally/doctrinally complex, and would not be settled in the bystander era. But it was disputed.

The leading case to see university facilitated student activities/injury cases through a different lens was *Mintz v. State of New York*,[66] a 1975 New York appellate court decision and one of the earliest crosscurrent cases. That case involved the periphery of university facilitated activity injury cases as it involved an extra-curricular, overnight canoe trip on (dangerous and unpredictable) Lake George in New York State.

Early one May, a time of very cold lake water and changeable weather, a group of students set out on Lake George, as part of an "overnighter" sponsored by an intercollegiate outing club. A bad storm blew in and students were drowned in the lake. Because the intercollegiate outing club had a university charter, the university became a defendant. Nothing in the *Mintz* decision suggests (or even seems concerned) that the university did more than *encourage*, indirectly, the activity as an extracurricular activity. There was no hint of university custody and only very limited control. There was little to no university supervision, as such, of the particular outing in question. *Mintz* featured far less college involvement than the academic field trip situation in *Beach*.

The *Mintz* court dismissed the case against the university, but for very different reasons than *Bradshaw, et al. Mintz* determined that "all reasonable and necessary precautions were taken to guarantee a safe outing."[67] The court noted that the club had conducted outings for ten years without significant incident and had taken many precautions on this particular occasion. Among other precautions, there was a motor boat escort, and there were veteran canoers on the trip. Canoes were equipped with lights and experienced canoers were given the more responsible posts. The accident occurred in pre-Weather Channel 1966: the weather

---

66. 362 N.Y.S. 2d 619 (N.Y. App. Div. 1975).
67. *Id*. at 621.

forecast did not foretell of anything dangerous to come. And *Mintz* emphasized that the students were not babies in need of close supervision (as would be the case *in loco parentis*). Under these circumstances, *Mintz* ruled that the unforseen weather—not the university—was the "proximate cause" of deaths.[68]

Mintz did *not* say there was no duty, or that a duty arose only under special circumstances. Even with the tenuous thread of control over such activities, *Mintz* acknowledged duty, but emphasized facts which showed there was no *breach* of duty that would be the legal cause of harm. Simply put, the university avoided liability because it exercised reasonable care in its involvement in the trip. The university did not avoid liability because it assumed a no-duty posture relative to safety precautions, but because it acted responsibly in attempting to make the trip as safe as possible. *Mintz* is distinctly modern in its analysis and uses accurate tort analysis. The result in *Mintz* is also correct from a policy standpoint and in keeping with the responsibility a good university would feel in encouraging field trips/outings by professors and students or student organizations.

In essence *Mintz* said: "Yes, you have a duty to use reasonable care towards students in extra curricular activities. But you *did what was reasonable here* (and perhaps more) and you could not have foreseen this ferocious and unusual (unpredictable) storm. Sometimes accidents just happen, and this is that case." *Mintz* is a classic example of the fact that duty alone does not create strict liability, nor insurance, nor a responsibility to babysit students. Legal liability is a complex of several variables. Duty is just one variable. Duty is not *in loco parentis*. It is possible to have shared legal responsibility and not be liable legally.

Why did *Beach,* another field trip case with far more supervision than *Mintz,* not do this type of analysis— the ultimate result was the same? The answer is that some courts are reluctant to rule as a matter of law (meaning no jury) that there is no proximate cause or breach of duty (negligence) present. *Mintz* is unusual in that courts sometimes say that a totally unforeseeable sudden storm is an "unforeseeable intervening cause," cutting off liability. This is basically a particular rule of causation that law students learn and memorize. It is a legal idiom (and one that may be waning in light of modern weather forecasting for many storms, but that is another matter). So *Mintz* represents the unusual case where there is no proximate cause because the *judge*, not the jury, says so. In any event, the reasoning in *Mintz* is correct otherwise. A university should avoid liability for student injury on a field trip/outing facilitated by the university not because it has no duty to plan reasonably for the safe conduct of the trip but

---

68. *Id.* at 620-21.

because it in fact takes reasonable precautions. No-duty paradigms *encourage carelessness, distancing,* or *inattention* by administrators and invite injury.

At one time there was another legal no-liability "idiom" that was far more important to student/activity injury cases than the *Mintz* weather rule. It related to alcohol. Not long ago, American courts held that a voluntarily or negligently intoxicated individual was the sole proximate cause of harm caused to self and others. The rule appeared in cases involving liquor served in a bar to persons who drove off and killed or injured others or themselves. Because the individual drinker was considered the *sole* proximate (or sole legal) cause of injury, the bar, bartender, etc., were *not* "legal" or "proximate" causal agents and were thus not liable. Non-drinkers were not liable. However, courts who said bars and bartenders were not liable were meticulously careful not to say there was no duty; instead they thought in terms of the lack of legal or proximate causation (like *Mintz*). In essence, the drinker was the worst actor, not the bar owner or bartender. Courts were not praising bad bartenders who overserved drunken drivers, just exonerating them.

These rules have faded, and it is now common to impose liability on bars and bartenders who overserve adults or who serve minors. Yet, alcohol-caused deaths and injuries occur in so many ways. Not all liquor injury problems come out of bars. When liquor is purchased outside a bar (say at a convenience store) or consumed privately, courts have been more hesitant to impose liability upon such vendors or "social" servers. For instance, so-called "social hosts"—private cocktail party hosts for example—have traditionally escaped liability. Once upon a time, the same proximate cause rule protected them as well as professional bartenders and commercial bars. But when the proximate cause rule died, even social hosts were potentially vulnerable to liability.

Most courts filled the gap immediately with no-duty rules for social hosts for social policy reasons. Professional and commercial vendors of liquor for on premises consumption—bars and restaurants—were subject to duty regarding liquor serving, but virtually everyone else had no duty (there were some important exceptions, the biggest one of which was giving someone who was visibly drunk a dangerous item like a car). The law had moved from a *no-liability*-for-liquor-related injury rule (except for the drinker), based on no *proximate cause as matter of law,* to a new paradigm: Duty for certain commercial vendors, *proximate cause questions for the jury regarding these vendors* (example: I overserved you at noon, and you killed someone in an accident at 11:00 p.m.), but *no duty,* therefore *no liability,* for most others. Courts chose the duty/no-duty paradigm because it offered them the opportunity to select which cases would be subject to litigation (discovery, trial, appeal, etc.) and which would not.

Instinctively, *Beach* reacted to the student's injury in that case as an *alcohol related* injury in a non-commercial, non-bar/bartender setting. Thirty years earlier, the case would have been dismissed properly under proximate cause rules in most jurisdictions because the voluntarily intoxicated student would have been the sole proximate cause of her injury as a matter of law. To the extent that her complaint was that she was permitted to drink in a way that caused unreasonable danger, she would have been part of a much greater class of injured individuals who could only look to the drinker for legal redress. Since in that case *she* was the drinker, she would have had nowhere to turn. Because in the era of duty/no-duty for liquor related injury the once all powerful proximate causation argument was no longer available, *Beach* did what most courts in that period did. Anyone other than commercial vendors for on-premises consumption—bars and bartenders—was not subject to legal liability (no duty) for liquor related injuries if they served a drunk, knew someone was drinking, or even facilitated or promoted drinking activities. Wine with dinner, a private cocktail party, an office party with beer, a fraternity party, and even a university sponsored event with liquor (*Bradshaw*) were treated in the social host category (no duty) as contrasted with the bar/bartender category. Hence, *Beach* thought in terms of duty to the student. The legal result would have been the same decades earlier, but using a different rationale.

Indeed the point—a critical one for understanding the entire bystander era and its paradoxes—that should not be lost is that *Bradshaw, Baldwin, Beach* and *Rabel* were *all* liquor related injury cases where injury did not come from commercial bars and bartenders. To the extent that they reflect no-liability results for non bars/bartenders, the bystander cases are unremarkable cases of their period as liquor injury cases. These cases were on the periphery of the more common social host cases—football party with beer; drunk friend drives off and kills another motorist—and these courts chose the no-duty approach, although they did not overtly connect these cases to specific liquor duty/no-duty rules as such. Instinct led these courts to no-duty results—after all the courts had said no duty in almost every factually similar case. Yet it is instructive that these courts chose legal doctrinal *rationales* (the end of *in loco parentis*, the birth of student freedom, *etc.*) which were very *atypical* of social host cases. The courts focused more on lack of custodial control than on protecting social hosts. As liquor cases, even in the bystander era, these cases saw something unique about the student/university relationship and university life. Even these courts were not willing to *justify* college-aged liquor culture but were (like courts in the proximate cause era) willing to exonerate colleges from liability for special reasons. Like species on the Galapagos islands, university cases—particularly university liquor cases — took on a *sui generis* life. Only a trained eye could detect the distant genealogical connections and the special adaptations to a unique environment. *Bradshaw, Baldwin, Beach* and *Rabel* signaled the continued unique legal treatment of university life and its risks, even if the uniqueness was still in its infancy. These cases were a prominent stage in the development of the basic theme in university law in the 20th Century — the special application of general tort and liability rules to university culture.[69]

Some final points about liquor liability and social host no-duty rules. In most cases raising the question(s) of liquor related injury which occurred as a result of conduct *other than* that involving bars and bartenders, courts have often made two critical observations. First, in some cases liquor liability is imposed on bars/bartenders by *statute*. To the extent that the legislature(s) had chosen not to extend liquor liability to other parties, a kind of immunity existed by legislative inaction as to those parties. Second, social hosts (really most entities other than bars and bartenders) had no duty because of policy reasons and social forces which outweighed the policies in favor of imposing liability. In essence, courts deliberately provided an immunity for social hosts.

Immunity is subtly different from no duty in that it connotes that a *protection* is afforded for policy reasons, even though the actor is engaging in otherwise unreasonable conduct. No one praises someone who knowingly serves a drunken friend another beer with full knowledge that he will soon drive home. It is not what a reasonable, prudent person would do. When the law says that host has no duty to the innocent mother who is injured in the subsequent car wreck, that is not a court's way of condoning or praising the host's behavior. It is only saying that private drinking is so pervasive, so hard to regulate, etc., that it would be inappropriate to assess liability on a private person who does not ordinarily insure for that type of risk. Rightly or wrongly, that is *all* that courts are saying when they protect social drinking.

In the 'bystander' era, then, when a student activity became "wet" in some way, courts were likely to side with a university, as they would with other social hosts, even as they in essence saw colleges as special social hosts. But when the situation was "dry," the courts began to acknowledge duty and the circumstances under which a university could be liable. While *Bradshaw* and *Beach* (liquor cases) talked about the loss of

---

69. The approach that these courts took set the stage for recent legal developments that question "lack of control" arguments in student drinking cases. By casting the legal line in terms of "no-control" as opposed to "social host" as such, the bystander cases have made it much easier to challenge modern university efforts regarding student drinking.

custody and control, *Mintz* spoke of duty owed and how it can be satisfied. The paradox of these cases (and all of the cases of the era) was rooted in alcohol tort law and the not so easy task of flushing out the new legal relationships of student and university. Courts took it a case at a time and instinctively and typically found no duty in alcohol cases and duty in others. University personnel and students were forced to try to make sense of this.

In *Bradshaw* and *Baldwin* the courts reached issues of student alcohol related injury occurring in vehicular mishaps *off* campus. It would have been fascinating to hear these courts on another troubling issue: who would have won if an innocent non-student were injured in the community by student activities which carried over into the community? Suppose a pregnant mother driving to a supermarket had been struck and seriously injured by the drag racers in *Baldwin*? To what extent would a university be liable for injury occurring off campus to non-students if the university in some way facilitated danger on campus? Most likely in that era, courts would have deployed social host type reasoning. Today, however, social mores and the law of alcohol responsibility are shifting.

Such cases are thankfully still quite rare. Students are usually the victims or victimize themselves or other students. But as college drinking takes to the streets, we can only expect more such injuries. For example, when unruly students riot in the streets for beer parties, innocent citizens may be hurt and their property destroyed. Or, as college students move drinking off campus, we can expect a rise in driving accidents. Again social host or other no-duty rules may protect universities in these cases (as proximate cause rules did in another era).

There are other ways in which danger spills into the community. By far, the leading case to address the unusual problems of dangers which carry off campus was a case involving predatory sexual assault/murder — *Tarasoff v. Board of Regents of the University of California.*[70] The University of California, like other modern multi-service universities, offered psychiatric counseling on premises. In *Tarasoff*, a man in outpatient counseling with a psychotherapist confided his intention to kill a specific named woman. The threat was deemed highly credible and the psychotherapist alerted campus police. Campus police detained the man, but were told by the psychotherapist's supervisor to let him go on his way. No one called the woman to warn her that a danger was headed her way. The man killed the woman in cold blood. Until 1976, that would have been the end of the story legally (at least in term of civil liability).

---

70. 551 P.2d 334 (Cal. 1976) (*en banc*).

We have taken so many steps (and more are needed) to protect women from dangerous lovers and husbands, stalkers and predators, that it is hard to think back three decades when terms like "battered woman syndrome," "sexual predator," "stalker," *etc.* were not in common use. Prior to 1976 (yes, 1976) a patient could walk into a psychiatrist's office, outline a murder plan of a specific person set to happen in an hour, and even if the psychiatrist believed in all good professional judgment that the danger was real and present, the psychiatrist could legally sit by and watch the murder go down. This was considered nonfeasance—and the psychiatrist could be said to be a mere bystander. The lunacy of the then majority (nay, unanimous) rule that no duty was owed to anyone other than the psychiatrist's patient was changed forever and rapidly by the decision in *Tarasoff. Tarasoff,* in one form or other, since has become a majority rule imposing some responsibility on psychologists (and others) to use some care for certain endangered persons.

At root, *Tarasoff* (and later cases) said[71] that, in some instances, a university psychotherapist would owe a duty to an *off-campus, non-student* who became endangered from forces/individuals on campus. To oversimplify a bit, if you know who the victim is and she is not aware of the danger, you must warn her of the danger, if reasonable professional judgment would say that she is at risk. The university fought this duty all the way to the California Supreme Court. That court unanimously ruled against the university.

In the heart of the bystander era, an important seed was planted. If the university facilitates or knows of a manifest danger to an *off-campus non-student*, the university must calculate the possibility that courts will ask them to respond for harm caused or use reasonable care to protect off-campus interests. Universities increasingly were (and are) integrating their activities with those of the larger community. With this closer connection came new responsibilities. As we shall see in the next chapter, these responsibilities have developed in new dimensions.

The bystander era, then, was a complex and paradoxical post-insularity and post-*in loco parentis* period. The perception was common that universities were relieved of most if not all duties to protect student safety. But the cases defied that simplistic model. Strong no duty, bystander rhetoric—fueled by social movements on and off campus, the loss of confidence in law enforcement powers, and the resurgence of al-

---

71. The precise parameters of *Tarasoff* and its implications for psychotherapeutic practice are complex and there is considerable debate about the margins of responsibility. *See* Peter F. Lake, *Revisiting Tarasoff,* 58 ALB. L. REV. 97 (1994); Estates of Morgan v. Fairfield Family Counseling Ctr., 673 N.E.2d 1311 (Ohio 1997); Fraser v. U.S., 674 A.2d 811 (Conn. 1996).

cohol culture—were most prominent in cases involving liquor related injuries to students or by students. Yet equally powerful crosscurrents were at work: cases in which the university was held responsible to its tenants, to its business "customers" (invitees), for the activities it supported, and even to the community with respect to certain dangers exported off campus. It was a stage in the development of duty law: the idea of duty had been suppressed in the *insularity* era, but slowly rose in the bystander era.

This bystander era was a transitional era, however. The no-liability case law was rife with hard rhetoric and strained rationales. There was a vision of newly emancipated students who were now free to harm each other and be harmed: the vision was cold and left the university in a helpless role. Moreover, that vision was supported in some cases by legal reasoning with inherent flaws. The pro-liability cases were politically marginalized by the politics of university law. With some exceptions, even these crosscurrent cases were lacking in overall vision. Although *Mullins* discussed the duties of a university landlord, even that case did little to offer a significant comprehensive post- *in loco parentis* vision of university/student relationships.

Tarasoff, Mintz and other cases were written without much attention to the fact that they were *university* cases (*Mintz* is commonly cited in non-university cases; *Tarasoff* applies to psychotherapy generally, and only a small fraction of cases like *Tarasoff* come from university situations.) The bystander image—defective and contradicted—was the only significant legal image of its era. The duty era in university law was forming but had no appropriate legal image to support it.

The central question still remained then: "What is the nature of the student/university relationship?" The answers of the bystander period were incomplete, or in some cases, inappropriate. It was now settled that the student/college relationship was *not in loco parentis* (although some persist in incorrectly reading the crosscurrent cases of the bystander era as such). The bystander era settled that university/student relations would now be cast in terms of duty or no duty. Perhaps the university was best conceived of as a helpless bystander with no duty. Yet as compelling as that may have seemed in alcohol injury cases, it was hard to believe that image when the issue was fixing broken locks on lobby doors, sweeping sidewalks, getting a weather report before taking students on an icy lake, or turning your back on the off-campus victim of a deranged student. The truth is that sometimes the university did just stand by, but at other times it was a co-participant in an association of complex shared responsibilities. Bystander images could not suffice to replace the demise of *in loco parentis* and the fall of insularity. Such images could not do justice to the safety of modern college life in totality. What could?

V

Student/University Relationship(s) at the Turn of the Millennium— The Duty Era

The period since the early to mid 1980s has seen the fairly steady erosion of no-duty-to-student bystander case law and the rise of successful student litigation regarding physical safety on campus. Most courts still remain reluctant to impose liability on colleges in alcohol-related cases and will often limit student claims arising from obvious dangers. The recent case law is not obviously united in some apparently simple theoretical paradigm like *in loco parentis* or a bystander image; overtones of business law and some vestiges of the bystander era continue to inhabit the imaginations of judges. However, commentators have almost uniformly observed that a shift has occurred, even if they disagree on just what that shift is and what it will imply for the future. It is a time of transition. Concerned that university law is retrograding, several commentators continue to see recent developments in university law as a (feared or misguided) "return to *in loco parentis*." In fact, what has been occurring is the steady consolidation of the duty era in university law. Courts today enforce business-like responsibilities and rights while preserving some uniqueness in college affairs. Judges are increasingly willing to apply traditional negligence and duty rules to university life and activities and are increasingly less willing to view the university as subject to traditional insularity rules. Nonetheless, courts remain sensitive to the unique roles and circumstances that characterize the American college experience. There are strong indications that the image emerging from the process is one in which a university owes duties to students and students owe duties to protect themselves. The rules that will be applied will recognize that the university is a unique, if sometimes business-like, environment where *special* applications of more general negligence and duty rules are needed. The new image is one of *shared* responsibility and a balancing of university authority and student freedom. Duty is the vehicle which courts use to make this happen.

The commentators in well known secondary legal literature tell a surprisingly similar story of the recent trends in university law regarding physical safety of students. There are three major points of agreement:[1]

(1) *In loco parentis* was once the key paradigm for university law but is dead, should be dead, and should not "return";
(2) University legal responsibility for student injury is limited but is on the rise (as are claims). The period of the 1970s—early 1980s where the university retained significant legal protection is waning;
(3) Recent case law is difficult to understand, and needs a theoretical model—an image (other than *in loco parentis*)—to assist and comprehend developments in the law.

For the most part, the commentators disagree only on interpretations of certain historical cases and doctrinal applications and, significantly, on what the new legal vision is or is becoming. Despite significant disagreement on some points, though, the commentators all identify these three basic features of university law. Importantly, the commentators continue to call upon the courts to replace the vacuum left by the demise of *in loco parentis* with an appropriate new image. To the lament of the commentators, no single case is the *Bradshaw* or *Beach* of this generation. The current era is interstitial and transitional.

As we shall examine, there are subtle reasons (rooted in developing university duty rules), for the delay of the courts in the creation of a new image. Courts confront the law of student/university relations on a situational basis—one case at a time—and are demonstrably influenced by two counter-balancing notions. On the one hand, courts in the current duty era can see direct analogies between cases involving student injuries

---

1. As Zirkel and Reichner stated in 1986: "the college context is the only one in which the *in loco parentis* theory has undergone a clear rise and complete demise in our courts." Zirkel & Reichner, *Is the In Loco Parentis Doctrine Dead,* [Yes], 15 J.L. & EDUC. 271, 282 (1986). *See also* Szablewicz and Gibbs, *Colleges' Increasing Exposure to Liability: The New In Loco Parentis,* 16 J. L. & EDUC. 453 (1987). In the wake of the death of *in loco parentis* came cases like *Bradshaw*. Snow & Thro, Spaziano, and Hirshberg, *inter alia,* have argued that the current retreat from cases like *Bradshaw* brings a feared return of *in loco parentis*. *See* Brian Snow & William Thro, *Redefining the Contours of University Liability: The Potential Implications of* Nero v. Kansas State University, 90 EDUC. LAW. REP. 989 (1994); Jennifer L. Spaziano, *It's All Fun and Games Until Someone Loses An Eye: An Analysis of University Liability For Actions of Student Organizations,* 22 PEPP. L. REV. 213 (1994); Philip M. Hirshberg, *The College's Emerging Duty to Supervise Students: In Loco Parentis in the 1990s,* 46 WASH. U. J. URB. & COMTEMP. L. 189 (1994). The above commentators identify the complexity/confusion of recent case law and invoke images that could fill the void. *See* Stamatakos, *supra*; Jackson, *supra*.

and cases involving business responsibility, professional and amateur sports, and, in some instances, municipal liability for certain governmental operations. On the other hand, courts have always viewed the university as a unique environment which deserves some protection from rules which, while appropriate for some entities/activities, are not always strictly appropriate for universities. The university is not a government, nor is it a typical business (*e.g.,* manufacturer). The university has a special social mission. Finding the special application of general negligence and duty rules for the university context is a socratic process that requires back and forth dynamics and balancing. That process also requires the careful consideration of the policies and factors which should govern the unique college experience. Duty is an organic concept and needs to be carefully fitted: it is ill suited to fast, off the rack, solutions.

Ultimately, the value of a given court decision lies in the guidance it gives. But socratic dialogue-style patterns of cases—like Plato's famous dialogues—have a propensity to give imprecise practical messages. Concretely, for instance, an administration must decide through counsel whether *Bradshaw* or some other more recent contra-*Bradshaw* case applies: what do the apparent, if not real, inconsistences in the cases mean here, for this college in this situation? "Trends" in the law are hard enough to discern and work with (however untrue, the perception was that *in loco parentis* provided clear and predictable rules of decision and hence guidelines for university and student conduct), but this is especially so when there is a genuine lack of determinable overall vision. University officials and students are asked to step back from the brush strokes and be Monet, even when there is no real assurance that there is a painting at all. So the current situation may be a transitory phase of case law evolution, but it is one of the most difficult times ever in the history of university law for administrators. For good or bad, university law today on the subject of student safety and security is not simple.

. . .

In developing the law of rights and responsibilities of universities and students with regard to safety and security on campus, the courts have seized upon certain duty/special duty doctrines to deal with particular campus safety issues. The basic "strategy" (the courts do not openly collaborate, but training and experience guide them collectively down often predictable paths) is to relate a particular type of claim to particular duty rules and to solve problems posed by the "claim" within those parameters. Courts use divide and conquer tactics.

To understand the tactics, it is helpful to see the categories into which courts sort claims because they are not intuitive but are based upon specific historical/doctrinal developments in the law of duty. Courts typically break the questions presented into functional categories like these:

(1) Premises/landlord responsibility with respect to conditions on premises (like broken locks);
(2) Responsibility to control dangerous persons on campus and/or prevent harm caused by them;
(3) Responsibility regarding student activities (like chemistry lab, sports, field trips, etc.);
(4) Responsibility for student alcohol use and abuse.

These categories are *not exclusive*: a court might have to address a matter involving (2) a dangerous male student who was able to gain entry to a female dormitory (1) because a broken lock had not been repaired.

Moreover, the categories are not exactly sorted in the ways that a typical campus administrator might encounter or solve campus problems. Thus, a dangerous student on campus might be a student disciplinary panel problem *and* a dormitory assignment/safety problem, etc. Nonetheless, the law insists on *its* divisions, not those practically demanded for use by college officials (this is another reason why an overall vision is necessary: college officials have difficulty arranging legal doctrinal icons so as to quick-sort their problems and issues).

Critically, these legal categories do not reflect any sort of return to *in loco parentis* by the courts. No court discussing university and student duties states that current rules are parental responsibility based; indeed, courts often explicitly bend over backwards to state that current rules are *not in loco parentis* based. Moreover, the argument that courts are secretly or unwittingly returning to *in loco parentis* is specious. As we saw in Chapter II, were we to return to the era of *in loco parentis*—the era of insularity—the results courts reach would not be babysitting or parental liability results, but would rather be results which would tend to insulate the university environment from legal liability by the application of traditional immunities. Family based tort immunities—the essence of *in loco parentis*—were historically used to protect the university from lawsuits regarding discipline, regulation, and punishment of students. The irony of much of the bystander era case law was that in many ways it perpetuated (if reconfigured) a key feature of the era in which *in loco parentis* flourished—university immunity and insularity from legal scrutiny. The case law that drifts away from the no-duty rules of the insularity era is not a return to *in loco parentis*. It is a profound retreat from the era in which that doctrine flourished. The current phase of the duty era—lacking in a simple vision like that of *in loco parentis*—is susceptible to oversimplified attribution.

The reality, not especially dramatic, is that in each of the above areas university law regarding student and university duties and rights reflects the process of mainstreaming university law and tailoring general duty criteria to the specific and unique university context. Again, somewhat ironically, the roots of the duty era could be detected faintly even during the period of *in loco parentis* in the handful of cases applying charitable and governmental immunities to universities. The seedlings for current case law were the duty-based bystander era cases themselves. Bystander era cases replaced the immunity rules of the era of insularity with no-duty rules. Those cases made duty prominent in its negation; crosscurrent cases used duty more directly to impose legal responsibility. Today, the university community is governed as a duty community, with a complex allocation of rights and responsibilities. This allocation neither immunizes universities generally nor provides students with opportunities to foist their own unreasonable conduct or deliberate risks upon universities. The duty era is a *shared* responsibility era and in that regard does mark a departure from the major periods which preceded it. The prior eras have favored all-or-nothing style approaches in which only a student or a college, or no one, was *the* legally responsible party. The duty era is about a balancing of university control/authority with student freedom/rights and shared responsibility.

We now turn to a review of how the duty era is functioning in the various legal/doctrinal categories upon which courts rely.

Premises/Landlord Responsibility

As we have seen, a landowner has a duty to use reasonable care in the operation and maintenance of his premises for the protection of so called "invitees." Such a relationship is legally special. Universities are landowners, operating classroom, library, and office buildings, walkways, athletic and recreational facilities, parking facilities, cafeterias and bookstores, etc. Some questions are tricky, such as the university's responsibilities for premises like fraternity houses (many courts would say that a fraternity-owned house is not a part of university premises), but in the large, most of the buildings and grounds pictured in college catalogs are university premises. Students are invitees almost without exception as are employees of the college, and typically so are others who come as guests to the college's premises to participate in college functions. The roots of such premises responsibility first dimly appeared in the era of insularity, but premises responsibility substantially developed in the 'bystander' era and then solidified in the current 'duty' era.

Landlords, as special premises owners, owe similar maintenance responsibilities to their tenants, a sub-class of invitees; students in university—owned residential facilities are treated much like other tenants. The landlord/tenant relationship is also legally special and therefore imposes certain affirmative duties defined by common law or statute.

Among university attorneys the most well-known and often-cited university non-tenancy premises case is *Poulin v. Colby College,*[2] which was decided in 1979 in the heyday of the bystander era (as such, another crosscurrent case).

In *Poulin*, a man was injured when he slipped and fell on an icy hill at Colby College. To determine what responsibility was owed to the person on college premises, the court had to determine the man's "status" vis-a-vis the College. He had come to the college's premises to escort a college-employed maid to the dormitory in which she worked: he was not a student, nor an employee, but just a regular guy helping a college employee in icy New England conditions. Nonetheless, he was considered by the court to be like an invitee (note that the college did not actually invite him onto the premises) because in helping an employee of the College to get to her place of work safely, he had conferred a benefit on the university. The College therefore owed a duty to make its premises reasonably safe for him (and also to the uninjured maid, who as an employee was also an invitee).

It might seem odd that a leading university premises liability case is a *non-student* case. *Poulin* involved someone who was, for non-legal purposes, almost a stranger to campus (he was not a prohibited stranger or a "squee-gee man"; had he been, the matter would be different)[3]. *Poulins's* significance lies in where the margin is drawn. If the injured *non-student* in *Poulin* were entitled to reasonable care, then a person coming with a more palpable economic benefit to a college campus would clearly be entitled to reasonable care. For almost all purposes, students and their guests (like mom and dad) are invitees and thus owed reasonable care in premises maintenance and design. Cases solidifying *student* rights to premises safety came in great numbers on the heels of *Poulin*. Since *Poulin,* cases involving premises maintenance have held, *inter alia*:

- A university has a duty to use reasonable care to warn students of significant dangers associated with excavation.[4]

---

2. 402 A.2d 846 (Me. 1979). *See also* Isaacson v. Husson College, 332 A.2d 757 (Me. 1975) (jury question as to whether a college maintained premises reasonably); Shannon v. Washington Univ., 575 S.W.2d 235 (Mo. Ct. App. 1975) (jury can decide whether a university negligently maintained a walkway).

3. In cases where homeless people wander onto colleges and get hurt, they are owed a much lower standard of care because in most jurisdictions they are considered "trespassers," especially when efforts are made to keep them from the premises.

4. *See* Prarie View A & M Univ. v. Thomas, 684 S.W.2d 169 (Tex. App. 1984).

- Students are invitees and are entitled to reasonable care in premises maintenance.[5]
- A university can be liable for negligently installing a screen door in a student apartment when it leads to injury of the tenant or her child.[6]
- A college has the same duty that any private landowner has regarding removal of dangerous accumulations of snow and ice on its premises.[7]
- A university has a duty to maintain athletic facilities in reasonable condition—but not to prevent all student injury from participation in athletics.[8]
- A college must repair broken locks on common exterior entry doors in dormitories or face liability when a student is attacked in her room by an intruder who easily entered because of the broken lock.[9]
- A university has a duty to use reasonable care to maintain a safe parking garage, including fixing dangerous holes.[10]

A few points are critical with regard to these cases. First, no case views routine maintenance responsibility as a form of babysitting, parental responsibility, or strict liability. To the contrary, the cases uniformly require only *reasonable* care, not all possible care. A college does not have to foretell the future. A college does have to fix broken locks, repair windows, and fill in the pot holes in garages. These responsibilities are virtually identical to the ones which modern businesses (and in some cases cities) have today. Indeed, the university premises cases are routinely cited and quoted in non-university business and municipal cases and vice-versa. (*Poulin* is an example). If you were to ask a judge what the law of university premises responsibility is today, the judge would most likely answer, after looking at you a bit cross-eyed, that there are no special rules regarding university maintenance: universities must use reasonable care towards their invitees, just like any other business.

A recent case is illustrative of this point. In *Williams v. Junior College District of Central Southwest Missouri,*[11] a high school student enrolled

---

5. *See* Baldauf v. Kent State Univ., 550 N.E.2d 517 (Ohio Ct. App. 1988).

6. *See* Bolkhir v. North Carolina State Univ., 365 S.E.2d 898 (N.C. 1988).

7. *See* Mead v. Nassau Community College, 483 N.Y.S.2d 953 (App. Div. 1985); Goldman v. New York, 551 N.Y.S.2d 641 (App. Div. 1990).

8. *See* Henig v. Hofstra Univ., 553 N.Y.S.2d 479 (App. Div. 1990).

9. *See* Delaney v. University of Houston, 835 S.W.2d 56 (Tex. 1992).

10. *See* Malley v. Youngstown Univ, 658 N.E.2d 333 (Ct. Claims Ohio 1995).

11. 906 S.W.2d 400 (Mo. Ct. App. 1995).

in an auto mechanics course at the college (there was no special treatment because the student was a high school student). He was injured when he slipped and fell on the floor of the shop class. The evidence showed that a petroleum based substance had been left on the floor between classes. The instructor said that he inspected the floor before the injury occurred, but the jury felt that he did a careless job. In affirming an award of damages based on the jury's determination that a *duty* was *breached,* the appellate court made a point of holding that the duty was one of *reasonable* inspection. Just because something was done did not mean enough was done; just because not enough was done did not mean that everything possible had to be done. The instructor was in the best position to anticipate spills of petroleum matter that might not be obvious to a student or an ordinary and less experienced observer, especially because the instructor repeated the auto shop class throughout the day. As we shall see, things would have been dramatically different if a student had actually seen a huge oil spill on the shop floor; if the student knew the floor was slippery and walked on it anyway, his knowledge would have likely reduced or defeated his recovery if he had been able to avoid the dangerous area. The jury did not ask the instructor to babysit his students but rather just to do his job with reasonable care. Nor was the college strictly liable for any injury, no matter how careful it might have been in cleaning its shop floors. Responsibility here was identical to that of a business.

The second critical point is that when a university fails to properly maintain its premises (including student dormitories), it is no longer entitled to seek protection from the traditional immunities of (1) family, (2) charity, (3) bystander, or (4) government. First, for obvious reasons, no lawyer today argues a family immunity to protect university misconduct. Second, charitable immunities have largely been abolished and were never particularly strong with respect to premises maintenance regarding business properties.

Third, bystander arguments do not apply to invitees or premises. The invitee is in a special relationship with the college even if the problem is one of omission or nonfeasance.

Now, fourth, governmental immunities for public universities have not completely disappeared. Indeed, public universities still enjoy substantial immunity from private lawsuits regarding design and planning level decisions (*e.g.,* what type of dormitory to build; where to place it). However, public universities typically do not enjoy governmental immunity when they operate "proprietary" (business-like) activities such as parking garages, bookstores, etc., nor with respect to routine "ministerial" non-discretionary tasks, like fixing broken door locks or repairing sidewalks.

In fact, in situations where universities have attempted to push the notion that the public university is immune as a governmental entity too far, the courts have offered stern rebuke. The case which best illustrates this point is *Delaney v. University of Houston*.[12] In *Delaney*, the university apparently received numerous requests from female students in a women's dormitory to fix the lock on a dormitory entry door. The university did not repair the lock. The broken lock became the access point for a criminal intruder. In an argument that would shock the conscience of any parent and possibly deter students from choosing one university over another, the university seriously contended in court—under cover of alleged governmental immunity—that it had the right not to fix the broken lock, even after it was a source of danger *and fear* for female students (the university attempted to define the issue as being about the level of campus security it provided to its students, and then argued that police power issues are immune from private tort suit). The university also blamed the intruder as the sole proximate cause of the injury to the student and denied any shared responsibility for the incident.

The Texas Supreme Court—not exactly notorious for strong pro-plaintiff sentiments nowadays, rejected both arguments. The *Delaney* court held that the act of fixing a broken lock on the entry door of a student residence hall is not invested with the level of policy making and political judgment that would require courts to defer to the "political" (or discretionary governmental) process, nor was the issue one of campus security as an immunized police power function. Fixing a broken lock is a no-brainer—a simple and routine feature of providing a safe residence hall. *Delaney* basically said that a governmental university is not entitled to permit unsafe tenant conditions to persist under the umbrella of pretending to be using a kind of sovereign discretion. The university was severely chastised by the court for its attempt to avoid responsibility by seeking immunity from the consequences of its negligence in deferring the repair of a common entrance to one of its female residence halls.

In addition, *Delaney* took a very modern approach to the proximate cause question. There was a time under landlord-tenant law when the criminal intruder/attacker would have been considered the sole proximate cause of harm and danger and hence the university would have escaped liability. The notion that the deliberate criminal attacker was the determining cause was very much in keeping with the primary belief of police and criminologists at one time: crime, they thought, was a function of major index crimes and the way to stop crime was to punish such criminals. But, as Kelling and Coles (and others including James Q. Wilson, Mayor Rudolph Guiliani, and former N.Y.C. Police Commissioner William

---

12. 835 S.W. 2d 56 (Tex. 1992).

Bratton)[13] have now convincingly pointed out, that crime strategy failed.[14] One reason it failed was that it misperceived and disconnected the links between *disorder* and crime: failing to fix broken windows and locks facilitates major criminality.[15] Preventing crime by restoring order has had substantial success in places like New York's once infamous, but now safer, subway system.

Moreover, reducing disorder—fixing locks—decreases student *fear*. Fearful students (and those forced to waste precious study time repeatedly asking for routine maintenance with obvious safety parameters) are not learning. Fixing locks, as *Delaney* perceived, can stop crime and lead to a (real) sense of safety on campus, thus improving education. In that sense, the university community itself bears responsibility (proximate) for crime and danger in its midst. Reducing disorder is a feature of shared responsibility. The students did their part in *Delaney* (unlike some dorms where students deliberately disarm door locks after repeatedly being told not to do so), but in *Delaney* the university did not do its part. The rule in *Delaney*—that a public university must defend the reasonableness of its failure to perform maintenance which when unperformed enhances the opportunity of crime on campus—tends to prevent injury to, and fear of injury by, students.

Why would a university even argue such a counter-intuitive position all the way to a state supreme court, rather than admitting fault and agreeing to a monetary settlement to compensate a student for her injuries in such a situation? Surprisingly, the answer is that tort rules and procedures, and the professional responsibilities of lawyers, often encourage such litigation. Because of the way in which university law is created there is an incentive for a college to continue to litigate to the margin of responsibility up to the point where "bad" precedent could be made. Indeed, with a public university—and we are not talking specifically about *Delaney*—a very real political issue may exist as to how much to spend on very politically unglamourous buildings and grounds maintenance. The legislature may not want to give a school more money—particularly money without a political tag—and private donors often want to give money to *new* buildings and major renovations or restorations. A dollar spent on buildings and grounds maintenance (or on campus law enforcement) is a dollar that donors and university leadership typically wanted to go somewhere else. Sometimes only by *legally* requiring certain minimum maintenance

---

13. *See* WILLIAM BRATTON WITH PETER KNOBLER, TURNAROUND - HOW AMERICA'S TOP COP REVERSED THE CRIME EPIDEMIC (1998).

14. *See* GEORGE KELLING & CATHERINE COLES, FIXING BROKEN WINDOWS — RESTORING ORDER AND REDUCING CRIME IN OUR COMMUNITIES (1996).

15. The *Delaney* court held that the university's negligent failure to fix the broken lock provided the opportunity/setting for easy criminal intrusion and attack.

standards will maintenance and campus security dollars begin to take on new importance: a dollar not spent on required maintenance is many dollars more in litigation fees and injury awards, not to mention the potentially brutal public relations problems that can follow from failure to stop readily preventable injury. A public university then might actually be in the perverse position of *litigating against its students to protect them.* Such litigation is close to a win/win for a college officer/administrator. If you win the case, you can divert building and ground funds to popular activities like athletics, scholarships, or new libraries. If you lose, you can give the students a decent and safe place to live, and get the money you need to fix the problems at other dormitories on campus. Ironically, and paradoxically, there are times—as generals know well—that a loss is a huge victory. So while cases like *Delaney* could be the product of win at all costs litigation (and/or hubris brought about by substantial control by universities and their lawyers over what the law is and how it is perceived), there is the possibility that other motives are present. As Danny DeVito's wicked little hostile takeover character in the movie *Other People's Money* said, "I bring out the best in people."

The final, and perhaps most critical aspect of the recent premises responsibility cases is that they are a very conscious effort by courts to balance university responsibility with *students'* responsibility for their own safety. Early American common law stated that a person who was injured as the result of another's negligence could not recover *any* civil reparation for the harm done by the other's negligence if the injured person had himself been careless (negligent). That rule persisted into relatively recent times (well into the 1960s). But in the 1970s, the old "all or nothing" rule was abrogated in favor of a rule that apportioned liability for injury—and thus damages—between the parties, according to the extent that their fault (negligence usually) had contributed to the injured party's damages. The concept is called *comparative* negligence. It has been one of the most important changes in American negligence law. The doctrinal shift from the all or nothing approach of contributory negligence to comparative fault was an important legal step to a system of shared and apportioned responsibility. The all or nothing effect of a contributory negligence rule often unfairly barred the partial recovery of damages by an injured person. There was a windfall for the person whose antecedent negligence caused the injury if only blameless plaintiffs could sue. Such a rule caused the legal system—sympathetic to the plight of an injured person who might recover nothing from a negligent defendant—to employ strange rules and tactics to overlook the victim's own carelessness so as to grant her damages for her injury. These rules and tactics were then harsh on defendants because some plaintiffs received windfalls. The logical middle ground was to ask the parties to share responsibility for the injury and apportion it. Thus the typical faulty accident victim recovered something for her/his injuries[16] but would be asked to bear the relative costs of her own fault. Now, common sense and experience in a university community suggest that students are often architects of the problems that injure them and are — most importantly — sometimes the ones in the best position to help themselves. Sometimes students clamor for locks and the university fails to provide them; sometimes universities provide reasonably safe premises but confront students who foolishly take risks. Some of the most senseless acts of Bluto Blutarski-style self-inflicted injury inhabit university tort caselaw. Some students have taken the bystander messages too clearly and literally and have gotten intoxicated and jumped out of windows, or "expressed" elevators, or slid down slippery snow slopes without regard for personal safety, only to make sudden contact with obvious concrete poles.

In this context, the messages the courts are sending at one level are very clear. A university has a responsibility to use reasonable care to prevent premises/dormitory injury, but not to the extent that the danger presented is "open and obvious" to a student who voluntarily encounters it anyway or is created or enhanced by the student's own action (with reasonable alternatives available of course: the broken locks were painfully obvious in *Delaney*, but where would the women go?). A university can diminish or even defeat liability if a student is comparatively at fault, either by failing to use reasonable care for his or her own safety and/or by assuming a risk voluntarily and knowingly (especially an open and obvious danger) in the face of safer alternatives. A university may have a duty to maintain its premises, but it has ways to avoid liability. Courts are not reluctant to send the message to students that they are sometimes responsible for their own safety. The courts most often send that message when the students themselves are in the best position to avoid an injury.

Students have a responsibility not to be negligent in their conduct and must be willing to share or bear the consequences of their own voluntary, informed choices. Safety on campus depends on shared responsibility. The more reckless students are, the more an activity with known dangers should be guided and facilitated. Students may choose to accept attendant risks, and the more risk they assume, the more responsibility they bear. Just as Kelling and Coles note that citizens must increasingly understand the limitations of policing and know that they must take some responsibility to protect themselves, their families, their neighbors, and even strangers using the streets, so too college students must recognize that

---

16. In the period after the adoption of comparative fault, some courts have re-introduced the idea that a party who voluntarily proceeds in the face of a known danger can recover nothing at all.

they are not children of tender years. Students are responsible for their own safety also and are capable of comparative negligence or assumption of risk. The college student is a *legal adult* insofar as he or she is responsible to exercise *reasonable care* for her/his own safety and the safety of others and accept certain risks. Thus, in many situations, it may be said that the student is responsible for her own injury or the injury of another. And even in those situations where the college is negligent in some respect, such as in the allegedly negligent failure to barricade an excavation site, the student may be comparatively negligent in entering the construction area when the risk of doing so is unreasonable. Negligence law holds the college student to the standard of care that a reasonable person would exercise under the circumstances for their own safety. Damages resulting from a student's injuries should be reduced to the extent of that student's own careless conduct.

The law thus recognizes a significant responsibility residing in students to understand and deal with matters of their safety and the safety of other students and third parties. Where the college acts as a facilitator of student safety by actively educating students in ways of self-protection and civility toward others, the student who ignores the university's efforts can be held legally accountable for his or her own injuries or injury to others. In some cases, where the college has exercised reasonable care in facilitating student life, the burden of shared responsibility will fall legally upon the shoulders of a student.

For example, in *Banks v. Trustees of the University of Pennsylvania,*[17] a student who fell on university property sued the university and lost. This was no ordinary fall, however. She had encountered a fraternity protest blocking a pedestrian right of way and elected to scale a wall to bypass the protest. She was not as nimble as she supposed and fell. When she sued, the university successfully pointed out that a wall is a known and obvious fixture, which if one were to climb it, poses obvious risks (unlike the petroleum-based substance in the *Williams* case, *supra*, which even the instructor's inspection missed, and which would not have been apparent to a typical student). A wall is a wall after all.

The *Banks* court did point out two important things: First, the student had other, more reasonable options to get to where she was going. Had the student been faced with a fraternity meleé, or a Paris-island wall to scale, the matter would have been different. She did have a right to some reasonable path to her destination.

Second, the *Banks* court specifically noted that, even if a danger is open and obvious, a university (or any business) has a responsibility to use care

---

17. 666 A.2d 329 (Pa. Super. Ct. 1995).

to prevent danger if it is foreseeable that a student (consumer or business visitor) will, due to extenuating circumstances, overlook the otherwise obvious damage and proceed anyway. A very famous case[18] involving a K-Mart store illustrates the rule: A K-Mart customer passed some large, post-like barriers as he entered the store to make a purchase. He was injured by the barriers when he exited while carrying his large, bulky purchase. (The barriers were designed to stop vehicles from getting too close to the entrance and hitting pedestrians walking out of the store). The man obviously saw the barriers on his way into the store; but after he shopped, he either forgot about them or was distracted when he walked his large purchase out the exit door (which obstructed his view). What is open and obvious at one moment can become foreseeably less so under other circumstances:

> the modern majority rule is that a landowner is liable to an invitee on his premises if the landowner (1) knows, or should know of a condition that presents an unreasonable risk to the invitee, and (2) should expect that the invitee will not discover or appreciate the dangerous condition, or will fail to protect himself against it. Thus, the landowner may be liable where he should anticipate that an invitee might be injured by a condition, despite its obviousness. Such situations include those in which the invitee's attention is foreseeably distracted, or where the condition is unexpected or forgotten by the invitee.[19]

The *Banks* court determined that there was nothing to indicate—as in the K-Mart case—that someone would be so distracted. At the moment you climb a wall, you know you are climbing a wall; when you walk through a door, you may forget what is, or may be, on the other side (as anyone who has clobbered a loved one or the family pet by accident with a door while coming out of the bathroom can attest to).

What happens if a student does proceed (unlike *Banks*) in the face of a should-be-obvious danger, or proceeds into non-obvious danger when an alert person would hesitate? Again, the current legal answer is not a coddle-the-student answer, but a balancing of rights and responsibilities approach that emphasizes shared responsibility.

Two excellent examples are provided in two recent cases.

In *Weller v. College of the Senecas*[20] a student suffered serious paralytic injuries when he fell from his bicycle on campus. The injured student had elected to ride on a grassy path between some trees instead of riding on the paved path. However, other students had ridden off the paved path in

---

18. Ward v. K-Mart Corp., 554 N.E.2d 223 (Ill. 1990).

19. Robert Bickel, *Tort Accident Cases Involving Colleges and Universities: A Review of the 1995 Decisions*, 23 J.C. & U.L. 357, 363 (1997) (footnotes omitted).

20. 635 N.Y.S.2d 990 (App. Div. 1995). *See* R. Bickel, *supra*.

the area where the plaintiff rode, and the university (through its maintenance contractor) knew of these deviations from the paved path. The fall in this case was caused by impact with an exposed, but not obvious, tree root: the plaintiff did not know about the root until it was too late. (Tree roots are not necessarily common hazards on paths, even unpaved ones). So the danger was not "open and obvious." However, the court held that the student's failure to use care for his own safety could be used by a jury to reduce or eliminate recovery, even assuming some university negligence in the maintenance of the path. The fact that a student made what some jurors would consider a bad choice did not relieve the university of its *responsibility* but instead potentially relieved the university of some (or all) *liability*. *Weller* reminds us that in accidents sometimes no one is at fault, sometimes one entity or individual is at fault, and at many other times fault is shared. Responsibility for fault can thus be shared as well: just because you are at fault does not *ipso facto* mean that I am not. Legal rules in the university context sometimes openly acknowledge that apportioning responsibility is best. This is classic comparative negligence law.

Sometimes, apportioning responsibility or fault between the university and the student can be very tricky even for the courts, as is illustrated by the other case, *Pitre v. Louisiana Tech University*.[21] In *Pitre*, a rare winter storm covered the campus of Louisiana Tech with snow. In good form, the university had anticipated the storm and issued an appropriate bulletin including warnings (because many of these students were unfamiliar or inexperienced with heavy snow or serious winter weather). The bulletin encouraged students to enjoy the snow, build snow people, and sled in proper areas using good judgment. The bulletin also discouraged stupid, "X-games" style sledding, etc; "Do not sled into the path of cars, or on certain bad hills, or allow yourself to be dragged behind cars" (a popular, if stupidly dangerous, ploy). The bulletin was a classic example of how modern student affairs engages student activity: the bulletin was neither babysitting, parental, or custodial. It was not some draconian control missive: the bulletin of the *Gott-Hunt* era might have read "All students caught sledding will be expelled." Instead, the bulletin provided needed information and admonitions.

When the snow hit, it was a big one. Classes were canceled and several thousand students were trapped on campus. Earl Pitre, a student from Louisiana, decided to take advantage of the unusual conditions and went to an 85-foot hill. Louisiana is not exactly the land of sleds, saucers, or the luge, so students had to make do. Homemade sleds and cardboard, plastic signs, cafeteria trays (a sport once known at snowy Wellesly College as 'traying'), and even a toilet seat became makeshift snow/gravity

---

21. 673 So. 2d 585 (La. 1996).

conveyances. Pitre elected a large plastic garbage can lid. It should have been lots of fun; but sledding on steep slopes can be dangerous, particularly when one is sledding into a parking area with concrete light poles. On his eighth ride, Pitre struck a lightpole base and was paralyzed. Pitre had chosen, with some friends, to go downhill backwards (on your back, feet facing uphill), which is exciting but, as the author from Massachusetts can attest to, is guaranteed trouble. You cannot see what is coming and you almost always go head over back, or worse. As Pitre headed towards the pole, other students shouted warnings while jumping up and down, but it was too late.

At one level, the events of that evening were tragic and confusing. A student was seriously injured. Had the university done enough? Too much? Was the student at fault? Was this just an accident that happens? What is the appropriate balance between student responsibility for their own safety and university responsibility to provide safe conditions for students?

On these issues, the Louisiana court system predictably flip-flopped and finally settled the issue in a split decision (with a vigorous dissent) of the Louisiana Supreme Court that ruled slenderly in favor of the university. At the trial court, Pitre lost when the trial judge granted summary judgment (the judge believed that most of the facts were not in dispute; the real questions were what is the law) on the grounds that the danger associated with striking the concrete base of the light pole was obvious and apparent, and therefore there was no duty to warn Pitre or prevent the danger. On the first appeal, the intermediate lower court reversed the summary judgment and sent the case back for trial (believing that there were fact issues for a jury to consider). The trial was held and things went against Pitre again. On the second appeal, the Louisiana intermediate appellate court reversed (again) and determined that *both* the university and Pitre were negligent and should share responsibility legally under principles of comparative fault. The university appealed from the "split it up the middle" decision to the Louisiana Supreme Court.

The majority of that court sided—albeit narrowly and fact specifically—with the university and reversed the intermediate appellate court. The state supreme court recognized the typical duty owed to invitees/students to make university premises reasonably safe by either warning of danger or correcting it, *except* where a condition was as obvious to the student as it was to the university. If a danger is obvious to a student, the court reasoned, that is an important factor in determining whether the university's handling of the condition was unreasonable. A condition that is obvious to anyone and everyone, the court concluded, was not unreasonably dangerous and there would be no duty. The court clearly weighed a university's responsibility against the responsibility of students to watch out for their own safety.

In that vein—balancing of responsibilities and risks—the *Pitre* court determined that the concrete base and its light pole were "clearly visible" and "observable" to virtually all the sledding students: the parking lot was still lit and Pitre himself apparently had observed students slide past the light poles and also saw students collide with stationary objects.[22] It was, after all, a light pole and a large fixed, hard object. Because the light pole was so obvious and sledding is not unusually or highly dangerous (no more dangerous than hiking or skateboarding, two other popular student activities), the court reasoned that the general risk of injury was slight.[23] On the other hand, light poles prevent other accidents and attacks on students on typical days and nights in Louisiana when there is no snow (and even prevent injury during snow by illuminating an area). Moreover, the court reasoned that it would be burdensome on a university to *eliminate* this risk; for example: the cost of posting police at every possible point of injury during the storm would be too high. As such, the university did what was reasonable under the circumstances (*Pitre* is suspiciously similar to a duty *and* breach decision: recall that courts sometimes use duty in the combined sense of duty and breach).[24]

Pitre tried to argue that there were bases for duty other than a landowner/invitee theory. Unfortunately for him, once the court made its reasonableness/policy factor determination—balancing the risk of harm against the cost of its prevention—these arguments had no chance. If the university did what was reasonable, then it did what was reasonable under other duty theories. The Court did not protect the university from accountability for unreasonable conduct: it determined that the university did what was reasonable under the circumstances.

Thus, when Pitre argued that his status as a *student* alone created a duty on the part of the university to protect him from harm it was to no avail. The *Pitre* court recognized that Pitre's status as a student was relevant to the duty owed to him regarding conditions on university premises—so he is student/invitee wherever he goes on campus—but otherwise did not entitle him to care in the form of supervision, etc.

The university/student relationship, *Pitre* said, is not sufficient in itself to create a duty. Of course, it *is* the basis for the landowner duty owed. *Pitre* stated that a duty premised merely on a student/university relationship would be an *in loco parentis* duty; in this regard, *Pitre* could all too

---

22. *See Pitre,* 673 So. 2d at 591-92.

23. *See id.* at 591-592.

24. The university did have a responsibility to patrol areas used by unusually high numbers of students during the highly unusual storm—but the university did make reasonable efforts in this regard, and the presence of student affairs administrators or campus police might not have prevented *Pitre's* injuries.

easily be interpreted to fall into the trap created by *Bradshaw, Beach,* and *Rabel* when those cases suggested—in a historically false way—that *in loco parentis* once legally protected college student safety. *Pitre's* determination to say that student status itself does not create duty might seem gratuitous and even hyper-technical. But the point is clear: courts like *Pitre* wish to make certain that the law does not require the university to always follow students on or off campus to protect their safety. The point is often obvious since many on and off campus actions of students are beyond reasonable efforts of the college to monitor or guide. When courts say that a student/university relationship in itself does not create duty, remember that students are a unique set of invitees on campus who are entitled to reasonable, even affirmative, care. A university does not guarantee safety or provide the type of supervision of student activities that would be required for elementary or high school students. Thus, to the extent that there is a modern *in loco parentis* legal safety rule for K-12 students, it does not apply to college[25] students.

Pitre also tried to argue that a duty to warn arose because the university had sent an encouraging bulletin on snow activities to students and the campus police had some general, *ad hoc*, powers to use their judgement to intervene in dangerous student behavior. *Pitre* in essence argued that the university thus assumed a duty to him and facilitated his injury. The court disagreed: other students testified that the bulletin did not motivate them to sled. And the campus police were not legally required to stop sledding, just use good judgment. Critically, the court seemed of the view that the university's actions had not proceeded so far as to work a positive wrong or to show a particular assumption of responsibility to Pitre himself. That ruling is very much in line with modern rules regarding police duties to citizens. When police issue general warnings or police a beat, they do not typically assume special duties *ipso facto*. No doubt the *Pitre* court was influenced by the similarity of the problem to non-university police situations.

Pitre did not specifically relate its holding to the rules in the K-Mart case, but it is roughly consistent with them. Although the university knew of the danger, the court ruled that it could expect students to also observe the danger and protect themselves. It is easy to see where some judges might see it the other way. Excited students, late at night, might be tempted (and pushed by their peers) into overlooking danger, like a very last minute shopper on Christmas Eve might race down an aisle looking for one last gift. And perhaps at a commonly snow bound college with a

---

25. In recent K-12 education law, there is a doctrine of *in loco parentis* regarding student safety. These rules developed largely after the fall of *in loco parentis* for colleges and were never applied to college law.

hill leading to a parking lot, a university might place padding around concrete poles or even promote "traying" at safer locales. These might be inexpensive solutions. Perhaps a judge might view this type of question as more appropriate for a jury not the court. In essence, the dissent in *Pitre* argued that a jury should be given the opportunity to balance the relative responsibilities of university and student. The fact that a majority went the other way gives some indication that deference to university prerogatives still governs in many of the close cases. It is a precarious position of deference, one which universities could easily lose in the imaginations of judges.

In sum, *Pitre* is a tough case with a tough result and a tough message. If students fool around on campus, they risk literally everything. A university is *not* an insurer of student safety even though it does have responsibility for student safety on campus. In some instances, accidents do just happen or are attributable to students' own conduct (misconduct). Courts are aware of the need to place some responsibility for student injury on the heads of the students themselves. Courts are sensitive to the burdens that a university might face otherwise and to the almost infinite ways in which college students can get hurt. The other tough message is that the court was divided—and could easily have gone the other way (as had the intermediate appellate court)—on the shared responsibility of the university and its student(s) in this situation. A university could easily then lose a case like this one in the future if it were to fail to bring less than obvious risks to the attention of students and to take other reasonable steps to minimize the risk of injury.

The message of *Pitre* is then somewhat ambiguous, particularly for other jurisdictions in other contexts. Would the Massachusetts Supreme Judicial Court rule the same way if a Wellesly College student were injured in a 'traying' incident? Is *Pitre* a subtle message that there is still some protection for universities in the courts but that the halcyon days of insularity are over?

To conclude, when a student asserts a right to safe premises or dormitories, modern courts balance university responsibilities to students/invitees and student/ tenants against responsibilities of students for their own safety. The outcomes of the balancing process are not always easy to predict because courts must weigh various policies in each fact specific context to find an appropriate result. University duty to students as invitees or tenants is not parental, babysitting, or insurance—but there is a duty to exercise reasonable care. That duty is subject to the limitation that students do assume some risks of college life and must shoulder some (and in a few cases all) responsibility for their own safety. The premises liability/landlord-tenant cases of the current era are not heavy on images of what makes the university environment special or unique, although some vestigial deference to university culture can still be detected in the cases. In many ways courts treat universities like other businesses, and courts do say what university life is not—it is *not in loco parentis*, nor is it insular. The university, as any other business or landlord, has a duty to manage risks to student safety reasonably, and students are subject to legal requirements that they exercise reasonable care for their own safety. Safety is rarely an all or nothing proposition and neither the university nor its students should expect a windfall.

Dangerous Persons on Campus

The hottest area in university liability law in the modern duty period is the growing responsibility of universities to protect students on campus from dangerous persons who come from off campus or who come from the student ranks themselves.

The message of the cases in the preceding 'bystander' era was radically ambiguous on this issue. In cases like *Rabel*, the message was that there was no duty to protect a student from an attack by another (drunken) student on campus or in a dormitory. Yet without any attempt to make sense of the obvious incongruity, cases following *Mullins* found that a university had a responsibility to protect students from non-student intruders. The cases, when placed side by side, seemed almost unaware of each other and sent a paradoxical message to colleges: protect students on campus in dormitories from non-students, but do not protect them from each other. Incredibly, a student raped in her dorm by a fellow student was less likely to recover than one raped in her dormitory by a non-student intruder. Courts made no effort to explain—let alone justify or even recognize—this facially problematic difference in the protection of student safety.

The bystander era cases were beset by another powerful and ambiguous development—the rule in the famous *Tarasoff* case. *Tarasoff* imposed a duty to protect some individuals from foreseeable danger arising from university relationships with dangerous persons on campus. If a campus psychotherapist had a duty to protect a non-student off campus from a non-student on campus, what would happen if a known dangerous student attacked another student on campus (or someone else, off campus)? There was nothing in the language of *Tarasoff* to suggest that it was just an "export" case. Indeed, the case resounded with a broadside fired against preventable danger to (particularly) female students by rapists, stalkers and others who presented a danger to life or limb. The implications for campus safety were manifest, yet cases like *Rabel* needed to be reconciled with *Tarasoff*.

Currently, universities increasingly face responsibility for student injuries that arise from the presence of dangerous persons or groups on campus, whether the bad person is a student or not, whenever there is a foreseeable risk of danger and/or the university has a relationship with the dangerous person from which danger is predictable and imminent to a known or readily identifiable student. While in some cases courts speak of special relationships, it is clear that a relationship does not have to be custodial to be legally special for these purposes. It is in this area that university attorneys and commentators have perceived the biggest shift in decisional law in the post-bystander era. Again, there are intimations by some commentators that these cases are a return to *in loco parentis,* or strict liability. However, these cases neither ask a college to be Nostradamus nor to use every possible means to protect every student from attack. The danger to a student must be known or reasonably foreseeable by a university, and then reasonable care must be able to prevent such a foreseeable attack.

There is a substantial overlap in these cases with the landowner/landlord cases as to the legal doctrinal basis for duty. Universities do not actually encourage students or actors to attack students, so they are often cast in the passive, non-feasance role. As such, the legal question presented is typically one of special duty—affirmative duty or duty under special circumstances. Again, being a landowner to an invitee, or a landlord to a tenant, is an adequate special relationship to create an affirmative duty of reasonable care toward a student. Courts essentially view the potential or actual presence of dangerous persons on land or in a tenancy as a very special type of *condition*—a condition that makes the campus or residence hall unsafe.

Courts do see dangerous person cases as analogous to slippery floor cases, but also treat them differently in analysis, tone, and, ultimately, liability. Most of the dangerous persons or premises cases are non-university cases decided in the last 30 years.

In the 1950s and early 1960s a dominant rule of proximate cause would have determined, *per se,* that the dangerous person was the only party legally responsible, and that a landowner or landlord was not responsible to prevent the risk of harm from criminal intrusion. Modern courts, anticipating the work of Kelling, Coles, Wilson, and others, recognize that disorder facilitates crime and have fashioned the law accordingly. Today, the dangerous person on campus is not the sole proximate cause, even if he is a student or an off-campus intruder.

Since *Tarasoff,* courts have recognized that a relationship to a dangerous person—student or other—itself can be a predicate for responsibility under some circumstances. One can have an affirmative duty to protect even a stranger from certain foreseeably dangerous individuals. This responsibility is *in addition* to any responsibility owed to a student in a landowner or landlord context; because many of the incidents do occur on campus and/or in dormitories they thus trigger multiple duty theories.

. . .

Because *Tarasoff* makes special relationships so prominent in terms of duty and dangerous people, a digression on duty, students, and special relationships is in order. Most courts remain reluctant to say that a duty is owed simply because a victim or attacker is a student, although there is a growing voice in the caselaw to that effect. As we have said, being a student does not itself usually create a special relationship sufficient to impose a duty according to most courts of the bystander and current duty eras. Judicial reluctance to treat students as intrinsically special must be viewed in context, however. Students are in a special duty-creating relationship on campus (as invitees), in their dormitories (as tenants), when there is foreseeable endangerment (*Tarasoff*), and also when working on campus or for the college (employees). Students are also owed a duty of reasonable care when colleges undertake safety precautions but fail to perform them reasonably,[26] increasing risk or inducing students to rely on the college's undertakings or services. Thus, for most purposes students are in a presumptive duty relationship with a college because of special relationships or special circumstances.

So students are not in a special relationship with the university except when certain things they do or experience as students put them in a special relationship. It's all very Monty Python — "I came here for an argument — no you did not." Needless to say, this state of affairs is very confusing to college officials in the line of duty. If one were to restate the law today in these areas, it would be easy to say that "you have no duty to students, except when you do." Confusing? Courts have reached this state of affairs very methodically and interstitially by applying and adapting doctrines used in other contexts. To date, the courts have yet to step back and identify the collection of patches as a quilt. College law is in transition and the current post-bystander duty era will likely continue to evolve. The case law is close to critical mass in terms of identifying the legal *vision* of modern college and university relations, apart from simply offering a seemingly *ad hoc* collection of complex duty and special relationship rules.

. . .

---

26. According to the *Restatement (Second) of Torts,* a person or entity which undertakes a safety service for another person can be liable if the failure to perform that service increases the risk of harm, makes a person worse off, or induces that person to rely on the undertaking to her detriment. This is technically not a special relationship rule but an independent way to create duty under what we call "special circumstances". *See* RESTATEMENT (SECOND) OF TORTS §§ 323, 324 (1965).

Now the case which most university persons regard as the signal of the beginning of the end of the bystander rules, specifically regarding dangerous persons/activities on campus, is *Furek v. The University of Delaware*,[27] decided in 1991. For many, *Furek* brought the patches of responsibility together.

In or around 1977 (yes, 1977—university cases can take over a decade to resolve in the courts), the University of Delaware began to take note of students who were injured in fraternity pledging activities. The director of health services at the university specifically reported two injuries to the vice-president for student affairs and labeled them "hazing" incidents. The university then responded in writing by promptly admonishing fraternities about hazing. The Dean of Students issued a formal statement that hazing, including beating, mental and physical intimidation, forced games of humiliation, etc. would not be permitted *on* or *off* campus. In 1979, an assistant dean pulled the presidents of the fraternities in about matters involving disruptive behavior and hazing. Later, the Dean spoke to the campus about hazing deaths occurring around the country; the Dean made it clear that the university was willing to revoke the charters of any *Animal House*.

Yet, hazing went on at the university. A major breakdown occurred in policy implementation.[28] The campus police were not properly instructed concerning the university's position on hazing. There were formal policy statements and announcements regarding fraternity-related disorder and danger, but there was an insufficient plan of implementation. We know that "making it wrong" can actually play into the hands of perpetrators whose intentions are to engage in secret, prohibited conduct as a way to bond and gain control over others. A public statement by administration can actually *worsen* a problem like this.

In one sense, it certainly did. The campus police appeared hamstrung. Campus police officers (and other campus personnel) observed obvious indicia of fraternity hazing such as the marching of pledges with paddles, pledge "line-ups," and pranks. On a night just before "Hell Night," suspicious looking students were actually stopped by campus police, but no action was taken because there appeared to be no clear rules regarding such disorder for the police to enforce nor any effective instruction on how to use discretion in these matters. Had an individual campus law enforcement officer decided to use her discretion and seize a paddle or disperse a group, she perhaps would have risked a great deal—reprimand, lack of support from above, lawsuits, etc. Caselaw like *Rabel* would not have indicated the need to intervene; to the contrary, it would have counseled standing by.

---

27. 594 A.2d 506 (Del. 1991).

28. At least that is the inference to be gained from the appellate court's opinion.

Yet the link between disorder and the dangers of hazing is clear: seize a paddle and you may prevent a beating. You may also obtain more information to prevent other dangerous episodes and may set the tone that fraternity hucksterism is not permitted. Fix broken windows, as Kelling says, and the drug dealers move out. When Bratton arrested fare beaters in the Subway he caught criminals with guns and other dangerous things.

In the fall term of 1980, Furek pledged a fraternity. He entered "Hell Night"—a long hazing ritual featuring paddling, eating from a toilet, and being covered with food and other organics. This pointless ritual was exactly what the university had sought to prohibit. Here is why: one foolish fraternity member poured *oven cleaner* over Furek while he was blindfolded during a "ritual." Furek was chemically burned and scarred severely and permanently. Hazing has a way of getting way out of hand.

The *Furek* case squarely presented the question of how to deal with dangerous students and dangerous group activities on campus. The answer in *Rabel* and similar earlier cases had been that to have responsibility, a university must be in a special relationship with students premised on *custodial* control. *Furek* saw the question in a different light than *Rabel* and sensed that more subtle forms of relationships between students and universities exist in a modern era.

The Supreme Court of Delaware determined that:

- The university/student relationship is *unique* and it is *more than strictly educational* (a clear rejection of a fundamental premise of *Bradshaw* and *Beach*); the primary function of the university is to foster "intellectual development through an academic curriculum."[29]
- Many other aspects of university life are *"university guided,"*[30] including housing, food, security, extra curricular activities, and student life;
- Students are not *solely* responsible for their own safety simply because they are adults (the court saw no empirical or other support—as suggested in other cases of the bystander era—that university supervision was inversely related to the maturation of college students or that supervision and control of dangerous student activities would make for an inhospitable or educationally dysfunctional college experience);
- The fact that students may be adults does not make university concerns and efforts related to student alcohol use inappropriate (noting that in both *Beach* and *Bradshaw* the *students* were *not*

---

29. *Furek,* 594 A.2d at 516.
30. *See id.* at 518.

adults under drinking law); The university is in a unique relationship with students because of the "situations created by the concentration of young people on a college campus and the ability of the university to protect its students."[31]

Furek saw a very different vision of university/student relations than that of the bystander era. Students were often nascent or pre-adults. The university was not powerless. It could act without placing students in custody. It could facilitate and guide students into many of the circumstances which increase or decrease risk. *Furek* did not see the university as a helpless bystander but as guide and co-creator of campus life and student activities.

The legal principles that *Furek* used to reach its ultimate conclusion that the university had a duty to the student reflected the shift away from the affirmative duty/special relationship/custody concepts of *Bradshaw, Baldwin, Beach,* and *Rabel.* The duty of care in *Furek* arose not from special relationships, *per se,* but from ideas of "reliance" and assumption of responsibility/creation of risky conditions. Indeed, *Furek* was about starting something and finishing it properly when people (mainly students) have come to rely on what you have started.[32] *Furek* is about duty existing under unique or special circumstances: a college is not merely a passive educational repository for students, like parentheses in an equation, but is one of the most important variables and part of the functions. Colleges, according to *Furek,* often guide the creation of a community in which the college remains a major player in what actions or activities are promoted or discouraged. The college itself guides the level of safety which occurs on campus in the way a director determines how a play will be performed. Once the college "play" is in motion, there is an illusion that there is no director. If you see the director—or if you see too much of the director's hand in the play—the play is not working because the director must facilitate the vision of the playwright and the talents of the actors while keeping the expectations of the audience in mind.

In this vein, the *Furek* court held that the university had been committed to providing security on the campus in *general* and in *particular* had formulated general policies regarding hazing. In both these regards the university had undertaken to provide a level of security to students on campus and endeavored to eliminate hazing by fraternities. To the extent the university did not see its undertaking through, it could be legally responsible. Duty—to use *reasonable, not all possible care*—thus arose under the unique and special circumstances of the university's affirmative commitment to student safety in the context of long-term and well-known hazing

---

31. *Id.* at 519.

32. At its core, this is a fundamentally long-standing duty rule.

problems. Such a duty can be breached by a university when the campus police are given an ineffective implementation plan regarding an acknowledged danger, thereby permitting students to flagrantly disregard anti-hazing policies. This is not a campus policing failure but a university administrative policy failure. It would be as if the director refused to direct the final act of the play, and then blamed the actors for the play's failure.

There are some important points to recognize about the implications of *Furek* for the modern college. These points belong under three headings—reasonable care, not strict liability; student responsibility; and assumption of duty.

Furek: Reasonable Care, Not Strict Liability

The *Furek* decision does not impose strict liability nor does it require babysitting or seeing students in a custodial relationship with the university. The duty owed is *only* that of *reasonable* care. This means that, despite reasonable efforts, some students will be severely injured in hazing or other incidents. However, *Furek* sends an unmistakable message that a university cannot make rules and policies against hazing (etc.) and then do nothing to enforce them beyond verbal threats and admonition or fail to give campus police the authority and guidelines to enforce them through intervention. Moreover, it was apparent to the Delaware Supreme Court that non-draconian actions can reasonably prevent harm and discourage the unwanted behavior. Had the campus police seized a paddle and taken some names—a visit with an associate dean to follow—a life might not have been ruined. Instead, campus policies unwittingly facilitated negative behavior. Bad students learned quickly that the rules would not be enforced and drew good students and (wannabes) into their dangerous activities; the fact that the conduct was "wrong" only enhanced the motivations of students whose attitudes about hazing were precisely to act out secret, prohibited, or unacceptable behavior. The fact that the campus police appeared to students to be disempowered only accelerated the sense that students were in charge and there were no real rules. As any parent or businessperson knows, making rules and not enforcing them leads to trouble.[33]

Drinking is dangerous conduct; as we discuss in Chapter VI, college drinking is a major social problem and a major source of risk on campus.

---

33. Active intervention, rather than post-injury discipline, is often more effective risk management strategy. All universities have inherent, contractual, or governmental (constitutional) authority to restrict conduct that poses unreasonable risks to student safety. There is no need to return to *in loco parentis* to intervene and protect student safety.

There are no easy solutions or simple answers that we know of.[34] Nonetheless, we believe, like *Furek,* that there are some reasonable steps that universities can take to reduce risks from alcohol-related activities. Unlike *Furek*, many courts have thrown up their hands — no doubt recalling the futility of prohibition — at college drinking and its risks.[35] The issue, however, is not prohibition but prevention and reduction of risk. The social causes of drinking on campus (and off) may be beyond the control of a university but the consequential disorder and danger engendered by campus drinking is not. Grab a keg or take a paddle and hood, and you may stop a senseless act before it occurs.

We follow *Furek*, and a growing number of courts, in the belief that *courts cannot say — as a matter of law, categorically — that there are no reasonable solutions to alcohol and/or Furek type incidents.* Decisions like *Bradshaw*, *Beach,* and *Rabel* seem conservative because they protect university defendants, but they actually institute a stridently negative vision of students on campus and a negative view of attempts to restore reasonable safety and order on campus. *Bradshaw, Beach,* and *Rabel* became powerful visions of extreme student libertarianism.

Fundamentally, this is where much modern, pro-defendant tort reform disconnects from the university context. Protecting universities from liability in improper ways can actually *facilitate* extreme student libertarianism and needless danger and disorder that threatens student safety. To promote the growth of student personal accountability, universities must facilitate the conditions of order and safety which make higher education possible under conditions of acceptable risk. It did not take Nazis to clean up the subways of New York; it will not take a Mussolini to clean up American colleges. The vision of *Furek* is the faith restored in the possibility of reasonable solutions.[36] In the next chapter we sketch ways in which this faith can be made concrete.

---

34. In recent years, the authors have been told by many college presidents and senior administrators that they perceive drinking on campus to be the most significant problem in student affairs and that they are highly motivated to find legally sound solutions to the problem.

35. The *Bradshaw* and *Beach* courts could well be criticized for essentially advising universities to give up attempts to affect drinking by college students. Colleges and universities bought into these decisions for years, creating problems from which they are only now beginning to recover. Much of the delay in the response by the colleges to the problem of alcohol-related student injury was counseled by embracing *Bradshaw's* and *Beach's* no-duty/bystander rules.

36. The university of Delaware's own experience after *Furek* attests to this, as we discussed in Chapter VI.

Furek — Student Responsibility

Furek did not see a university as the solely responsible party in matters of student safety.[37] To the contrary, *Furek* is very much a *shared* responsibility case. In *Furek* both the student who poured the oven cleaner and the fraternity were responsible parties. In this sense *Furek* is at odds with cases like *Beach,* which assume that responsibility is a zero-sum game; shared responsibility does not diminish but can actually enhance student accountability.

Today, it is very common for courts to hold individuals and individual associations like fraternities liable for injuries negligently caused. For example, in a recent Mississippi case, a fraternity was liable both for gross negligence and punitive damages after a female student was forcibly grabbed against her will and thrown off a high railing into a shallow pool.[38] The court criticized the fraternity for failing to properly supervise the party, for maintaining the dangerous pool and for failing to comply with university alcohol and party rules. Holding individuals, associations, and distributors of alcohol liable was also a feature of the bystander era. Today, the cases are split somewhat on issues regarding the liability of national fraternities for their locals, but jurisdictions like Mississippi reflect modern courts' intolerance of bad behavior from various actors in the university community.

Moreover, a student victim is not always entirely blameless. A student who deliberately goes along with known unauthorized activities and fails to use care to protect himself faces hard questions — usually for a jury to decide in each case — regarding what, if any, offset any defendants are entitled to. Cases which have stated no-duty rules may thus be overreacting to plaintiff misconduct (*e.g., Baldwin,* where the students were clearly at fault). Recall that at one time a negligent plaintiff was entitled to nothing — a rule that is a great deal similar to no duty, at least in result. *Furek* does not disable affirmative defenses but merely states that a university can properly be considered as *one* of the responsible parties in an accident. There will be situations where student misconduct is so egregious that courts should bar claims as a matter of law. They should, however, make it clear that they are not saying that a college has no duty. Courts no longer need to say no duty, and doing so disserves the community.

---

37. Indeed, courts have never seen the university as solely responsible for student safety. Even high school students have been held responsible when failing to exercise reasonable care for their own safety.

38. *See* Beta Beta Chapter of Beta Theta Pi Fraternity v. May, 611 So. 2d 889 (Miss. 1993).

Furek—Assuming Duties and Ostrichism

One unfortunate consequence of *Furek* is the perception that if you become involved you become liable, so, the logic goes, it is better to be uninvolved or push the students and their dangerous activities off campus. This perception is part of a larger legal and social milieu in which the belief is that you are better off not to get involved. Popular culture of the 1990s seems obsessed with this theme. For example, the final episode of the popular *Seinfeld* series placed questions of deliberate indifference squarely on the table.[39] The question is white-hot in university affairs at the turn of the millennium.

"Assumption of duty" is a particularly scary phrase for university administrators (and university attorneys for that matter). It connotes, in legal effect, that when an actor (here the college or university) voluntarily assumes a duty not imposed by law, it is bound to carry out the duty with reasonable care and is liable for its negligence if it does not. Now, if an administration believes that the general rule for college law is a no-duty bystander rule (because *in loco parentis* is dead, etc.), there is fear that to affirmatively intervene in student activities, programs, conduct, etc. (even in ways that establish parameters which clearly reduce risk of injury) will lead to liability in the event of failure. The seductive option will be the temptation to not engage at all: be careful not to "assume" a duty that you would not otherwise have.

Major problems exist with this approach. First, as is evident even in *Furek*, most college and university administrators are not about to ignore student conduct or activities that invite danger (indifference is both counterintuitive and unlikely given their professional education and training). Following strategies of deliberate indifference is professionally distasteful and disempowering. It makes a career in college affairs like life in a Dilbert cartoon. Indifference is also hard to pull off: the active involvement of student affairs professionals, campus law enforcement officers, and other university administrators in student activities is an inherent feature of the modern college or university. Most importantly, deliberate indifference increases the chances that student injury will occur and thus enhances the likelihood of a finding of negligence. The best way to defeat a

---

39. In what might have been a truly pointless "Sein-off," the writers of the hit show chose to put a premise of the show on trial. The principle characters were arrested and convicted for being bystanders who deliberately mocked a man being robbed. They suffered a form of extreme disconnection—a world of face and fantasy—and at their esque trial it was shown that their lives were generally characterized by a lack of caring much at all about others or even each other. (Although Kramer once noted to Jerry that if he—Jerry—killed someone, he (Kramer) would "turn him in without hesitation.")

lawsuit is to avoid the injury in the first place. Finally, the strategy is now legally doomed to backfire because courts are much less likely to see a college as a true passive bystander and will more often see students and colleges in legally special relationships.

As to this latter point, only a small number of college and university programs are so disengaged from student life and activities that they could credibly be seen as having taken no affirmative steps to facilitate the environment in which risk occurs. Certainly, a college which features substantial on-campus housing, sanctions and regulates Greek life, and provides a panoply of student services including campus police, medical services, sports and recreation programs, and other co-curricular and extracurricular experiences and events has engaged itself in student life to a point where withdrawal or disengagement from student life and safety issues would be impracticable and unprofessional. It is not the creation of regulations alone which engages a college; it is the creation of a guided, facilitated environment which suffuses student/university relationships with a responsibility of reasonable care to guide student growth and development. Indeed, student affairs professionals see their role as student *development,* and thus have an inherent problem with legal rules which encourage disconnection or passivity in student/administrator relationships.

Another example is illustrative. As Arthur Levine points out in his new book with Jeanette Cureton, *When Hope and Fear Collide—A Portrait of Today's College Student* (1998),[40] the modern college student increasingly likes to party off campus in non-fraternity situations. In some instances, as in *Baldwin* (the drag race case), the activities begin on campus but carry on off campus. Colleges struggle with whether it is preferable to encourage students to stay on campus (increasingly, as Levine points out also, students do not live on campus) or to push drinking off campus (or *de facto* encourage that state of affairs.) *Furek* logic might seem to encourage an administrator to establish *de facto* policies that put college drinking problems in the lap of the greater community. The problem again—at the root of all bystander style legal solutions—is that the best way to avoid legal liability is not to avoid involvement with others but *to avoid the accidents, however caused, which might give rise to lawsuits.* The best way to proceed with student affairs/campus security is the way which will result in reasonable and tolerable levels of danger. Deliberate indifference results in the worst case scenario for a college: (1) students are injured, *and* (2) the university may pay damages in a lawsuit (3) and face potentially humiliating public relations problems. For the modern college, looking the other way regarding off campus drinking is a danger-

---

40. *See also* Arthur Levine, When Dreams and Heroes Died (1980).

ous option. There may be no easy solutions to how to manage college-aged drinking—but this does not mean that there are no reasonable measures to be taken. Deliberate indifference is not a reasonable solution.

Courts, like parents, are much less likely to view many modern universities as true bystanders. Courts are more likely to view colleges as co-creators of a campus, and even off-campus, dynamic. The cases which saw the university as a bystander were partially a throwback to the idea of insularity and/or belief in the futility of university control over student behavior, particularly drinking. But modern courts are often less influenced by the "rather myopic view" that "to control" someone requires custodial control or constraint.[41] As the Ohio Supreme Court recently stated in an extremely important non-university, *Tarasoff-* type case, "the duty to control the conduct of a…person is commensurate with such ability to control as the defendant actually has at that time…. In other words…there will be diverse levels of control which give rise to corresponding degrees of responsibility."[42] There is a growing sentiment that universities *have* done things, *can* do things, and *should* do things to prevent unreasonable student injury. Ostrichism is bad policy and increasingly legally suspect. Anyone who believes that *Furek* and cases like it encourage college ostrichism risks worst case scenarios. Reasonable solutions are not always obvious or easy, but more courts in the duty era will expect colleges to look for them.

For example, the typical first response to alcohol problems is a campus alcohol ban (whole or partial) and/or a crackdown on Greek, particularly fraternity, life. The solutions are oriented towards less subtle forms of control and have caused some students to react violently to them as perceived strong arm tactics. Some solutions have also facilitated off-campus drinking. There are effective alternative solutions, however. Student affairs administrators and campus police often confront a small and *recidivist* group of dangerous students who seem to delight in risky rituals and bullying others into problem behavior. A discreet group of students takes its toll on administration and the campus itself; they become the source of a disproportionate number of lawsuits, injuries etc. The larger student population makes its share of mistakes, but not as intensely and not with a focus to draw others down with them. These hard core students on campus resist overkill and some hard strategies. For example, when Greek life is exorcized and campus drinking is curtailed, these individuals can use their martyrdom to cajole drinking off

---

41. *See* Estates of Morgan v. Fairfield Family Counseling, Cts., 673 N.E.2d 1311, 1323 (Ohio 1997).

42. *Id.* (citations omitted).

campus. They often form quasi-criminal partnerships with less reputable off-campus drinking establishments (who comply with the law less and are notorious places of disorder). They sometimes do this with impunity, and in a strange way the college has unintentionally facilitated them.[43] An important strategy to impact abusive college drinking is to identify these individuals, disempower them, and separate them from the college environment if necessary. This is a more subtle way to control abusive and dangerous college drinking. It would be more effective than, for example, total campus alcohol bans.

This does not mean, of course, that all universities are responsible to operate as if they are the University of Delaware after a case like *Furek*. Courts will look to the unique situation of each college to assess *its* relations with *its* students. Thus, a pure commuter community college—offering classes in one building and no student life activities to speak of—will not be similarly situated to a residential college with substantial Greek life. Isolated rural colleges will be different from urban colleges, etc. The ramifications of duty assumed—the amount of care necessary so as not to be in breach of duty—will necessarily vary from college to college. But, *Furek* clearly signals the end of blind judicial acceptance of the notion that because colleges generally act reasonably regarding student safety, there is no legal duty to students. As students are injured in preventable ways, universities will lose the insularity which arose in part from the unspoken presumption that colleges generally do a good job of providing safe learning environments.

. . .

The spirit of *Furek* has been manifest in cases dealing with a most serious issue on modern campuses—attacks, particularly sexual attacks, upon students on campus. Overwhelmingly, the cases follow the *Mullins/Furek* approach.[44] Either by virtue of status as invitee, tenant, or someone to whom a duty has been assumed, students are owed reasonable care to prevent foreseeable attacks. Courts remain somewhat reluctant to impose responsibility for certain forms of peer sexual assault etc.,[45] but the different treatment of assaults by students vs. by non-stu-

---

43. Derrick Bell has observed that a law enforcement model breaks down when people identify sympathetically with the lawbreaker. Though Professor Bell speaks of the vulnerability of civil rights law, his observation also illuminates why criminal alcohol laws are so frequently frustrated.

44. Given the long-standing acceptance of *Mullins*, it would be a mistake to overstate that *Furek* broke new ground. It is, in many respects, not a novel case at all.

45. *See* Gebser v. Lago Vista Indep. Sch. Dist., 118 S. Ct. 1989 (1998); and *Gebser*, 118 S. Ct. 2000, 2007 (Stevens, J., and Ginsburg, J., dissenting).

dents seen in the bystander era is fast eroding. The major shift has been in *duty*, not liability. Universities still win— and should win—a significant number of cases, but they will be held liable for student injury if they persist in litigating on the basis of outmoded interpretations of post-*in loco parentis* doctrine or if lawyers counsel clients to generally avoid "assumed duty." The recent cases have abandoned almost entirely the notion that someone must be in a custodial relationship with the university as a precondition to university responsibility to prevent this type of harm.

The definitive recent cases demonstrating how courts will respond to dangerous persons on campus who sexually assault students are *Johnson v. State of Washington*[46] and *Nero v. Kansas State University*,[47] from Washington and Kansas courts, respectively.

In *Johnson,* a first-year student was abducted and raped near her dormitory on the campus of Washington State University. The university argued that as a public governmental entity, it was entitled to a form of governmental immunity. Usually, governments are immune from suit by private citizens over the negligent failure to provide *general* police protection.[48] This is known as the "public duty" doctrine, which means that a duty to provide police protection is owed to the public at large, but not to specific members of the public—a misleading position because there really is no duty at all (as no citizen can enforce the duty in a court). In essence, the university argued that it had no legal duty whatsoever to protect young women from abduction and rape—a throwback argument harkening to the era of insularity. A trial judge agreed, and dismissed the case.

The Washington court rejected this argument. The *Johnson* court agreed that duty did not arise from notions of *in loco parentis,* or even from the fact that the victim was a student; however, duty *did* arise from the fact that the student was an invitee/tenant of the university. As such, a duty was owed to her, irrespective of some public duty doctrine. The public university could not hide under the cloak of being a government agency or functionary to avoid using reasonable steps to avoid sexual attacks on students.

The duty owed to the student was thus exactly that owed at a private school to a student or to any invitee/tenant. If the location of the premises or prior criminal events make criminal danger foreseeable, the university has a duty to provide reasonable—not all possible—security. *Johnson*

---

46. 894 P.2d 1366 (Wash. Ct. App. 1995).

47. 861 P.2d 768 (Kan. 1993).

48. Lawyers often associate this rule with *Riss v. City of New York*, 240 N.E.2d 860 (N.Y. 1968), which as such is a majority rule. The *Riss* rule is subject to powerful exceptions, however. Among other exceptions, a duty does attach to a private citizen if the police assume a duty to a particular person or class of persons (as in sending a crossing guard to an elementary school).

adopted the modern rule that a criminal attack or intrusion is not the sole proximate cause of harm. A university landlord can be a (concurring) proximate cause if criminal attack is foreseeable.[49]

Johnson did not say that the university was strictly liable. A jury would have to decide whether unreasonable acts or omissions of the university landlord significantly contributed to or created the opportunity for the assault and whether or not a criminal attack was reasonably foreseeable. The university certainly could not prevent all attacks and would not be responsible if there were no reasons—apart from general background criminal activity—to suspect and foresee danger to its students.

Johnson represents the application of general business/landlord rules to a university. It is *Mullins* and follows *Kline v. 1500 Massachusetts Ave. Apt. Corp.,*[50] the seminal non-university, landlord duty case. Some commentators on higher education law are suspicious of cases like *Johnson* (and *Mullins*) as returning to *in loco parentis*. Again, they miss the mark. Even today, parents do not have a tort duty to protect their children from merely foreseeable criminal intrusion or attacks. If they did, imagine the lawsuits from children whose parents move to high crime areas or dangerous buildings. While commentators argue about straw men like a sup-

---

49. The rule is explained by the *New York Court of Appeals in Nallan v. Helmsley-Spear, Inc.,* 407 N.E.2d 451 (1980), a case arising when a union member was shot in the lobby of the defendant's office building while there to attend a meeting. Citing the *Restatement Second of Torts,* § 344, the court observed:

A possessor of land who holds it open to the public...is subject to liability...for physical harm to [a business visitor] caused by...the intentionally harmful acts of third persons [e.g., a criminal], and by the failure of the [landowner] to exercise reasonable care to (a) discover that such acts are being done or protect them against it. The court emphasized that the landowner is not liable merely because of the presence of criminal activity. Rather, the victim of an attack must show that crimes on the premises were sufficiently related to the conduct that caused plaintiff's injury to encourage a reasonable landowner to take precautions against future attacks. If the landowner knew or had reason to know of such prior crimes in the building and further found that the landowner should have anticipated a risk of harm from criminal activity in the lobby, it properly could have gone on to conclude that the defendant failed to make the premises safe for the visiting public. The fact that the 'instrumentality' of harm was the criminal conduct of a third person does not preclude liability where the criminal activity was itself foreseeable and reasonably preventable. Where that plaintiff can show that the presence of a lobby attendant or security guard would have likely reduced the risk of an attack, the landowner may be held accountable.

50. 439 F.2d 477 (D.C. Cir. 1970) *Kline* ended one aspect of a nasty slumlord era; *Mullins* brought pro-tenant rules to campus.

posed return to *in loco parentis, Johnson* and other cases are charting a "business" tort law path for colleges, rightly or wrongly.

Nero is *Johnson* and *Mullins* with a twist. *Nero* deals with the more legally controversial problem of dangerous persons *who are students* and who attack other students. The problems of dangerous *students* are always at least binary: how to protect other students and how to deal with the problem students themselves. *Nero's* facts presage what may come onto campuses with a vengeance if we do not act soon. High school murder sprees are not just problems of secondary education (for example, gangs[51] are already present on some campuses as outsiders and as students). Moreover, some of today's high school students bring drugs, guns, violence, fear, and disorder with them when they come to college as students.

In *Nero*, Kansas State University assigned a male student to a dormitory. One month later that student was accused of raping a resident student. The male student was reassigned by the university to an all-male dormitory and instructed to stay away from certain areas. The academic year came to a close and summer session began. The problem: only one residence hall was available and it was a male/female dormitory. Despite the fact that he had been removed and boundaried and was awaiting criminal trial for sexual battery, the student was given a spot in the summer dormitory, perhaps because of the university's fear of depriving *him* of *his* rights.

Shana Nero, a transfer student from Oklahoma, was also assigned to the summer session dormitory. She was unaware of the presence of a charged felon in the dormitory, and was she not aware of the male student's prior history or status. She was sexually attacked by this male student in the basement television room where the two were watching television. It is the type of situation that makes parents sick.

Once again, a trial court—no doubt reading *Bradshaw et. al.*—held that no duty was owed to the student by the university. The Kansas Supreme Court could not stomach that result. The *Nero* court reviewed the bystander era cases—including *Bradshaw* and *Baldwin*—and noted that those cases were different. In those cases, *Nero* said, the injured students asked the courts to impose a general obligation on colleges to prohibit underage drinking on and off campus. Like a city police department, there was no general obligation of a college to enforce regulations, although *Nero* did question those cases in light of countervailing authority.

Nero instead looked to *Mullins* and *Furek* for duties regarding student safety. Universities actively manage student housing. Reasonable care is owed to tenants, including, as in *Johnson*, reasonable protection against foreseeable attacks. The duty is not based on *in loco parents;* students pay

---

51. *See* Gragg v. Wichita State University, 934 P.2d 121 (1997).

for housing just like residential tenants, and do so in a market in which colleges compete against private landlords. The fact that a decision to house a student is "discretionary" does not mean that there are no consequences for a college once assignment is made. The college may have the power to place an alleged rapist in a dormitory, but once they do, they must use reasonable care to protect other students (and that student).

Nero held that the placing of the students in the coed dormitory presented issues of fact for a jury to decide. The jury could consider what the victim knew and whether she was lulled into a false sense of security. The court realized, as *Estates of Morgan* did, that one way to control dangerous students on campus is to give appropriate warnings or information to potential victims so that they can protect themselves.[52] Again, the questions were ones of reasonableness and foreseeability.

A few points about *Nero* are worth noting, as it raises important issues about assignments to dorms and even classes and co-curricular activities. The points revolve around the fact that the attacker was an "alleged" rapist at the time of dormitory assignment and that there was but one summer residence.

A potentially dangerous student on campus does have rights, but we must be careful not to overstate these rights. For one thing, removing the male student from housing was not the only option in *Nero*, although it was the best option. Students could have been warned of the presence of a potentially dangerous male student, for example. More importantly, however, denying or terminating student housing is not a matter of high constitutional scrutiny (in contrast to, say, racial classifications) but a matter of ordinary discretion. Certainly, a student is entitled to some appropriate process regarding cancellation of his dormitory lease or contract — but

---

52. When concern for student peril is evident, common law privacy rules, as well as federal and most state statutes and regulations regarding student records, permit the sharing of information about dangerous behavior between or among institutional officials in the "need to know" chain. *Tarasoff* says as much directly, even where counseling relationships exist, when a client is a danger to an identifiable victim; and federal statutes and regulations governing the privacy of student disciplinary records permit disclosure of information contained in such records to a person employed by the University in an administrative, supervisory, academic or research, or support staff position who has a legitimate educational interest, if the official needs to review the record in order to fulfill his or her professional responsibility. *See e.g.,* Family Educational Rights and Privacy Act (FERPA), 20 U.S.C. § 1232g. The sharing of information certainly compromises privacy, particularly when campus police reports are made, since police records not protected by educational records privacy acts may be subject to disclosure to local authorities, etc. However, information sharing may be critical to the safety of a student, and is a vital aspect of university responsibility, when consistent with case law and legislative protections of privacy.

there is nothing in the idea of due process (look back at the language of *Dixon*) which requires *undue* or *too much* process. A student being removed from a dormitory is not being *convicted* of a crime, but a decision is being made on policy grounds to offer or resolve a lease arrangement. Such a decision does not require anything like criminal trial in full battle dress. To the contrary, it would be absurd to give that much process. Indeed, to do so pragmatically denies other students *the process they deserve* to protect their life and liberty interests in safe dormitory housing. Too much deference to process "rights" can be as bad as too little — *Nero* is the flip side of *Dixon*.

There is the very real problem of identifying which students are "dangerous," particularly in light of prior or alleged criminality. A sizable number of students have traffic tickets, DUI's, petty theft, drug possession, vandalism, etc. Serious crimes of violence are much less common. Moreover, colleges have some information about students but certainly not all. Much of what is gathered by a college comes through an admissions process not designed to root up criminals, as such. *Nero* tells administrators that there is a duty to consider future danger, but what does this mean?

For guidance on these hard questions — what to look for, who to flag as dangerous — colleges can look, again, to business employment case law. Businesses are faced with the same duties. What do courts tell them?

The message in the business cases is much clearer. First, do *reasonable, customary* research of individuals. In the university context, where admission is often selective, it is often reasonable to believe that the vast majority of students are not serious known threats and that, if you ask, much of their criminal history will emerge. (An unfortunate reality is that many criminal courts still allow children to seal their juvenile records, or expunge them making it difficult or impossible for colleges to get accurate and complete records and giving students the false belief that they are entitled to answer questions about criminal history untruthfully). Colleges can attempt to get around the problem in some cases by insisting that all records be provided whether sealed, expunged, purged, etc.) As such, there is reason to believe that courts will not ask colleges to do much more than they already do. One caveat: what the university *knows* about dangers to student safety it must use reasonable care to *share* among its various areas of operation. Thus campus police, student affairs administrators, and others must have clear direction and must be mutually aware of action to be taken in specific situations. *Furek* essentially assumed (whether true or not) that the campus police knew students had paddles and hazing-gear and that therefore the university administrators had actual or constructive knowledge of the likelihood of dangerous hazing activity in violation of university policies on hazing. Courts will assume generally that information is shared and used and not forgotten or unused. This may be the greatest 'burden' of *Nero*.

The second message of the business cases is that the criminality which is *relevant* is *similar* criminal behavior that would alert a reasonable person to further danger of that kind.[53] This means that students who have been caught speeding or shoplifting generally pose little threat of violence on campus. Students with multiple alcohol, drug, and violence convictions are problems.

Nero and other university cases are most concerned about serious physical violence on campus (a shoplifter might steal a ring from the bookstore; a speeder might hit a student's car in a parking lot) and will respond to that. A person criminally charged with an on campus rape requires the attention of university administrators, and sound judgment must be exercised regarding the risk presented to other students, employees, etc.

Finally, *Nero* asks the question of what to do with the bad student— won't he or she sue if mishandled? The unmistakable message of the cases is that universities must responsibly prepare themselves for dangerous students on campus. A bad student is no longer a legal "oh-my-gosh" but a predictable feature of modern university life. Ask any dean of students, student judicial officer, or campus law enforcement officer. This means that universities must be proactive rather than reactive just like modern businesses which are used to this particular shift. Proaction can actually avoid harm and lawsuits.

For example, we have noted as have we have traveled to various universities that many campuses deal with a sexual batterer on campus by requiring a female student to complain and be willing to assist in the sometimes lengthy process of student conduct code/sexual harassment adjudication. The procedures are (1) aimed at establishing guilt or wrongdoing, (2) usually cumbersome, and (3) ask female students/victims to become *de facto* private attorneys' general for the benefit of security on campus. There is a perception that this is the best or even the only way to deal with disorder and danger. Luckily, again, this is not the law. Dangerous students can delay the process, and even take advantage of the fact that these procedures are costly and draining on faculty, administra-

---

53. For example see *Nallan v. Helmsley-Spear, Inc., supra,* 429 N.Y.S. 2d 606 (N.Y. 1980), holding the owner of a Manhattan office building liable for the shooting of a business visitor in the lobby when the lobby attendant was away from his post. The court held that the fact that there had been more than 100 criminal incidents in the building, including several assaults, in less than 2 years meant that the owner should have foreseen the likelihood of harm from criminal activity in the lobby unless adequate security were provided.

tion, student, *and victim* energies. However necessary some process is, the investigative process must be suited to fast and safe interim solutions. When the issue is not guilt or expulsion—but immediate safety and the loss of limited temporary privileges—due process permits much less process and permits different kinds of process. Again, this is the message of *Dixon*.

For example, an appropriate student affairs administrator, perhaps in consultation with a campus law enforcement officer, can decide after expedited review that a *potential danger exists* and that a *reasonable interim* solution is to relocate a student. If college protocols appropriately determine specific aspects of disorder and danger with regard to protecting the limited interests at stake, they can protect all students more quickly and efficiently. However, if the college has an ossified and cumbersome conduct code procedure and an inflexible sexual harassment policy, it is likely that it lacks the process needed to deal with the problems of imminent danger. This is a guaranteed recipe for danger and costly lawsuits. The lawsuits colleges will see—sooner or later—will be by a student/victim (like *Nero*) who was harmed while the college fiddled with process that exceeds constitutional/contractual minimums for purposes of restoring order and safety.

It is true that expedited process to restore order and safety on campus will draw fire from some students and even some civil rights groups. Litigation will ensue. One key survival of the era of insularity in college affairs is the fear of litigation that permeates college administration. Levine reports that many student affairs administrators express concerns over litigation. The truth is that the modern university has lost its legal insularity and can expect to have its disputes reach courts of law. Lawsuits should be avoided but not at all costs. *It is better, we say, to pick your lawsuit if you are a college.* If college action risks litigation, would it be better to defend a lawsuit from a student rape victim, or to defend a lawsuit from a dangerous student denied access to a dormitory who challenges the process used?

A lesson can be learned from advocates of community policing like Kelling, Coles, and Bratton. As they point out, restoring order will challenge some individuals' senses of "liberty." Instead of fearing litigation, rules and procedures should be designed with the expectation that they *will* be litigated and tested in the courts. In the area of campus law, courts following *Dixon, et. al.,* have afforded universities tremendous space in which to facilitate order through appropriate and adaptable process. Universities have often promoted an anti-law culture—a deep holdover from the era of insularity. The opportunity that is missed is that the law is an ally in the restoration of order and safety on campus—not an enemy. Treating law on campus like an enemy, however traditional, is foolish—

courts will not show 1950s style deference to universities. Defensive, reactive litigation will be counterproductive. Armed with the law on their sides, universities can more readily exercise *meaningful, balanced authority over student affairs.* In the *Dixon* era, universities learned that to exercise authority that was not lawful discredited their overall authority; it is time to adopt the positive message of *Dixon* and its progeny. A *facilitator* university—as we discuss here and in Chapter VI—works with the law, not against the law as if law were a background obstacle to be satisfied before the real work of a college can be done. Yoda says "use the force, Luke," not "comply with the dictates of the force Luke, and then do what you want."

By *engaging* the legal system—working *with it rather than against it*— it is more likely that after courts establish clear parameters, process oriented litigation will die down, if it ever occurs in the first place. For one thing, if the system works well it will often work correctly—truly dangerous students will be dealt with quickly and efficiently. Those students later convicted of crimes or conduct code violations will be in a relatively weak position to contest less intrusive *intermediate* decisions like denial or reassignment of housing. Indeed, the awareness of such procedures alone can create a deterrent to some criminal students to enter certain living arrangements at all. Embracing some kinds of potential litigation rather than others can reduce overall risks and campus cost of litigation. And save some lives. A *Nero* campus—wrapped up like an enchilada in its own reactive procedures—is a safety and litigation time bomb.

A final point about *Nero* relates to the unusual problem of access to the university by *convicted* criminals. In some instances, individuals have done their time and state law may actually facilitate the return of a criminal into society *via* university programs. In short, colleges may be forced to consider some individuals for matriculation who might raise real red flags. Of course, not all individuals would be of such concern—white collar criminals, check fraud artists, and perhaps even *some* drug and alcohol offenders. Again, "criminality" does not always translate into foreseeable danger any more than lack of criminality precludes it (we all cross the street to avoid a dangerous person without first checking "rap" sheets). But sometimes past criminality does connote future danger. On this point there has been little litigation and hence little guidance from the courts.

The leading case, *Eiseman v. State of New York,*[54] is not a clear directive. In that case a former convict was enrolled at a New York college and attacked a student. The university was not held liable. The New York

---

54. 511 N.E.2d 1128 (N.Y. 1987).

Court of Appeals indicated the state's interest in reintegrating a former convict into society—allowing him to enroll and reside in the university community—could outweigh the state's general interest in student safety. As a matter of civil rights law, that ruling remains highly questionable. Now, in an unusual but important twist of fact (and fate), the university had no actual or constructive knowledge of the convict's dangerous propensities. *And*, the student-victim *was* aware that her assailant was a convicted felon (thus she was not a *Nero* victim). Most likely, *Eiseman* chose to protect the university from dubious social/legislative policy and from the university's own *reasonable* ignorance. The case might have general applicability, say, if the FBI placed a student on campus in witness protection, but no college should read *Eiseman* as *carte blanche* regarding dangerous felons. The court's holding does not mean that colleges cannot or should not work to rehabilitate society's offenders: just that they should generally know who they are dealing with and use reasonable precautions for student safety.

Furek, Johnson and *Nero* are the leading edges of a discernable group of cases which follow a consistent pattern. Duty is owed if danger is foreseeable from prior indicia of dangerousness or assumption of duty and reasonable precautions could prevent harm; the university does not always breach the duty owed, and in some instances the predicate conditions are missing (lack of foreseeability). Courts hint at (higher) duties that may be owed by contract but usually apply typical tort rules nonetheless.[55]

In sum, recent cases have determined that:

- A university, as a landlord, has a duty to provide and maintain minimum reasonable security measures in student dormitory rooms (*see Cutler v. Board of Regents*, 459 So. 2d 413 (Fla. Dist. Ct. App. 1984); *Nieswand v. Cornell Univ.*, 692 F. Supp. 1464 (2d Cir. 1988));
- A university has a duty to protect students in residence life because the university has supervisory control over residential facilities and certain aspects of student life (*Duarte v. State*, 148 Cal. Rptr. 804, *vacated,* 151 Cal. Rptr. 727 (Cal. Ct. App. 1979) (unofficially published opinion);
- When a state university receives complaints from dormitory residents about strange persons in the hallways, men in women's bathroom facilities, and there have been numerous

---

55. For example, *Savannah College of Art & Design v. Roe,* 409 S.E.2d 848 (Ga. 1991), *overruled by Sturbridge Partners, Ltd. v. Walker,* 482 S.E.2d 339 (Ga. 1997), suggested that contract rights can alter minimum tort requirements; the Savannah case is the view of only a few judges to that extent.

instances of robberies and trespass, the university, like any private landlord, has a duty to use reasonable care to prevent abduction and rape of a student. Failure to lock outer doors can be sufficient to support breach of duty under such circumstances (*Miller v. State*, 478 N.Y.S.2d 829 (N.Y. 1984));

- A college can be liable if a student is sexually attacked by an intruder who hid in untrimmed foliage near a stairway (*Peterson v. San Francisco Community College*, 685 P.2d 1193 (Cal. 1984)).
- A university can be liable when a security guard negligently fails to properly respond to a threat on a student's life by an identified student assailant (*Jesik v. Marikopa Co. Community College Dist.*, 611 P.2d 547 (Ariz. 1980)).

The cases indicate how simple acts of maintenance such as locking doors, quickly fixing broken locks, trimming bushes, and challenging observed dangerous behavior can forestall crime and send a message that order—not conditions of criminality—exist on the campus. Implicitly, courts have begun to accept the Kelling/Coles/Wilson/Bratton notion that order maintenance measures prevent serious crime. Courts do not view inadequate maintenance as some vindication of a students' liberty interest. To the contrary, safe premises are a condition under which student freedom can be exercised and foreseeably dangerous persons can be thwarted.

The cases impose *reasonable* care responsibilities only and hence colleges do win and should win many cases. Consider the following cases:

(1) In *L.W. v. Western Gulf Association*,[56] a student was raped by another student while unconscious in her room. She had become intoxicated at a party and her attacker (with others) brought her back to the room. The court dismissed the action against the university because of lack of foreseeability. There had been no complaints about the student/attacker and no one had felt threatened by him or complained about him. The court specifically pointed out that a university has a duty not to "facilitate criminal acts," but a rape is not foreseeable simply because it is foreseeable that some students consume alcohol and have consensual sex.[57] General background risks do not themselves create duty, except with respect to simple maintenance items that prevent obvious dangers. Factually, *L.W.* is not *Nero*.

(2) At Carroll College in Montana, a college employee (it could just as easily have been a student) was shot by a homeless man. The homeless

---

56. 675 N.E.2d 760 (Ind. Ct. App. 1997)
57. *See id.* at 763.

man went to the college chapel first and raised Cain. He was drinking, had a gun in his pants, and hollered and banged on a pew during the Priest's preparation for Mass. The priest escorted the man from the chapel but did not have him removed from campus or notify the police. The man went to the college cafeteria and shot an innocent employee. The case went to the jury (hence the duty issue was alive) which brought back a verdict for the college. The Supreme Court of Montana affirmed, holding that the College had been the super safe sanctuary many imagine colleges to be up to this point: there had never been a serious problem caused by a homeless person and the College had been free of rapes, murders, assaults, and armed robberies.[58] The jury recognized a duty of care but heard all the evidence and found that college employees had handled the matter appropriately given the past history of safety on campus.

(3) In *Gragg v. Wichita State University*[59] a woman was shot and killed while attending a 4th of July fireworks display on campus. The Kansas Supreme Court—which had just decided *Nero*—affirmed a summary judgment for the University. There had been no shooting or violent assault resulting in death on the campus for a quarter century, and the assailant was unknown to the university. There was evidence of gang related activity in the area, but the university had developed a security protocol and had deployed more than 80 police offices for the event of approximately 20,000 persons. The University had done what was reasonable.

(4) Two recent decisions of intermediate California appellate courts are likewise notable. *Tanja H. v. Regents of the University of California*[60] and *Crow v. California*[61] are two cases where athletic team members attacked other students on campus. In both cases, the universities escaped liability for the peer attacks.

In *Tanja H.*, a young woman was sexually attacked by members of the university football team. The attack was the result of alcohol suffused activities on campus. The *Tanja H.* court determined that although the drinking was prohibited by university rules, the university was considered to be limited in its power to enforce drinking rules given the specific privacy rights students enjoyed in their rooms. More importantly, the attack was a spontaneous assault, not specifically or readily foreseeable. *Tanja H.* effectively conceded that while attacks may be generally foreseeable, the culture of student privacy rights would not allow reasonable efforts to

---

58. *See* Peschke v. Caroll College, 929 P.2d 874 (Mont. 1994).
59. 934 P.2d 121 (Kan. 1997).
60. 278 Cal. Rptr. 918 (Ct. App. 1991).
61. 271 Cal. Rptr. 349 (Ct. App. 1990).

prevent this sort of assault. In finding no duty to the student the case turned, as other cases, on foreseeability, and the reasonableness of what would be necessary to stop such atrocious acts.

The *Tanja H.* court also had to grapple with the fact that there was a broken light bulb in the stairway and agreed that a duty to repair defects which facilitate crimes exists. However, the court believed that the broken light did not have a meaningful nexus to the particular attack. In this vein, *Tanja H.* did correctly establish that not all maintenance problems are in fact or proximately the causes of injury. Otherwise, a clever plaintiff's lawyer could point to any number of unrelated defects as a way to force a time consuming jury trial. Courts will be reluctant to permit a victim to put the entire university on trial in this way. This is a major purpose of causation requirements in negligence law.

Tanja H. does represent a somewhat disturbing concession, however, to unlawfully prohibited underage drinking in dorm rooms and the predictable problems of date rape (and worse) that it can facilitate. The court is empowered to draw its own conclusions, but there is no doubt about the foreseeable connections between such disorderly drinking and more serious crimes, particularly against young women. "Hedging" on the issue of the university's responsibility in situations of known alcohol abuse in residence halls, *Tanja H.* emphasized the fact that the victim was herself engaged in unlawful consumption of alcohol (thus she was not blameless). In this regard, *Tanja H.* represents a judicial antipathy to student plaintiffs who are themselves participants in alcohol consumption. There are strong hints of historical no proximate cause, assumption of risk, and comparative negligence theories at work in the court's opinion. Thus, we question the efficacy of *Tanja H.* on two grounds. To the extent that *Tanja H.* represents the idea that date rape/gang rape on the heels of campus drinking is unforeseeable and/or is unstoppable, the case is bad social policy and will not likely survive. As we argue in Chapter VI, we have a responsibility under modern tort rules to reclaim our campuses from the kind of dangers which have been unfortunate signatures of the modern college era. Moreover, the undercurrent that students—even vulnerable underage freshman students who have never lived away from home—assume the risks of college drinking, *including possibly gang rape*, is another faulty concession to extreme models of student freedom. If the price of absolute privacy in a dormitory room is gang rape, it is clear that initiatives must be designed which grant reasonable protection to privacy, but restore safety and prevent such horrible scenarios from recurring. We respectfully believe that *Tanja H.*, while carefully reasoned, is somewhat out of step.

Tanja H's sister case is *Crow v. California*, which is more in line with modern trends. The victim was an adult male student drinking beer in a dormitory. He ended up being punched-out by a college athlete. *Crow* noted that there was no claim that the university knew or had reason to know of the particular risks in this dormitory. Reasonable care could not have prevented this attack. As *Crow* indicated, if the athlete/aggressor had been a known danger to others, the matter would have been different. The difference between *Crow* and *Tanja H.* is subtle but important. Reasonable steps, we believe, do exist to prevent *Tanja H.* occurrences; dormitory fights are a fact of life and when they simply spontaneously erupt, it would be usually too much to ask any university to prevent them. Reasonable efforts cannot prevent all violent human encounters (even Navy S.E.A.L.S. need M.P.'s).

The conclusions to be drawn from the recent explosion of cases involving dangerous persons on campus are at one level very simple. Universities consistently have a legal duty to provide reasonable protection for students on campus and in dormitories. Duty is not liability, however. To hold a university liable under negligence law, a student victim must establish that the danger was foreseeable in more than a general sense. The danger must be reasonably apparent (like overgrown bushes near an isolated dormitory entrance) or a pattern of behavior must establish and define the risks. Moreover, the risks must be capable of being mitigated by reasonable efforts on the part of the university. Student-victim misconduct is relevant, especially when that conduct is disorderly or includes improper uses of alcohol: as we discuss *infra*, cases still tend to skew around this issue of alcohol in favor of no university liability.

Bradshaw logic is still evident in some duty-era case law. *Tanja H.* is a prime example of this. Yet there is a powerful *Furek*-like crosscurrent regarding foreseeable alcohol misuse. As passive, libertarian attitudes regarding under aged student drinking change in society, cases like *Tanja H.* are vulnerable to reconsideration.

Courts in the duty era have decided cases one at a time and they have patched together the following legal rule scheme. Student/university relations are not, *per se*, special. However, most student relationships with a university are sufficiently special to create duty. Duty exists from:

- -residence in a dormitory, with respect to safety there;
- -presence on a campus, with respect to safety there;
- -actual or constructive knowledge of a dangerous person who foreseeably endangers a student;
- -assumption of duty by acts which show an intent to protect or lull students into a sense of security;
- -contracts with students.

Overall, there is a tendency to analogize university case law to *business* case law. *Universities* have a general legal similarity to *businesses*.

The paradox of the cases is that courts virtually say that student/university relations are special, but some still back away slightly ("I really, really like you" or "Ditto" vs. "I love you"). Why? Courts see two variables at play. First, the student/university relation is important but, second, so is the *scope* of that relationship in terms of *time and space* and the *intentions* and *understanding* of the students and the university. Courts treat and think about businesses this way. Duty in the business and university context both have distinct qualities of time and space requirements. As such, it makes a difference whether a student is attacked in a dorm on the eve of final exams or attacked at a bar in another city during holiday break. Duty fades as one moves physically farther from campus and its students and university activities;[62] being a 'student' is a four (or more) year moniker and is not itself solely determining of duty. While a student would reasonably expect some protection in an off-campus internship, some student activities are too far removed from the institution to be within the scope of the relationship. As American courts have begun to place universities under duty scrutiny, they have done what they have always done—take it one step at a time. The steps have accumulated in recent decades and suggest that university law regarding dangerous persons and student activities is on the brink of reaching critical mass. In essence, the courts have basically come to say that a student/college relationship is special so long as injury occurs within the scope of that relationship.[63]

Liability for Student Activities (Curricular, Co-Curricular etc.): The Scope of the University's Duty to Instruct and Supervise

The cases in the duty era firmly support the idea that a duty to use reasonable care exists to manage and supervise curricular and co-curricular activities, including internships, externships, field trips, and study abroad.

---

62. For example, in *Ramsammy v. City of New York*, 628 N.Y.S. 2d 693, (*appeal denied* in part and *dismissed* in part, 663 N.E.2d 916 (N.Y. 1995), a security guard at Yeshiva University found a man (non-student) sleeping in his car near the campus. It was alleged that the guard woke the man up and told him to drive away even though he was visibly intoxicated. A person (non-student) was hit by the driver and sued the university. The court said there was no duty to a non-student off campus under these circumstances—no special relationship. The court pointed out that the guard had no power to arrest the driver and the 'encounter' was off campus.

63. As such, many courts have cautiously viewed dangerous drinking as "on your own time" and not within the scope. We see shifts in this attitude ahead, particularly with respect to dangerous drinking by underage students who are first timers away from home.

Again, the duty is one of reasonable care not insurance, and colleges have significant ways to avoid and limit potential liability in these areas based on ideas of assumed risk and comparative negligence.

With the fall of charitable and governmental immunity, duties to provide reasonably safe classroom instruction (physical injuries only—courts routinely reject educational malpractice claims) became readily enforceable, even if instances of injury and lawsuits were rare. Where reasonable care has not been used, liability can follow. Universities have been held liable for injuries in chemistry labs and physical education classes, for table saw injuries in a scenery class and injuries in aeronautics courses,[64] for example. Indeed, the rule of reasonable safety has been extended to community college classes taught off campus on other premises.[65] The duty is *not in loco parentis* and is *not* based on any argument that the student/instructor relationship is custodial. Any actor—business or college—has a duty to use reasonable care in its actions and activities. There is no need for a special relationship in such circumstances, any more than the driver of a car would need a special relationship with other motorists and pedestrians before that driver would be required to use reasonable care. However, students assume the ordinary/inherent risks of the classes they take, and a student's failure to use reasonable care can diminish or defeat recovery.

Curricular activities that are inherently physical, such as certain physical education classes, and field trips are now numerous and diverse and are governed by basically the same rules whether it is a weightlifting course or a school sponsored rock climbing class. Students assume the ordinary and obvious risks of such activities. There is no duty to protect against inherent, obvious, or primary risks of such activities. But students do not assume the risks of (1) reckless or deliberate and intentional behavior compromising safety, (2) hidden (or non-obvious to them) or non-ordinary dangers and (3) that an institution will take a student to a level of risk that the student is not capable of handling without proper instruction and guidance. Perhaps the best expression and explanation of the shared responsibility in student activity is contained in *Regents of the University of California v. Roettgen.*[66] In *Roettgen*, a student was killed in a rock climbing class. The court determined that rock climbing is a dangerous sport with some very obvious dangers. Rock anchors can fail and cause falls, which cause injury or death. These are the apparent or ordi-

---

64. *See* Bickel, 23 J.C. & U.L. at 374 n.128.

65. Delbridge v. Maricopa County Community College Dist, 893 P.2d 55 (Ariz. Ct. App. 1995).

66. 48 Cal. Rptr. 2d 922 (Ct. App. 1996).

nary risks of an extra-ordinary activity. The instructor(s) had a responsibility to place the anchors carefully (which they did—but the anchors still failed) and to keep the students within their range of capabilities (which they did).

Roettgen was very particular in its reasoning process. The responsibility of the student for his/her own safety and the responsibility of a college for non-ordinary risks were considered in light of the nature of the activity, its risks, and the relative experience of a student. To find the balancing of responsibilities, *Roettgen* explained the rule in the context of the fact situation:

> [p]laintiff relies on cases involving student/instructor relationships and those involving commercial recreational operations in urging that defendant owed Mr. Roettgen a duty of care simply because he was enrolled as a student in defendant's commercial venture. *The determination of duty in the student/instructor or commercial recreational operation cases turns not on labels given to the sporting participants, but instead on the facts surrounding their levels of experience and/or their relationships to one another in the activity resulting in the plaintiff's injury.*[67]

Roettgen represents the belief that sporting or recreational activities, even when academic in nature, should be governed by flexible rules that focus on the activity rather than on a "label." If you take students on a Kayak excursion as a part of a geology course, be prepared to respond at the level of responsibility reasonable for that activity, not to some abstract or special student/university relationship. The rule explained in *Roettgen* is appropriate for field trips, study abroad programs, and, in fact, most instructional activity that mixes inherent risk with aberrant or unusual risk. The basic idea is that students do assume certain risks, but the university has responsibility too. *Mintz* is consistent with this vision of shared responsibility as are other cases.[68]

This again does not always require a so-called special relationship. A special relationship *can* create *affirmative* duty where none exists, but negative duty—the duty to use reasonable care to refrain from injuring others by your acts, actions, and activities—*does not require a special relationship.* If this were not so, strangers and many others would be "free game" as it were. In *Beach* and *Bradshaw* (especially *Beach*) the university was an active facilitator of the activities which caused harm. In *Beach* the activity was a *required* field trip. Even in *Bradshaw*, the class picnic was sanctioned and facilitated by the university. The universities

---

67. 48 Cal. Rptr. 2d at 925. (emphasis added).

68. *See* Delbridge v. Maricopa County Community College Dist., 893 P.2d 55 (Ariz. Ct. App. 1995).

were not strangers just standing by. Both *Beach* and *Bradshaw* doctrinally overreacted to the problems of student alcohol use by giving a *de facto* immunity to the universities via a no-duty to rescue rule. Unfortunately for university law, both cases could have used and applied well accepted legal rules to reach the same results. This legacy of *Beach* and *Bradshaw* still carries forward into the duty era: some courts follow the logic of *Beach* and *Bradshaw* uncritically and fall into the same trap.[69]

Beach and *Bradshaw* are also out of step with the duty era cases regarding student activities in another way. Those cases require *custodial* control before a duty attaches. The presumption they make is that (1) nothing short of "custody *and* control" of students will work and (2) it is not reasonable for a modern university to exercise *custody* over college students. We agree with the latter assertion in most circumstances, but the first assertion is fundamentally flawed.

Responsibility for Student Alcohol Use

All four of the important no-duty era cases were alcohol-related injury cases: *Mullins* and other crosscurrent cases of the bystander era were *not* alcohol cases. Even in the duty era, cases involving beer and liquor weigh substantially towards no college liability. In cases like *Beach, Baldwin,* and *Rabel,* students assumed almost all the risks of alcohol use—on campus, off campus, and even risks associated with other students who were drinking. *De facto,* many courts are still convinced of this. In essence, courts treat alcohol use on campus like a dangerous college sport, with known and obvious dangers. Unlike other college "sports," however, courts have often seemed to place few safety parameters on liquor abuse and are willing in some instances to take extreme positions such that students effectively assume all risks—even gang rape in a dormitory—when they consume alcohol. College life has assumed over the years, *de facto,* the character of a no-liability social drinking community.

There are several reasons why a no-liability pattern has followed college drinking from the era of insularity (immunity) to the bystander era (no-duty) to the duty era (no liability, usually for lack of specific foreseeability and/or because reasonable care could not prevent the incident from occurring). One major reason is the continued adherence to legal rules which treat liquor liability within narrow boundaries. For example, social hosts have historically not been subject to lawsuits, and most courts still adhere

---

69. *Beach* and *Bradshaw* spill over onto *Dixon* as well. Many university administrators seem to believe that extreme civil rights were granted by *Dixon,* as suggested in the bystander cases.

to this rule. Another reason has been a sense of futility: college-aged drinking, like subway graffiti, seems an inevitable feature of college life. Charles Homer Haskins, writing in the 1920s on the rise of universities from antiquity, did not overlook the featured role of alcohol in the earliest accounts of student life.[70] It is as if college and liquor go together. There is a picture of John Belushi as Bluto Blutarski from *Animal House* where Bluto stands wearing his "College" sweater and has a dazed, confused, post/pre-alcohol visage and a vacant "why? and where is the next beer?" look in his eyes. This type of vision has become an icon of post-secondary education. Ernest Boyer has reported that alcohol is the drug of choice.[71] In two books, Arthur Levine describes the power of the bottle on campus. Courts have taken specific judicial notice of this culture. In 1998, students on several college and university campuses rioted when liquor privileges were curtailed or revoked. Courts are loathe to make rules that will fail; fighting campus liquor culture, it has been argued for years, is futile.

Yet another reason is that many plaintiffs/victims have not been sympathetic victims to the courts.[72] In cases like *Beach* (though not in *Rabel*), it is the drinking student who seeks refuge in tort liability. For example, in *Albano v. Colby College*[73] an underage member of a college tennis team was hurt on an annual trip to Puerto Rico following his excessive consumption of alcohol, which the coach specifically prohibited. Courts see powerful paradigms of assumed risks and contributory negligence as appropriate to bar recovery in such situations. In most states today, even when liquor liability flows against a defendant, rarely can the drinker sue for her injuries. Tort liquor liability rules generally operate to protect third parties not drinkers.

Thus, case law in the duty era remains demonstrably skewed. When a sexual assault occurs, or a laboratory experiment explodes, or defective premises cause injury, students have a solid chance of recovering.[74] When

---

70. CHARLES HOMER HASKINS, THE RISE OF UNIVERSITIES (1957).

71. Boyer, *College* 201 (1987).

72. The way courts view the parties to a lawsuit affects the application of legal rules. *See* HENRY STEINER, MORAL ARGUMENT AND SOCIAL VISION IN THE COURTS: A STUDY OF TORT ACCIDENT LAW (1987).

73. 822 F. Supp. 840 (D. Me. 1993).

74. The court in *Furek* saw a hazing, not alcohol, case. Courts and legislatures seem much more willing to create duty rules regarding hazing than for perceived alcohol-related injury cases. *See e.g.,* Florida Statutes, § 240.262 (1997), which presumes that "willing" participation in hazing is "forced." Of course, *Furek* facts represent a scenario that is a common one in an alcohol culture: most hazing incidents have alcohol at center stage or in the backdrop. *Furek* signals that courts may look past the alcohol immunities by recasting the legal problems in terms of other duty issues.

liquor is in the mix, potential college liability wanes considerably, although there are significant cases which impose liability like *Furek*. If the courts see the question presented as premises/dormitory safety, assumed duty, and/or control of dangerous persons, a student will fare better than if the claim is that liquor caused or facilitated the injury. Yet, with the increased occurrence of abusive and binge drinking described by writers like Levine and the occurrence of riots over beer, these results are likely to be re-examined again. We sense a pending shift in attitude towards college drinking in the courts.

Still, courts have rejected college liability for student liquor injuries in the following circumstances:

> The Colorado Supreme Court found that a university was not liable for injuries suffered by an intoxicated student as a result of his use of a trampoline at a campus fraternity. The court insisted—similar to *Bradshaw*—that a special relationship be shown. (*University of Denver v. Whitlock*, 744 P.2d 54 (Colo. 1987));
>
> In *Hartman v. Bethany College*, 778 F. Supp. 286 (E.D. Pa. 1992) a college freshman claimed that because she was a minor, the college had a duty to prevent her off-campus drinking. She lost;
>
> In *Booker v. Lehigh University*, 800 F. Supp. 234 (E.D. Pa. 1992) a female student admitted she voluntarily consumed significant alcohol before she fell on a rocky trail as she went home to her sorority. She asserted that the university had a general duty to control student consumption of alcohol on campus and that the breach of this duty caused her fall. She lost. The court did note, however, that if the university, not a fraternity, had served liquor or otherwise planned or purchased and supplied liquor, the result would have been different (an interesting observation, given the facts of *Bradshaw*);
>
> A student was killed riding a motorcycle on a public street after drinking at a fraternity party. The university was not liable. (*Millard* v. *Thiel College*, 611 A.2d 715 (Pa. Super. Ct. 1992));
>
> Several students have become intoxicated and have been attacked suddenly by other students. In the absence of more specific foreseeability, the courts have held that the university (or fraternity) is not liable. (*L. W. v. Western Gulf Assoc.*, *supra*; *Tanja H.*, *supra*; *Motz v. Johnson*, 651 N.E.2d 1163 (Ind. App. 1995));
>
> In an unusual case, a college freshman "got wasted" off campus and after taking some sort of a beating, stumbled into a commuter rail platform and collapsed, in need of rescue. As a drunken trespasser, he was not entitled to immediate assistance by the railroad (*Rhodes v. Illinois Cent. Gulf R.R.*, 665 N.E.2d 1260 (Ill. 1996).

The cases add up to a fairly consistent picture—even including arguably contrary cases like *Furek*. The mere fact that a university regulates alcohol use has not created a specific duty to particular individuals. While alcohol dangers are *generally foreseeable*, specific foreseeable danger will be necessary to attach liability for a particular student/victim. In the courts, bad boys and bad girls deserve what they get for themselves: even under-age drinkers are rarely afforded the benefit of the doubt. Other parties, like the liquor vendor, are legally responsible for harm. As to alcohol culture on campus (and off), the university has remained a significant bystander.

Despite these rulings, however, there have been notable shifts away from a no- liability approach to student alcohol related injuries. For one thing, courts like *Furek* and *Booker* place accountability on a university if it supplies liquor, plans the activity, etc. *Furek* rejects the culture of non-enforcement of liquor/hazing rules. For another, courts have begun to consider that certain aspects of campus fear and disorder—many of which facilitate drinking related injuries—are themselves subject to duty and liability. Finally, courts have moved subtly away from categorical no-duty rules to less categorical, more fact intensive, "foreseeability" and "negligence" rationales. Cases like *Booker* are hollow victories for a college: win this one, but what the courts say in *dicta* will inevitably force a change in college alcohol culture.

More fundamentally, the basic reasons courts have inclined to no liability results are coming under more debate in social policy circles.

First, there has been a steady increase in responsibility for liquor injuries beyond the traditional bar and vendor categories. Importantly, some cases are now holding employers and businesses liable for liquor injuries arising from company parties. Also, some courts are relaxing the notions of what it means to "furnish" liquor to a minor. In sum, social mores about drinking and liability are shifting, and the law is shifting too.

Second, there is a sense of urgency about liquor problems on campus. It may not be realistic (or desirable) to have prohibition on campuses. However, as we explore in Chapter VI, there are effective techniques to affect some of the most dangerous aspects of disorder that are connected with alcohol use. The university is not a bystander, and it is not helpless—there are reasonable solutions.

Third, attitudes are shifting towards the young women and men who are both victims and drinkers. As cases have made the press, there is an increasing sentiment from the public and parents that *general* risks of alcohol culture are *specifically* foreseeable and that students are not solely responsible for alcohol-related injuries. Parents and the media see that students are being injured, attacked, raped, and killed as a result of an alcohol culture and will likely not continue to accept the argument by colleges that the dangerous behavior and risk of injury—including assault—that results from alcohol abuse on campus is beyond the college's control.

. . .

The duty era is an era of transition. It is a period that features a powerful judicial alignment around "rules of duty" — particularly familiar business and liquor liability rules. The messages of the cases seem mixed: *e.g., Tanja H.* plaintiff loses, *Furek* plaintiff wins. One fact appears clear: The duty era has effectively ended almost all aspects of college insularity except with respect to alcohol use on and off campus. The pendulum has swung away from extreme student freedom models. The duty era has been an implicit search for a balance between university authority and student freedom and for shared responsibility for student/safety risk. Yet, it is still legitimate to ask what, if any, images are evolving from modern decisional law. What kind of environment is being created? Who will assume the risks and responsibilities of college life in the next generation of higher education in America? How will the balance of student/university responsibility for the risk of college life be struck?

VI

The Facilitator University

The law of student safety has evolved in four discernable periods in the 20th Century. First, the university was insularized from legal norms.[1]

---

1. Nancy L. Thomas recently wrote of the development of law on campus:

In 1960, nine attorneys representing 15 campuses held a retreat in Ann Arbor, Michigan. Their theme was "The Function of House Counsel at State Universities." At the time, no body of "college law" existed, and members of this small group saw a need to examine legal problems and solutions common to their universities. When they met again in 1966 to consider *in loco parentis* and student rights, they distributed one handout fewer than 15 pages long.

Today, this group (called the National Association of College and University Attorneys, or NACUA) has grown to more than 2,700 attorneys who represent nearly 1,400 campuses. NACUA, which averages 40 new members a year, provides continuing legal education for university attorneys by producing publications and sponsoring frequent seminars. Its annual conference lasts five days and offers sessions on more than 50 subjects. At last June's conference, NACUA distributed large notebooks containing some 10 pounds of materials, resources, and references.

Over three decades, the field of higher education law has evolved from an informal "interest" to a complex and sophisticated legal specialty. West Publishing Company, the primary publisher of judicial opinions, publishes the *Education Law Reporter*, which includes a comprehensive descriptive-word directory of college and university topics. Once considered "immune charities," colleges and universities are now living the curse, "May your life be full of lawyers."

The presence of attorneys on campus has been met with mixed reactions. To some academics, attorneys are trusted advisors and key members of an administrative team. To others, they are naysayers or "Monday morning quarterbacks," are unnecessarily confrontational, or wield too much power. To most, they cost too much.

Sometimes the negative reaction to attorneys is simply a response to their too frequent role as messenger, warning of problematic situations and legal hazards. Other times, an institution has, regrettably, selected an attorney who is unnecessarily cautious, confrontational, or domineering, or who is a mismatch with the institution's culture and needs.

Nancy L. Thomas, *The Attorney's Role on Campus—Options For College and Universities, Change* (May/June 1998 at 35).

Institutionally, it was legally immune because the law recognized its status as surrogate parent,or government or charity, subject to minimal legal scrutiny. In the second era, emphasizing civil rights on campus, universities lost immunities based on *in loco parentis* when students won civil rights on campus. Students became "constitutional" adults—entitled to basic constitutional protections—regarding a university's authority to conduct searches, regulate the content of student speech, restrict the rights of students to associate (based on political belief, etc.)—and requiring fundamental due process for students accused of misconduct. Later, during the third phase—the bystander era—governmental and charitable immunities likewise eroded, although a new form of protection rooted in no-duty-to-rescue rules emerged. As a result of the second and third eras, the university was required to treat students with procedural regularity in matters of discipline but could legally stand back from many student safety concerns, particularly student-on-student violence and faculty negligence in the form of inadequate supervision of students. There were instances when colleges had responsibility for student safety, but a new immunity appeared briefly in the bystander era—an immunity based on the historical common law right to be a "bystander" to a "stranger's" injury or peril. In retrospect, it was a strange analogy; but the 1960s and 1970s were unusual times beset with a great deal of social upheaval. In part, bystander rules arose as a triage approach to sudden upheavals on campus. Legally, the university began to distance itself from students: elaborate procedures replaced familial interactions, and the university went from helpful charity and/or benign governmental entity to a kind of stranger. From the ashes of the fallen era of *in loco parentis* and from the cold night of the bystander era, the duty era has rooted today in modern university law as the fourth era (although it was certainly immanent in the bystander era). The duty era imparts complex legal images—as we saw in Chapter V—and it often paints an ambiguous image of the modern university and its students. In this chapter we describe the way that the new duty era will reshape student/university relationships.

One feature of the duty era has been that a variety of images of the modern college and its students have been shaped and discussed by courts and commentators. This plethora of images is emblematic of a time of both education law and tort law in transition. Table 1 sets out, in brief form, the most commonly stated university/student relationships with some brief parenthetical information on the relationships that we develop further on in this chapter.

Table 1

The university is...	The student is...
"Business/Producer of Educational Product" (a dominant view)	"Consumer" *(Id.)*
"Parent/Babysitter" *in loco parentis* (almost universally rejected) (sometimes considered instead of a positive description—"college is *not* a babysitter")	"Child/Minor" *(Id.)* *(Id.)*
"Bystander"/"Stranger" (the dominant idea of *Bradshaw* et al.)	"Uncontrollable/Stranger" *(Id.)*
"Insurer of student safety" (overwhelmingly rejected with "parent" etc. and sometimes considered as an alternative to being a "bystander." Duty era cases distinguish this "strict liability" from duty.)	"Protected/Insured" (confusion over the differences between strict liability, duty and insurance. Subtle mistakes about "moral hazard.")[2]
"Landlord" (Prior to 1960, almost unheard of as such; major development/recognition in recent cases) (similar → *landowner*)	"Tenant" "Resident student" (There are many creative ways to describe a dormitory or residential student tenant, but courts treat them basically the same) (similar → *invitee*)
"Custodian" (used in K-12 caselaw, but rejected for law in bystander era, except when college actually brings children into programs. Suggestions that this was the role of the parental, *in loco parentis* university, although there is no caselaw support for this idea)	"Persons in custody" (never used)
"Education/In a purely educational role" (limited role/no educational malpractice)	"Pure student"[3] (the student comes to college *only* to be educated in class)

2. The term "moral hazard" is an insurance term of art with a common sense idea tucked inside. Insurance law is concerned that the existence of insurance will facilitate and encourage increasingly risky or deliberate misconduct. For example, the existence of life insurance could create some perverse incentives to kill someone. Or, if students were truly insured against their own stupid acts, there could be an incentive to engage in risky behavior without fear of significant financial consequences (particularly if you are hurting someone else). Insurance law has an array of techniques to combat these problems, which, were a university an insurance scheme, could be very effective. Tort lawyers (surprisingly) remain largely ignorant of this, and there is great rhetorical effect in overlooking such issues.

3. This view, a reaction to the abatement of *in loco parentis*, that the student/university relationship is purely educational (as an alternative to custodial) was an attempt to recreate insularity of university conduct from legal scrutiny, since claims of educational malpractice were and still are for the most part summarily rejected by courts.

The university is...	The student is...
"Supervisor"	"Supervised"
(sometimes used negatively as similar to custodian; in recent times used, as in *Mintz*, in regard to field trips, etc.)	*(Id.)*
"Employer"	"Employee"
(In some cases, a student is actually employed by the college).	(student enjoys legal status of appropriate category of worker; can include Workers' Compensation).
"Manager/Organizer of student life activities"	"Participant"
(An idea, associated with *Furek*, that a college co-creates the environment on campus)	(not a consumer, or employee; one whose conduct is channeled guided or directed but not dictated)
"Fiduciary"	"One to whom fiduciary duties are owed"
(sometimes referred to in certain financial/educational/confidential relations situations)	(hints of relationships like banking and trusteeship where one relies on the ability and authority of the other; sometimes confidential)
"In a 'special' relationship"	"Person entitled to 'duty' because of special relationship, or not, for lack thereof"
(by virtue of being a landlord, a premises owner, or having some relationship to dangerous or endangered persons: because of misinterpretation of *Bradshaw* et al., often used inter-changeably with duty, as if duty *only* exists when a special relationship exists, which is false. Technically, special relationships are only necessary when a university is being entirely unconnected and passive, which courts in the duty era are increasingly less likely to see. Reluctance to see university relationship to student as *per se* special, but most aspects of student life are special or infused with duty.)	*Id.*
→ "Charity"	"Beneficiary" *(Id.)*
→ (A feature of the *in loco parentis* era)	*(Id.)*
"In a unique or delicate situation"	"In a unique or delicate situation"
(seen by university attorneys, and administrators, as synonymous with *in loco parentis*)	(a throwback idea to the era of insularity; a view that student relations are too sensitive for a heavy handed legal system; perceives law as bad, or dangerous.)
	(alternatively, a sense that business paradigms are not adequate or appropriate.)
→ "In a contract relationship/promisor"	"In a contract relationship/promisee"
(Many courts say that the student/university relationship is based in "contract", although most of these cases deal with financial, procedural, civil, and intangible rights)	*(Id.)* (*student* is typically contracting party, not parent)
"A public governmental entity"	"A citizen/student"
(once a source of near total immunity, now a source of limited immunity, but includes constitutional responsibilities of a government to provide "due process" "equal protection" etc.)	(Student falls back to "consumer" image, if activities causing injury are similar to what businesses do, yet still retains substantive constitutional and procedural rights, etc.)
"In transition from industrial age to technological age"	"Caught in transition where hope and fear collide"
(Levine's thesis)	*(Id.)* (unsure, unsteady, fractal community)

The university is...	The student is...
→ "Facilitator"	"Responsible student"
(our term, drawn as a synthesis of the various modern images)	(A balance between the *in loco parentis* student and the completely 'free' student). university and student legally share *responsibility* for student safety; university is neither strictly responsible for student safety, nor insulated or immune from legal accountability for its operational negligence.)

University administrators face a perplexing—sometimes conflicting, other times overlapping—array of images. A decision to treat a student as a "customer" can conflict with less expansive responsibilities for that student's well being. On the one hand, a student is a "tenant", but on the other hand, a university lawyer counsels against getting too involved in student peer conduct in residence halls lest liability result. The array of complex legal rules is bad enough: the variety of competing images animating those rules makes it nearly impossible for a conscientious college administrator to do the job without fear of walking into a crossfire. The facilitator university model is primarily designed to offer a *comprehensive, adaptable legal and practical model* for university/student safety affairs. It is the "Windows" which arranges (and discards) the various "icons," as it were.

The facilitator model is both the sum of the valuable parts of the images and also greater. It is principally aimed at establishing balance in college and university law and responsibilities. It is particularly valuable to first examine the various images and place them on a continuum from most "university authority" to most "student freedom" oriented. The views sort into a distinct pattern.

Table II graphically depicts what can otherwise be gleaned from the images themselves. One thing that is clear is that many conceptions fall rather narrowly to one extreme (leaving a hole in the middle) *or* span a very wide range in encompassing the center. Thus, the images either provide too much university authority (or too little), too much student freedom (or too little), or encompass wide extremes of both, sending impossible to manage messages regarding who is responsible for what. Most images are either too extreme *or* too wide.[4] Balancing the rights and responsibilities of universities and students is a process of both eliminating extremes and defining an appropriately wide center. The facilitator model generally prefers less expansive positions because it is fundamentally a vision of *shared* responsibility, and a wide grant of freedom or a heavy dose of authority will often disempower the college or the student.

---

4. Charlie Brown once observed to Linus that although winter days are shorter, they are wider.

Table II

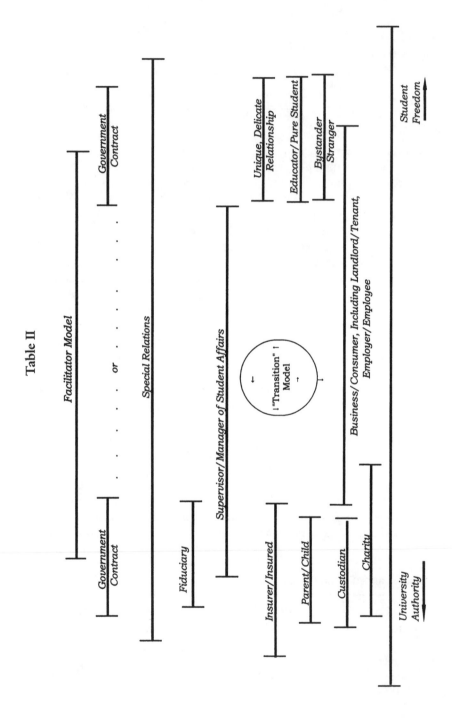

The other noticeable feature is that the more recent dominant images, particularly business/consumer images, trade extreme outcomes for center-oriented solutions. An inclination towards the balancing of university authority/control and student freedom is underway. However, center-oriented but still wide views tend to be too wide. For example, courts using business law decide cases which some university attorneys feel push too much toward university control dimension (hence the feared return of *in loco parentis*) — yet courts also decide cases involving "business law paradigms" which provide significant "student freedom," notably in alcohol related cases.

A final and related feature is the sense of transition, described in part by Levine. There has been some rather significant image shifting in university law in the last forty years. The motion is somewhat pendulum-like, and there has been a *dramatic* swing from almost total university control to radical student freedom oriented images. Today, a trend to more moderate balancing approaches is underway. The motion at times is also circular or overlapping. For example, special relationships images are intimately connected to "business/consumer" images. Courts often use one set of images without adverting to competing images in play in other cases. The transition in images is mirrored in students themselves: they too are restless, hopeful, often intoxicated, complex, fearful, endangered, even explosive.[5] The movement in images regarding university law reflects some profound questions about the nature of college education and the fair rules for student safety and the security of the learning environment. The facilitator model is the appropriate model for the transition and beyond.

A. Looking at the Images of the Legal Relationships Between Student and University

Each of the images of student/university legal relationships has its inherent strengths and weaknesses. The perspective of the facilitator college builds upon the various images and discards weaknesses inherent in them. It is helpful, in this regard, to sort the analysis of each image and its strengths and weaknesses roughly in sequence from models of the insularity, civil rights, bystander, and duty eras, respectively. However, some of

---

5. Today's students are also disappointed in the way they have been perceived and characterized by schools and society throughout their education. We have told them who they are. And we talk as if we almost *expect* them to abuse the legal freedoms they have gained in higher education.

the images span epochs or do not necessarily associate with one period, so this method is more of an approximation.

(i) Insularity Era Images

1. Parent/Babysitter/*In Loco Parentis*/Child

These were some of the dominant images of the era of insularity, and they have since been rejected. The belief of courts since the bystander era onwards has been that modern college students would not accept parental control nor would such a level of control be appropriate for the modern university. Students today are seen as "adults" (or better yet "non-children") even though some come to campus below the age of majority, and many are below the legal drinking age. A major weakness of the "parent" view was based in common-law doctrine of the insularity era—that the college as "surrogate parent" had nearly limitless power over students. The image was oriented to strong control paradigms; when universities exercised extreme and unreasonable (unconstitutional) "discipline" in the 1960s, the courts reacted and rejected parental imagery.

Although the parent/child view is largely dead as such, there are concerns expressed that it will return (some commentators suggest that the increasing recognition of university duties could lead to a return to "date calls" and curfews for female students[6]), and there are emerging indications that the legal system believes that students need some guidance. The parent/child model had little sense of nuance. Under an *in loco parentis* legal paradigm, a six-year-old, a twelve-year-old, and an eighteen-year-old were all seen as children. The image was not adaptable to age, experience, maturity, context, intelligence, etc. From parents' and educators' points of view, it is important and necessary to make such distinctions. For example, a barely eighteen-year-old college freshman who spent high school years in a highly structured and protected home environment may have a difficult time with pressures in the freshman year.

College students (although aging on average, as Levine points out) feature strong numbers of tweenagers *and* true adults (second career, part-time community college students for example). Colleges with large numbers of tweenagers (certainly the places with the most alcohol-based risks) must cope with a developmental reality. Many of these students (but not all) are not fully mature and responsible adults. Some of them are away from home and parental influence for the first time. Others have only limited experience on their own. These newly emancipated students often ag-

---

6. *See* Snow & Thro, *Redefining the Contours of University Liability: The Potential Implications of Nero v. Kansas State University,* 90 ED. LAW REP. 989, 998-99 (1994).

gregate into large groups and social pressures can build. These individuals need some guidance but not "Mr. Bear" or lock downs. Otherwise, college students are easy prey for irresponsible behavior, particularly if ringleaders form within the student body who facilitate unreasonably dangerous patterns of behavior.

The parental legal model has demonstrated that there is a need to revise strictly linear, sharply divided categories of development. There is not one magic moment when a person stops childhood and enters adulthood as such (June 6, 1944 and similar dates excepted). The need for guidance never ends truly but is certainly necessary in these critical tweenager years.

This type of guidance differs from strict control and discipline, where the parent makes all the life choices. A typical college student makes significant social choices throughout the four-plus years of higher education in the context of a highly dynamic, intellectually and emotionally charged social environment. Consultation with appropriate college administrators, trained and dedicated to provide guidance, is very important. Tweenagers need more than strangers to facilitate their own choices. It is critical that they learn to choose for themselves and to bear the consequences of their decisions. But these choices must be guided. Profoundly good and bad choices can be illustrated and challenged. Information, assistance, and affirmative efforts to raise civility are necessary. For example, today many young males and females drink heavily, and account for radically disproportional numbers of victims in automobile and pedestrian accidents. Criminality is, and remains, high in these groups. These manifestations play out on the college campus — they may begin and end there, or spill over to the community. A legal rule which requires choosing between the extremes of female curfews or date calls and no university responsibility at all regarding student conduct outside the classroom places unreasonable restraints on vital aspects of the appropriate student/university relationship. Such all or nothing rules almost never work, legally or socially.

Our social system historically once had significant mechanisms in place to transform the adolescent into mature adulthood. In the industrial age, the primary mechanisms were army, new family *(e.g.* the 1950s marriage), workplace, *or* college. A trend began in the 1960s and is evident today: more post-adolescents make the transition to true adulthood *through* college. College in the 1950s *mimicked* the highly disciplinary climate of army and workplace (example: professors, armed with threats of lost deferments, were very similar to drill sergeants). But the college lost its quasi-military/workplace/family authority in the 1960s and *then* was asked to shoulder an ever-increasing burden of more college students (of all ages).

As a society, we must fashion law to address these crucial years in a person's development. A major failure of society in its transition from the industrial age has been the failure of university law to identify and then address the tweenager issues created in the context of college life. The 1998 riots over beer focused everyone upon the fact that there are deep problems on the college campus. There is an in-between stage that social institutions must address—or else. Families do play a real role for many students—the parent, grandparent, good aunt, or older sibling, et al. who represent the guidance of elders—*but a legal paradigm that prevents the educator or education administrator from performing this role for fear of being sued, or which encourages a "look the other way" attitude in situations where guidance or intervention is necessary to the students' well-being, is seriously flawed.*

Letting eighteen to twenty-year-olds kill themselves because of liquor is as much an abdication of an opportunity to facilitate as is Dean Wormer-style control. Underkill and overkill show no sense of subtlety. Parents with small children are simply one kind of facilitator: the tactics for a five-year-old differ for older children, and so on. As with Yoda and Obi Wan Kenobi, active guidance gradually fades into observation as the young person matures. There *is* an in-between.

A facilitator is a two-directional entity. Facilitation is socratic. Yoda chides Luke not to encounter Darth Vader—"you're not ready." But Luke is warned. If Luke were a child, he would be grounded; if he were an adult stranger, Yoda would not be involved (Luke's friend Biggs never sees Yoda but could have used his guidance). Yoda charts the middle path—inform, guide, teach, chide and observe. In the end, it turns out that Luke was not ready in the sense that he lost his hand, yet it was precisely that loss which teaches him the "lesson of the cave," the real power of the force. Luke defeats Darth Vader *and* resurrects his father by learning these lessons—compassion and responsibility—that Yoda could not teach. Such lessons, at some level, must be experienced to be learned. Do or do not, said Yoda. Luke had to learn it for himself in his own experience. Yoda also *learns* that in a very important sense Luke *was* ready—the timing was perfect. Had Yoda just met Luke, taught him nothing, and let him face Darth Vader, Luke would be dead and Yoda would be a bad bystander. If Yoda fully trained Luke like a Jedi Knight robot-killer, Darth Vader would be dead *and so would Luke's father*. Little gained, nothing learned, especially if Luke turns into another killer. Yoda needs to find the *middle* path for Luke, Darth Vader, and himself. Once Luke has mastered the tests, he now stands next in line as a master facilitator. *Star Wars* is just a movie (although a powerful set of images for today's students who grew up with them), but it can depict in an idealized way what is still appealing to many about the period of *in loco parentis.* Tweenagers, like Luke Skywalker, need magnificent guidance—not control or apathy—to succeed in life. The task of facilitating is at once difficult and essential. It is what the current generation probably gets less of than any previous generation; their paradox has been that they have peace and prosperity, but they often report closer relationships with liquor than college administrators.

2. Insurer/Insured

This image actually first appeared in the bystander era but was used to describe a perceived consequence of *in loco parentis*. The idea was that a university had agreed to guarantee a safe environment or pay if injury occurred. *Such a system has never existed,* but like Camelot, it is a powerful icon.

The weakness of this view is that it places no responsibility on students for their own safety or, at least, seriously diminishes it. By knowing they are "insured," students would be encouraged to displace the costs of aberrant behavior on the university. The burden on the finances of a university would then be catastrophic, *or* the university would have to reinstitute draconian control, *or* both. The allocation of risk and rights/responsibility would be drastically skewed.

Of course, insurance does not function quite the way courts have described it in university law regarding student safety. Nonetheless, there is a kernel of truth to the way courts see it. Students generally lack adequate insurance to protect themselves from other dangerous persons, and they do not always have adequate health and medical benefits in the event of *Furek*-type injuries. This means that there is little loss spreading, and loss allocation can be dramatic in a tort suit—all student or all university. Moreover, an insurance mentality is often a loss-avoidance, pro-active mentality. In this regard, universities could use more of an "insurance mentality." Workers compensation insurers have been very successful in reducing claims *and* injuries with pro-active, loss reduction programs. By analogy, better education of faculty, staff, and students regarding the scope of their shared responsibility for safety (in typical scenarios) and more resources devoted to safety implications of activities (facilities maintenance, campus law enforcement, safety technology, etc.) could avoid student injury and litigation. Sometimes the simplest strategy, when pro-acted, is most effective. This is the mind-set of an insurer. Bystander and parental universities are legally *re*-active. In the bystander model, the incentive is to avoid liability by non-involvement; this is a counterproductive and legally risky incentive. The duty era increasingly fosters *pro-active* college administration, although there is still a distinct tendency for a campus to modify risks only *after* the first tragedy (note how even duty law still encourages this in some cases with its forseeability requirement.) So while bystander courts attacked the idea of an "insuring" university— rightly so for some purposes—there are *aspects* of the insurance image which could help to balance risk and responsibility and thus reduce risk.

3. Custodian

Like the insurance image, this strong image is very much a product of looking back on the *in loco parentis era*. K-12 students are considered to be in this type of relationship.[7] However, the cases do not, nor have they ever, applied the notion of custody to college students to create duty or liability; instead, some 'bystander' era courts stated that custody would be necessary for duty but that custody did not exist. The idea of a custodial relationship with college students is a legal straw man. The rhetorical effect of the bystander decisions was to suggest that, both practically and legally, the only forms of *control* that would work would be *the most draconian forms of control*. The phrase "custodial control" usually refers to patients in sanitariums, prisoners, and others held in a confined space and/or heavily guarded. The college was never like a sanitarium or a prison, so the analogy has had a *reductio ad absurdum* feel to it.

However, by engaging in such hyperbole—that the only possible control is the control of a prison guard—bystander courts set the stage for other courts to see the need for a more nuanced approach to control. "Control"—sometimes thought of as necessary for "special relationships"—and hence "duty," can be exerted in other ways. For example, one way to control behavior is to eliminate options or offer alternatives to undesirable conduct. Importantly, the law has evolved to ask individuals (and thus colleges and universities) to exercise *only that degree of control they actually possess*.[8] To exercise crowd control, for example, police do not take all in the crowd into custody. And control, does not connote a guarantee of success; we often ask who was 'in control' at the time of an accident, and not oxymoronically. In a university setting for example, a student can be controlled without expulsion, incarceration, or institutionalization. One way to control a dangerous student attacker—as in *Nero,* for example—would be to remove him from a dormitory and thus eliminate numerous options for attacks.[9] Just like criminal intrusion, you can control it, but sometimes you cannot stop it. The custodial image requires an extreme degree of university authority as a predicate for involvement,

---

7. The doctrine therefore has applicability on the college campus—e.g., during youth camps—insofar as it has imposed a duty on schools to supervise elementary and secondary level students who come to campus. *See* Rupp v. Bryant, 417 So. 2d 658 (Fla. 1982).

8. *See* Estates of Morgan v. Fairfield Family Counseling Ctr., 673 N.E.2d 1311 (Ohio, 1997).

9. Of course, if a student presents imminent danger to self or others, he may be subject to detention for purposes of evaluation by competent mental health professionals. All colleges and universities are aware of such procedures, and many have utilized them.

which is inconsistent with the college environment today and, for the most part, with college even in the era of insularity. It is worth remembering that even when colleges called in the national guard in the 1960s and fired into and over students, these actions failed and then backfired.

4. Charity

In the era of insularity, the idea that a private college was a charitable organization was a powerful way to avoid duty-based liability for injuries to students.[10] Calling a college "charitable" augmented university power and authority and left students legally powerless. It also disempowered students politically: like challenging the Girl Scouts, there was an air of ingratitude to challenging a charitable educational organization.

The charity model crashed for universities when other charitable organizations lost immunities. Courts today rarely recognize significant charitable immunities. Thus, today, no one argues that a college is a charitable institution when the issue is student safety. The defunct charity image, however, contained a kernel of wisdom. By viewing the (usually private) university in this way, the university took on the look of an institution with grand aims, public goals, and transpersonal missions. In short, as a charity the university was aspirational, more public and not simply some private agreement or limited voluntary association. Colleges served their own communities *and* a greater public interest. The loss of this sense parralled the change in the image of the public university as a governmental entity.

5. Governmental Entity

In the era of insularity, the public university was protected from student lawsuits over safety issues by governmental immunities. It was an arm of the state and was making important policy decisions on a macro and micro level. University decisions on most matters were insulated from judicial intervention on behalf of private citizens. The extreme deference to governmental authority declined appreciably after World War II, and in the civil rights era the governmental aspects of university life shifted from emphasis on the power and authority of a college to its responsibility to treat its citizen/students with minimum fairness.

Lost, it seemed, was the idea that the university existed as government (or charitable organization) for the greater good, with a public, transpersonal mission. The fall of this government image (or its transmutation)

---

10. For those who would argue that *custodial* duty relations existed in the era of *in loco parentis*, it is worth noting that truly custodial duties, when exercised by a charity (a sanitarium, for example), were generally actionable and not subject to the immunity of more ordinary charitable activities. Had students truly been in custody, the law would have recognized special duty-based safety rights.

set the stage for strong "private rights" notions. In fact, the success of due process and civil rights litigation in the 1960s spurred on an equally powerful idea that the *private* university was *contractually* responsible for rights owed publically. The fall of governmental power notions facilitated the rise of student consumerism and the image of the college as a business.

6. Contract

For over a century, courts have sometimes said that the essence of the student/university relationship lies in contract law. The image pops up even today, although most of the tort cases no longer even mention such a predicate. It is thus one of the most elusive and enduring images in university law. Contract imagery smacks of freedom and voluntary associations, and also limitations on authority.

In the era of insularity, contract notions served important college authority functions. Authority arose from *contract* with parent and/or in delegation of authority from the state and from the social contract. In much the way that governments prior to John Locke would trace the divine rights of kings, the courts would meticulously establish the authority to insularize university affairs through contract and delegation. Contract was related to ideas of sovereignty—sovereignty of government, family, and voluntary associations. The cases virtually never saw the contract image as a way to empower students or as a protector of their rights. Students were the subjects of "sovereign jurisdiction," not its architects.

Eventually, however, contract images, like governmental images, transmuted into rights conferring images in two ways.

First, contract thinking was used from the 1960s on to review and restrain private college authority. The contract was now between *student* and university, and was a special contract deserving of special rules of construction that sometimes favored student rights. These rights were (and are) invariably economic and intangible rights—rights to associate, rights of fair process, etc. Contract images, like government rights, shifted quickly from university authority to student rights and freedom images.

Second, the contract image began to view the student in a business/consumer relation, an image that first rooted in the bystander era and has dominated the duty era since. Still, somewhat paradoxically, some courts imagined a contract relationship but began to talk more and more extensively in the language of torts. The facilitator model that we advance makes quick sense of this apparent contradiction.

The strengths of the contract images are related to their weaknesses. Courts like to view colleges as a special form of voluntary association, and the pull of contract in this sense is obvious. Yet in the insularity period, the contract was more like indentured servitude for a student. In later periods, contract law required special adaptation to work. Students were given take it or leave it deals on the universities' terms and were often not well informed of all the ramifications of their agreement. Moreover, the public seemed to be dealt out of the equation. Was college *simply* a private experience between college and students? Had college lost its "noblesse oblige" and become merely a tool of private aggrandizement? Unintentionally, contract laid the groundwork for certain forms of disorder, particularly as students came to see themselves as radically empowered consumers.

(ii.) Civil Rights Era Images

The dominant images of the Civil Rights era cases were the government/contract images. The significance (as in (1), (5), and (6) above) was in the *shift*. Suddenly, the student became a citizen with constitutional rights and/or a contracting party with basic entitlements to fair treatment. These images were used to empower students and promote student freedom paradigms but were generally restricted to the concern for fundamental constitutional rights and commercial fairness. The focus was on intangible and economic rights, not safety rights.

(iii.) Bystander Era Images

A great deal of bystander imagery was negative and passive. Courts were anxious to say what universities were *not* and what they could *not* do. Images of eras past- -whether real or straw men—dominated. As we have seen, many courts rejected parent/babysitter/*in loco parentis* images, refused "insurer" (strict liability) ideas, and decried "custodial" images (that were in use by them in elementary and secondary education), and some courts simply ignored the expanding responsibilities of charitable organizations and/or governmental agencies for operational negligence that caused injuries. University was *not* mommy, not the "Rock," not the cuckoo's nest, not the Girl Scouts, and not big brother; the university would not hold hands, nor indemnify, nor control, nor accept the mantle of some benign greater public purpose. The university had a limited role to fill—it was an *educator*: Otherwise it was—legally—a bystander to student "strangers." Insularity gave way to two-dimensionality.

1. Educator

One of the most powerful legal ideas to emerge in the bystander era caselaw was that the college had a limited mission—to educate. The purely educational role was narrowly conceived as classroom instruction, etc. but not as education in any larger sense (as in socialization). This image saw the college as only marginally involved in non-catalog affairs. Fraternities, college drinking, extra-curricular activities, almost all off campus events (whether curricular or not) were not "purely educational." The responsibility was, then, to provide reasonably safe classroom instruction, etc. Of course, since there was (and still is virtually) no legal remedy for educational malpractice in college—the purely educational vision of college was in the nature of immunity *not* duty thinking.

The purely educational college model was a radical affirmation of student freedom and a very narrow vision of university power. The university could decide with impunity who got "A's"; otherwise students could do almost anything without the college being legally accountable. Actually, the courts would say that the college had the *right* to enforce regulations regarding student conduct but did not have legal *responsibility* to do so. As in *Rabel*, the university could have rules regarding drinking and fraternities but did not have to enforce them. This was a subtle message to colleges, but it became very clear in its implication. The college had the legal right to construct a paper utopia but no duty to manifest it; the college had no duty to enforce the rules and actually had legal incentives not to do so. *Courts told colleges, "You cannot control these students," and college attorneys translated this to mean that if you try too hard (and "assume a duty") you just might be liable if, despite your efforts, students are injured. The idea that a college is purely educational became a judicial invitation, with the active encouragement of legal counsel,[11] to be a bystander.* It also became an invitation to market campus safety to the public in unrealistic ways.

A legal model that sees the university as having no legal relationship with its students outside the classroom—one which sees the student/college relationship as purely educational—fails in at least two major respects. First, it enlarges student rights by allowing students to exercise so-called student freedoms to the point of the unreasonable endangerment of other students. Second, such a legal model fails to impose any sense of shared responsibility in matters of student/university relations because it precludes a balancing of university conduct and student con-

---

11. Many college and university attorneys, in fact, supported the desires of student affairs administrators to assume responsibility in matters of student safety but were constrained by their understanding of the major cases of the era (about affirmative and negative duty—misfeasance and nonfeasance). In doing their jobs, university attorneys were aware that if the university were to have "no duty" regarding student injury, judicial rules of procedure permitted student personal injury lawsuits to be dismissed as a matter of law. The bystander courts baited lawyers to seek this line of defense as it held the promise of marginal legal scrutiny of university affairs.

duct in matters of student safety and well-being. An "all-or-nothing" model simply fails to recognize that the college or university and the student both have some control over the safety and security of the learning environment.

An all-or-nothing, education-only legal paradigm discourages active university efforts to create a sense of civility in student affairs beyond the mere enforcement of rules and regulations. Gary Pavela observes that university efforts to teach students civility must reach past disciplinary rules, regulations, and process. A legal model that makes student affairs administrators fear that their intervention will produce a bad legal consequence for the university is a model under which efforts to teach students civility are doomed to failure.

Courts in the duty era have not often challenged the idea that the college is purely educational on its face. Instead, they decide cases that place more than narrowly drawn educational duties on the college. The image of a pure educational college has failed. Yet, it has never been overtly discredited. Courts accept that colleges do have an educational role but see it in the wider context of college life. Even purely educational images cannot really disregard safety concerns because education is only possible under conditions of reasonable safety.

2.   Bystander University/Uncontrollable Students

(i) Strangers

Bystander ideas are to student freedom what *in loco parentis* was to university authority. The bystander university gave students their education and provided "formal" regulation. Otherwise, students were free from university control. The freedom was really the freedom of a college from lawsuits regarding student safety. The freedom was also a chimera: bystander case law empowered radical libertarian behavior at the expense of other student's liberties. On balance, true freedom and the value of freedom declined.

As the bystander era emerged, it centered around no duty rules and a perceived lack of special relationships. With the fall of charitable, governmental, and familial immunities, the courts embraced a strange analogy—they began to view college life in terms of *rescue* law. There was a sense that college had gone bad. It seemed that hordes of young revolutionaries, demanding to be grown ups, had descended on colleges and overwhelmed their support systems. The students did not want guidance and control and would not accept either. The college was placed in a state of siege and triage.

That image, like all of the images, had a kernel of truth. The baby-boom generation was (or is) a demographic force of historic proportions. Happy families of the 1940s and 1950s did not foresee that they were creating the largest class ever of teenagers, tweenagers, and yuppies for future decades. When this group went to college in record numbers and hit political critical mass, traditional colleges were strained, perhaps overwhelmed. As an *intermediate* response to a *temporary* transitional phrase, the bystander era reflected the way that American courts typically treat nascent enterprises or enterprises in a developmental stage—substantial legal latitude is allowed at first. Examples of similar legal protection were: railroads, automobiles, consumer products, and polluting industries; even the computer industry has had this protection in fledgling phases.

There was very clear concern—expressed in *Bradshaw et al.*— that liability for student safety would deal a crushing financial blow to modern colleges. An immunity defined in terms of "no-duty-to-rescue" was appropriate, or so the courts thought. In what were perceived as unusual and transitional times, courts ruled that students should bear a significant responsibility for their own safety. To be sure, injury to college students is preventable only if students exercise reasonable care for their own safety, but the bystander image was faulty because it promoted the university's abdication of *its* responsibility to exercise reasonable care. Any sense of balance or shared responsibility was lost in the context of a rescue doctrine. The image cemented duty analysis—tort analysis—making it the prominent way to legal-speak college and university law. The seeds for this approach existed in the era of insularity, but university law could have gone in other directions besides "duty."

With duty analysis came a special focus on special relations. The bystander image was loaded towards the idea that duty exists only if there is a special relation. In other words, the rescue image was especially associated with some of the most peculiar tort rules that exist and pushed people to view the college as a passive receptacle, non-acting and almost invisible apart from classroom instruction. "The college" became nothing more than an educational entity in the strict sense of the term. Students were actors, active not passive, and were seen as the primary vehicles of dangerous or endangering behavior.

Bystander imagery has been immensely powerful. Levine and Boyer each describe how increasingly distant college administration has become from student life. When the college is an outsider to student life and safety, there is a sense of alienation and disconnectedness which breeds and replicates. Thus, the sense of a college system itself eroded under the bystander rules: the various processes of the "community" were independently operating variables. The very idea that a college *is* a community, still popular with faculty, also faded.

Decisions like *Bradshaw, Rabel,* and *Beach* fractured the law into two views of the student/university relationship. Some courts like *Mullins* rejected no-duty rules. This feature of the bystander era continues to throw some courts off track. There are remnants in the 1990s of the mistaken belief that duty exists only if there is a *special* relationship, particularly a *custodial* relationship. As a matter of law that is flatly false: duty exists in a variety of circumstances, and for tort lawyers, duty premised on special custodial relationships is just a small subset of the whole of duty law. However, if a court perceives that a college is just a passive bystander to *uncontrollable* conduct, the unusual rules become more prominent. *The facilitator university, however, is not routinely passive and does not accept the idea that because some student injury is inevitable all reasonable and positive avenues of protecting student safety are shut off.* In other words, both bystander and facilitator models believe in "duty" but just draw different conclusions of fact about the role of the college and its true power.

3. Landlord/Tenant/Landowner/Invitee

The politics of university law have successfully downplayed the dual-personality aspect of the bystander era. The bystander era birthed cases like *Mullins* as well as *Bradshaw*. The bystander era — dominated by the "university as stranger" image — was also a time when the university incongruously began to be perceived by many courts as a landlord and premises owner. Truly, the concept that a college is a business was rooted there. Prior to that time, the college was like a charity, a government, or a family to courts — strict analogies to business and business law were generally not used. The idea that the college was a business or landlord was, at least on its face, flatly inconsistent with the bystander image. Courts made no attempt to reconcile this dissonance, and even today a split of authority is occasionally evident. A few courts here and there treat *Bradshaw*[12] as if it existed in a vacuum.

---

12. Consider the poorly reasoned 1997 decision of the 10th Federal Circuit Court of Appeals (includes Utah) in *Orr v. Brigham Young University*, 1997 U.S. App. Lexis 6083 (3/31/97 10th Cir.) In fairness, the decision is an unpublished decision and is not binding precedent by rule of the court. This is good, because the case is wrong. In *Orr*, a student athlete complained that the BYU football staff injured him. As the court related:

Orr's complaint alleged that BYU football coaching staff and athletic trainers failed to provide adequate medical care for a series of back injury episodes he suffered while playing college football for BYU. He claimed that BYU's coaching staff placed enormous pressure on him to continue playing while he was hurt, which further exacerbated his injuries. Orr advanced several theories for holding BYU liable for his back injuries. He theorized that BYU owed a duty of care to him based on the special relationship created by this status as a student athlete at BYU; that BYU's conduct created a situation in which playing him would cause him harm, thus imposing on BYU an affirmative duty to protect

In one sense, these images were positive and realistic steps for students and invitees. Colleges could not offer slum tenant conditions or fail to perform routine premises maintenance. Students were still responsible for

---

him from injury; that BYU allowed its trainers to practice medicine without a license; and that BYU breached its duty of care to him in its diagnosis and treatment of his medical injuries.

Id. At the trial court level, summary judgment was granted on the claim (one claim was voluntarily dismissed). The trial court's decision was affirmed by the Court of Appeals on the issue of duty (there were obvious questions of breach, causation, and plaintiff's assumption of risk, etc.). Thus the only question raised was whether there was a *duty* to the student. Because the law controlling was Utah law, the *Beach* case controlled. The court rejected the plaintiff's claims generally, based on *Beach*:

> The rule Orr contends for would result in a broad, nearly unprecedented expansion of duty...for Utah's colleges and universities. At present, the boundaries of Utah law are defined by the Beach [sic] case, which rejected the claim that colleges and universities owe a special duty to their adult students, even when the students are participating in university-sponsored activities. As a federal court, we are reticent to expand state law in the absence of clear guidance from Utah's highest court, or at least a strong and well-reasoned trend among other courts which Utah might find persuasive, in favor of such expansion. See Taylor v. Phelan, 9 F.3d 882, 887 (10th Cir. 1993) (declining to expand concept of special relationships between police and citizens beyond bounds created by Kansas courts); see also Great Central Ins. Co. v. Insurance Service Office, Inc., 74 F.3d 778, 786, (7th Cir. 1996) (innovations in the law are better sought in state court than in federal court). We find no indication, either in the Utah courts or in a trend developing elsewhere, that the Utah courts would impose a duty on BYU based on a special relationship, under these circumstances. The district court properly granted summary judgment on Orr's claim that BYU breached a duty created by a special relationship between himself and BYU.

Id. (emphasis added). The case was clearly a simplistic reaction to *Beach*. A federal court can safely hide behind a state supreme court decision. However, the *Orr* court missed the game entirely. For once thing, the *Orr* allegations were different. In *Orr,* the plaintiff contended that he was pushed into service—that the university took affirmative steps that placed him in a position of danger. This would have been the equivalent of an allegation that a professor encouraged a student who had been drinking to walk near a dangerous cliff. Orr's claims contained obvious allegations of *misfeasance* that *do not require (even in Utah courts) a special relationship*. Moreover, the court acknowledged only one case on point, but overlooked the holdings of cases like *Mintz, Nero,* and *Roettgen.* In modern terms, the *Beach* case is unwinnable today in perhaps most states, even Utah itself. What is worse is that even if it were winnable, *Orr* would be readily distinguishable.

Admittedly, *Utah* may very well agree with the result in *Orr,* as it features some unusually harsh anti-victim tort rules. We wonder whether Orr and his family ever realized that if he played for a school in New York his claims might have been successful? Frankly, we find the Utah rule completely out of step. *Orr* represents what can happen if bystander-type thinking goes too far.

ordinary and obvious risks. However, as these rules were to become more powerful vehicles for student safety litigation, there was the chance that student/college relations would become similar to those of customers to shops in a shopping mall. Was college nothing more or other than the collection of various business responsibilities?

(iv.) Duty Era Images

1. Business/Consumer (Special Relationships and Duty)

By far, this is the dominant current conception of modern university relations, if one aggregates the cases. Although dominant, business images do not convey a complete or completely adequate picture, however. In re-imagining the student/college relationship through business law, modern courts only rarely see the college as just a bystander: some harm is inevitable on campus, but the no-liability logic of modern cases is much more oriented towards lack of foreseeability of risk by the university or assumption of risk by students—not college passivity or lack of power. Courts are quick to pick up on business analogies to campus problems and to apply the law of torts to those subjects.

(a) Specific Relations

Colleges play various business roles to students—landlord, landowner (premises maintenance), employer, and administrator or supervisor of student activities actively managed or facilitated by the college. A prominent feature of business relations in other environments is that they impose significant tort/accident responsibility. Not only does a business have a general duty to avoid actions and activities which foreseeably cause unreasonable danger, but invitees, tenants, consumers, and others are also owed *affirmative duties* because they are in special relationships with the business. Applying business rules to the student/university relationship forces the college as a business to use due care affirmatively to minimize the risk of student injury, within the scope of the business relationship. But this alone is not enough. Traditional tort law also says that whenever the university *acts* it is responsible to use care. For example, when the university in the *Nero* case affirmatively assigns students to a summer residence hall, it is legally responsible to use reasonable care to avoid placing students in positions of unreasonable risks. Therefore, when the university knows that a student is awaiting a criminal trial for rape, it is fair to ask whether a reasonable person would assign that student to a coed residence hall and thereby facilitate access to residents in common areas of the dormitory like hallways, laundry rooms, and lounges.

Because many business law cases do arise in situations of affirmative duty, there is a strong connection between business law and the law of special relationships. Some courts and commentators confuse this a bit and assume that because special relationships are a feature of business/college law, duty is owed only under special circumstances.[13] Let us make this perfectly clear: *Universities can owe duties to their students on and off campus irrespective of whether there is a special relationship of any kind. Legal special relationships only potentially enhance responsibility to include affirmative duties to proactively prevent harm even when caused by third parties, non-negligent forces, and/or students themselves. Special relations are not prerequisites to duty, per se, but only prerequisites to certain kinds of duty to take affirmative action. Custodial relations are only a subset of special relationships.* This is basic tort law.

Confusion on these points has led on occasion to bad court decisions and misguided secondary commentary. It is a seductive and easy mistake to follow the logic of *Beach* or *Bradshaw.* Of course, courts are free to fashion law anyway they please. But if courts are making distinct tort rules for colleges, they should say so in plain terms. Moreover, a facilitator model permits courts inclined to protect universities as a matter of law to do so with more correct rules of decision. As we develop *infra,* there is a better, more straightforward and candorous way to do what some courts wish to do when they use special relationships analysis to protect colleges. A decision which is correct for the wrong reason still hurts university/student relations.

A business law/consumer mentally has some additional advantages and disadvantages. For example, colleges now often employ administrators increasingly adept at risk management strategies to deal with campus risks of all types. To some extent, this is an excellent development, except that the campus is not exactly like a corporate workplace. As Gary Pavela has pointed out, many student affairs personnel view students not as fully mature adults, but in a liminal stage between life at home and work.[14] Risk management strategies designed for the workplace are not always tailored to student life situations. For example, certain alcohol problems at college campuses are more difficult to manage and are more dangerous than analogous problems with businesses and residential tenancies. A business strategy may fail because college problems have unique difficulties and re-

---

13. There is an intuitive reason to conflate special relations with duty in the business context as well. Particularly in the dormitory context and in many instances of premises responsibility, courts use special relationship analysis as a proxy for the idea that being a landlord or a business premises owner is much like carrying on an ongoing activity in which omissions are like misfeasance (active misconduct); the failure to fix a broken lock in a dormitory is like a driver who fails to apply the brakes not like a stranger who refuses to jump in a lake to save a drowning swimmer.

14. 7 Synthesis No. 3, at 531.

quire special solutions. Risk management consultants and risk underwriters who are acutely aware of the special nature of student life situations know this and encourage appropriate approaches to risk management.[15]

(b) Shared Responsibility—Strengths and Weaknesses of Business Law

The business/consumer model is very appealing to courts for some obvious reasons. For one thing, business law is familiar territory to courts. Universities can be treated like other businesses, without special legal rules. For another, that model supplies an array of rules which often balance university responsibility with student responsibilities. An experienced set-design student who disregards a professor's clear instructions and admonitions not to use a power saw that is obviously broken, and who is thus injured while cutting a piece of scenery for a theater class on his own time, will have no valid claim for damages from the university. On the other hand, if a first-year undergraduate student who has never before experimented with certain chemicals is burned while conducting an experiment without proper supervision by the instructor, she may have a valid claim that the university shares some responsibility for her injuries. Other models of university law feature extreme allocations of risk and responsibilities. Courts have a penchant for balancing approaches and thus have come to prefer business law solutions for colleges over many other approaches. The essence of business law images and rules is, in sum, a search for the reasonable center. Nonetheless, business/consumer images have still suffered from "width" problems. Some business law decisions are very protective of consumers. In the college context, commentators accuse these decisions of urging a return to *in loco parentis*. Other business-style decisions are criticized for not doing enough to protect students. In other words, business law-type decisions are not particularly sensitive to the balance between college and student responsibility *as such*; the balance of authority and freedom struck for colleges under an unqualified business paradigm mimics too strictly the approaches that courts use for malls, furniture delivery businesses, restaurants, etc. And so, there are complaints from both ends that business law applied to universities goes too far in both directions. There is a sense that there is something very appropriate about aspects of the duty era using business law-style rationales, but there is also a sense that results are sometimes skewed and that certain rationales are not always fully appropriate for unique college envi-

---

15. *See, e.g., Managing Liability,* a monograph series published by:
United Educators Insurance Risk Retention Group, Inc.,
Two Wisconsin Circle
Suite 1040
Chevy Chase, MD 20815.

ronments or situations. The facilitator model adapts business law to the unique university community and to each college uniquely (a community college may have different responsibilities than a traditional four-year college with teenage students).

The key to the reconciliation of business law approaches and higher education law lies in the resolution of problems with the analogy to business/consumer paradigms. Students are not ordinary consumers buying a sandwich or shirt. Students buy into a lifestyle in many cases. Housing, friends (roommates), meals, sports, activities, education, etc. often are all "purchased" in one transaction which is most like building a complex set of option contracts (except different). In addition, a great deal is offered on a take it or leave it basis. Shauna Nero was in no position to bargain for more safety; women students in *Delaney* begged for an entry door lock to be fixed to no avail. The student/university relationship is an unusual consumer relationship at best. Once a student has purchased an education, the power over the deal shifts radically in favor of a college. (For what it is worth, this problem animates the arguments for a fiduciary model. The idea there would be that a college would still be responsible to deal with students in good faith and trust. That model has not caught on, but the core idea is an aspect of a facilitator model.)

• • •

Levine and Pavela both note how students openly view themselves as consumers.

Pavela writes:

> The momentum for greater student rights was accelerated in the late 1970s and 1980s by the consumer protection movement. Students began to see themselves as "customers" seeking services — a view reinforced by federal and state legislation protecting student privacy, and requiring that 'consumer information' about financial aid, campus security, and other services be made available to applicants for admission.[16]

Students have increasingly looked upon education in terms of "comodification." Arthur Levine has eloquently described the exact same phenomena and supported them with his surveys.

In *When Hope and Fear Collide*, Levine devotes an entire section to what he calls "A Consumer Mentality,"[17] and the theme permeates the book. He describes the causes and consequences of consumerism. First, Levine points out that "consumerism is not new on college campuses;[18] it

---

16. Pavela, 7 SYNTHESIS 530-31.
17. See Levine *supra*, at 50.
18. *Id.* at 51.

was evident in the late 1970s (the bystander era). The "new con-sumerism" of today, Levine describes, is specifically targeted at colleges and universities, and students today bring to campus a true consumer mentality: "[t]heir focus is on convenience, quality, service and cost."[19]

This consumerism has been fueled by the changing demographics of the college. Most students are now "non-traditional": about half work or go to school part-time and a small percentage (less than 20%) are 18-22 years old going full-time and living on campus.[20] College, as Levine describes it, is not typically a central life focus as it once was for so many of us — it is just one activity, and often work and families are far more important.[21]

Students are thus, to some extent, naturally growing more and more apart from their campuses.

> [Older], part-time, and working students, especially those with children, often say they want a different type of relationship with their colleges from the one undergraduates have historically had. They prefer a rela-tionship like those they already enjoy with their bank, the telephone com-pany, and the supermarket.
>
> Think about what you want from your bank. We (the authors) know what we want: an ATM on every corner. We want to know that, when we get to the ATM, there will be no line. We would like a parking spot right in front of the ATM. We want our checks deposited the mo-ment they arrive at the bank, or perhaps the day before. And we want no mistake in processing — unless they are in our favor. We also know what we do not want from our banks. We do not want them to provide us with softball leagues, religious counseling, or health services. We can arrange all of these things for ourselves and don't wish to pay extra fees for the bank to offer them.
>
> Students are asking roughly the same thing from their colleges. They want their colleges nearby and operating at the hours most useful to them, preferably around the clock. They want convenience: easy, accessible park-ing (in the classroom would not be at all bad); no lines; and polite, help-ful, and efficient staff service. They also want high-quality education but are eager for low costs. For the most part, they are very willing to com-parison shop, placing a premium on time and money. They do not want to pay for activities and programs they do not use. In short, students are increasingly bringing to higher education exactly the same consumer expec-tations they have for every other commercial enterprise with which they deal.[22]

---

19. *Id.* at 50.
20. *See id.* at 49.
21. *See id.*
22. *Id.* at 50.

According to Levine, the new consumerism is deeply related to the rise of "me" values.[23]

Faculties and administrators, however, tend to cling to notions of community in favor of marketplace.[24] The student "consumerism" is part of a growing divide between what faculty and staff perceive and desire and what students (particularly historically non-traditional students) perceive and desire.

There are deep problems with the consumer image and strict business law applications. While these images are better in terms of shared responsibility and safety than predecessor images, they need tailoring to function well in the unique college community. First, if students are consumers, then they should be entitled to get what they want and pay for. Levine points out that we have given them this, for example with grade inflation. When universities have canceled beer privileges, students have rioted violently: as consumers paying more money than ever, they feel entitled to get what they pay for and be left alone. Students who view themselves as consumers often assert the very radical and libertarian aspects of freedom which the bystander cases described. In short, when applied to colleges, strict business paradigms tend to polarize student conduct.

As a *legal* liability approach, business law applications actually tend to *divide* campuses and responsibility. Business law sometimes divides responsibility, rather than thinking in terms of shared responsibility. In many business settings it is the consumers' job to look out for themselves only and the business shoulders the responsibly for all shared risk. For instance, it would be odd to ask one-time visitors to a theme park to do much more than the obvious to protect their own safety. To obey the rules works well. However, a dormitory or college campus is a familiar place to students; asking for shared responsibility, such as asking all students to keep the landing door locked, is appropriate.

The growing divide has serious safety consequences. Levine describes the growing gulf between administrators and students. The phenomenon bears a strikingly similar parallel to the divide between police and citizens described by Kelling, Coles, Wilson, and Bratton that has forced a major rethinking of traditional police strategies in cities. In cities, police assumed too much responsibility for what citizens should do as a community for themselves. Citizens withdrew from the community. In both cases—campuses and cities—disorder, danger, and fear have been products of the gulf created by *legal paradigms that de-emphasized shared responsibility*. Business rules, like bystander rules, tend to emphasize "freedom" and "me" instead of *community* and *shared responsibility* on campus. Business law categories often say "college is responsible for this, students

---

23. *See* Levine, When Hope and Fear Collide 53.
24. *See id.* at 52.

for that" with somewhat less emphasis on *shared* responsibility than is appropriate. So, while business law has served student interests in many ways by introducing some notions of shared responsibility, a purely business campus does not meet all the basic safety needs of many college students. *More* shared responsibility is necessary and appropriate.

Restoring community values—shared responsibilities—on campus can make campuses safer and less violent places. Business rules work well to promote safety at K- Mart, but young people on campus do not *live* at K-Mart or even spend significant amounts of their lives there. Business rules work well for pure commuter colleges, perhaps, but not major residential campuses which require more than the division of rights and responsibilities in a shopping mall. A consumer has little investment in making a store safer for others; every student depends on other students for safety on campus.

A business community campus is not the safest campus. It is a safer campus than a bystander campus but still facilitates some unreasonable risk because it emphasizes too much consumeristic thinking and not enough shared community thinking.

2. Fiduciary

Perhaps sensing that courts tend to see universities as businesses with business duties, some commentators have suggested that college is a different kind of business imbued with "trust." A "fiduciary" model would reimagine the college in a "trusting" relationship in which the college would act for the benefit of the student in a wide area of concern related to college educators.

Fowler and Goldman[25] have advocated such an approach. Goldman describes his view:

> All of the elements of a fiduciary relation are present in the student-university relationship. It is no small trust-no small display of confidence to place oneself under the educational mentorship of a particular university. The value of an educational experience is directly affected by the school's conscientious, faithful performance of its duties-duties which are directed toward the student's benefit.... In addition to often making confidential disclosures about his background, his health and his financial situation in applications for admission and [financial] assistance, the student is

---

25. *See* Gerald Fowler, *The Legal Relationship Between the American College Student and the College: An Historical Perspective and the Renewal of a Proposal*, 13 J. L. & EDUC. 401 (1984); Alvin L. Goldman, *The University and the Liberty of its Students—a Fiduciary Theory*, 54 KY. L.J. 643 (1966).

expected to confide in course and career counselors who are appointed by the university.... In making these disclosures, the student reposes confidence in the school's skill and objectivity.[26]

It is an image of confidence, counseling disclosures, and the gaining of trust.

Courts have not embraced the view. The power in such a view lies in the fact that it treats the college/student relationships as unique and as more intimate and connected than ordinary business relations. It is, however, a view which relies upon greater university control/authority and significantly less student freedom and responsibility. A fiduciary view is not a shared responsibility view as much as it is a shift in one direction on the continuum. Several commentators have made these points, and Stamatakos makes them most eloquently:

> The fiduciary model recognizes the trust a student places in the institution she attends. In response to this trust, a legally stringent standard of conduct is imposed upon the university.
>
> However, the fiduciary model is not practical. Whenever the student-college relationship is implicated, an institution must justify all actions affecting the relationship with fully-defensible explanations. Further, placing a fiduciary responsibility on institutions reduces students' responsibilities. This state of affairs compromises the institution's ability to foster responsible student decision-making and mature behavior. More damaging to the fiduciary model, however, is judicial resistance towards its adoption. To date, no court has characterized an educational institution as owing a fiduciary duty to its students. Thus, even if the fiduciary model were theoretically tailored to sound dimensions, the model has failed to be viable in practice.[27]

In a similar vein, Munch argued even in the 1960s that such a model would reduce student accountability.[28]

Although we treat the fiduciary model as a duty era image, in fairness it has roots in the other periods. Perhaps the best way to describe it is as a survival of or successor to *in loco parentis*. If a parent dies, a child may come under guardianship and/or have her fate decided in large measure by a trustee. Trustees and trust officers traditionally have exercised roles in the lives of well to do individuals even significantly past the age of majority. In an odd way, they play some roles a parent might play to children and even adult offspring in their tweenage years. The law of fiduciary rela-

---

26. Goldman, *supra* at 671-72.

27. Theodore Stamatakos, *The Doctrine of In Loco Parentis, Tort Liability and the Student-College Relationship,* 65 IND. L.J. at 471, 478-79 (1990) (footnotes omitted).

28. *See* Christopher H. Munch, Comment, 45 DEN. L.J. 533, 535 (1968).

tions was a natural place to look when the parent died. Its judicial unpopularity as a general image lies in, among other things, its allocation of responsibilities. It is not a centrist, shared responsibility view. It is a view that courts use mostly in economic and intangible, not safety, relationships. On the plus side, its core value lies in its recognition that many students require something special from college life to mature safely and productively.

(iii.)   Images of Transition and Facilitation

In the next section we explain the images of transition and facilitation along side appropriate legal rules for the modern university.

A. Facilitator University/Transitional Times

It is a time of transition in university law in almost every sense. The law has been moving from one set of legal rules to another. The duty era is still evolving in the courts and will continue to do so. Public attitudes towards campus safety have recently shifted to significantly less tolerance for alcohol and drug abuse and their related disorders, dangers of travel abroad, sexual assault, etc. There is a growing concern—particularly in light of the 1998 beer riots—that the campus is out of control and has become unreasonably dangerous and improperly ordered. These attitudes and fears produce changes in the legal rules that define the shared responsibility of the university and its students for student safety and campus security.

In addition, it is a time of transition in higher education itself. As Levine describes in *When Hope and Fear Collide*:

> There are rare times in the history of a society in which rapid and profound change occurs. The change is so broad and so deep that the routine and ordinary cycles of readjustment cease. There is a sharp break between the old and the new. It is a time of *discontinuity*.[29]

Levine describes only two such break points: the industrial revolution, which transformed America from an agricultural nation to an industrialized nation, and now. As Levine points out, "We name periods of profound change only in retrospect."[30] We are experiencing tremendous demographic, economic, global, and technological change, and there is a sense that major social institutions of the industrial age are failing—politics and government, public education, manufacturing and service industries, the health care system, family, church, many professional sports, and

---

29. LEVINE at 151 (emphasis added).
30. LEVINE at 153.

law and lawyers (including tort law *and* tort lawyers).[31] Even Disney World has become a target of political activism. Everything once sacred, sanctimonious, and solid has come under fire (or is scandalized) it seems. As our friend John Polise has said, it seems as if "there are no adults anymore."

Levine believes that the "emerging order is unknowable and unrecognizable"[32] and that there are profound tides of loss and frustration in American culture (road rage? beer riots?, etc.). Levine argues it is "fantasy" to describe our society as it will be seen in the future.[33] College and students are caught in this period of "unceasing, unknowable change."[34] College life is straddling two worlds, one of which was once familiar, and one which is emerging but is still unfamiliar. It is no surprise that the law itself reflects this profound shifting.

It is not just a time of transition in law, higher education, and culture — it is a time when college students are experiencing those changes personally, politically, and legally. Levine describes students who personally are frightened because of change, concerned about their security (especially financial), sexually active but isolated, heavy drinkers, overworked, lonely and tired, typically weak in basic skills but able to learn from their instructors in ways that the instructors often do not make use of, distant from college administrators and instructors, pragmatic, careerist, idealistic, altruistic, and surprisingly optimistic; politically they are more diverse than ever and also more divided and separated, consumer oriented, disenchanted with American politics and most major social institutions, oriented away from centrist political attitudes, liberal in social mores, focused on local issues than global, and socially conscious and active.[35] In his summary, Levine saw these students as "[d]esperately committed to preserving the American dream"[36] but often unsure of what this would mean for them and whether they would be able to manifest it. They have the frightened optimism of D-Day soldiers: they will hit the beach believing they will win but nonetheless are unsure of the outcome and their own futures.

The notions that this generation of students is a group of slackers or just consumers misunderstands who they are and what they need. Levine argues that education in this transitional period should serve four basic things, and it is intriguing how these needs relate to law.[37]

---

31. *See* LEVINE at 152-53 from whom we borrow liberally.
32. *Id.* at 153.
33. *Id.* at 154.
34. *Id.* at 154.
35. *See* LEVINE at 156-57.
36. *Id.* at 157.
37. *Id.* at 157-60.

1. "Hope" — many students feel forced to give up their dreams and study subjects they hate, like law and finance, when they do not have to do so. Without hope, students can experience ennui and divide, isolate, and intoxicate themselves. Lack of hope breeds physical (and spiritual and emotional) danger.

2. "Responsibility" — many students feel that financial, personal, and career security and responsibility are inversely related. As consumers, they tend to feel they are purchasing something for themselves. There is a common sentiment that they pay more than ever for a college/university education of more uncertain value — top dollar for a less valuable commodity. There is less of a sense of owing to others and even the college community itself. We have seen this in law school in some disconcerting cheating situations: the small number of students who cheat feel so entitled to promote their professional security that they cheat in blatant, easily detected ways and show only the remorse of someone who has lost an opportunity (even parents sometimes reinforce this attitude by threatening groundless litigation in the face of serious ethics breaches). Cheating is seen by them as just a business risk. The lack of accountability is mirrored by colleges themselves when they pursue protracted litigation over whether they have a duty to fix broken doors in women's dormitories.

Decades of legal polarization and extreme allocations of responsibility have destroyed a sense of shared responsibility. The consequences are serious for campus safety: a community which tries to deflect responsibility instead of sharing it tends to make narrowly drawn, "cover yourself" decisions that further short term interests only. Irresponsible campuses are physically dangerous places. Campuses without significant sharing of responsibility are irresponsible environments. The paradox of responsibility is that even if "blame" is fully allocated, it may still be necessary to *spread* the blame because in some domains only shared responsibility works.

3. "Appreciation of Differences" — Levine describes campuses where students disconnect and separate to social groups. They also tend to hold politically divisive views and consensus is weak. Legal rules have historically facilitated this. Students overcame extreme exercises of college power (like summarily dismissing black students for protesting segregation) by gaining constitutional rights. In response, certain courts recreated a legal community of students asserting "unpopular" political aims into a community of uncontrollable rebels. This image gave way to the image of the student consumer, "competing" with other students for "business" goodies. For example, when a disabled student is provided with reasonable accommodation pursuant to the Americans With Disabilities Act, it is not uncommon for some other students to complain that the accommodation is not fair to them. They see college opportunities in a zero-sum relationship. Because the law has imagined college life in powerful zero-sum business law, freedom oriented terms, it has

facilitated not community, but disconnectedness. College life has decreased in shared community values steadily since the end of the era of insularity. The law has encouraged this change.

4. "Efficacy" — Students need to know that they can make a difference. But there is a tendency to believe that making a difference is almost impossible. Students believe it is only worth it if you can become President or CEO — but even if you get there, a dysfunctional system will disempower you. Levine also declares that modern students tend to think and act locally, not systematically or globally. Again, there is an intriguing correlation between the law and the senses of disempowerment students experience and express. Students were viewed as "uncontrollable": for many their introduction into the world was via institutions that courts often described as "powerless."

The image of the disabled father/government/parent/college cemented in bystander cases, has given way to "duty" notions in which "power" is channeled cautiously and in narrow ways. Courts still sometimes "tenderfoot" around universities, hinting at their lack of power and seizing on that at times to deny liability (recall *Tanja H.*, where the California court made significant assumptions about how little power a college has to prevent rape). Even in the duty era there is a strong strain of pessimism about preventing student injury.

A sense of loss of efficacy is a principal cause of disorder and danger. Consider again cities like New York, which fell into a period of gloomy acceptance of status-quo disorder and criminality. There was a sense that problems were rooted in social forces beyond the control of government and individuals. Recent events have shown this to be false: by targeting specific acts of disorder, crime and fear can be reduced. If we can revitalize cities, we can restore campuses to higher levels of safety. Restoring a sense of efficacy — that individuals do make a difference, that they *are* the difference — is a major task. Too often, misguided legal arguments have kept colleges from getting about the business of actively working to restore safety and security to the learning environment.

. . .

It is worth mentioning that American law also creates a sense of disempowerment in the way that it imagines causation. Despite modern scientific arguments, American Courts choose conceptions of causation that are largely scholastic, medieval, Aristotelean, and Newtonian. In tort law, negligence causes harm only when an action can be specifically linked to a particular consequence *or* when an *inaction* by " X" occurs under very special and limited conditions. Tort law assumes that if "X" acts, or intends to act, without specific linkage to harm (or in the case of omission, also without special connection) there is no "wrong" or "responsibility." (Courts make throw away arguments that there are "moral" duties—moral duties are not enforceable as such—in a few cases, but that only reinforces the point.) It is said that no harm has been *caused* by "X." Harm just happened. The injury was just an accident. And, when one acts positively, whether causing specific gain or supplying general but unknown gain, tort law confers no benefit on the actor. There are no legal incentives to act better or for the *undifferentiated* good. What is caused is only specific linked *negative* consequence.

These legal senses of causation fly in the face of common sense *and* modern theories of causation. For example, a random act of kindness, like offering directions to a stranger, can prevent a crime from occurring. And repeated negligent acts that cause no specific harm create an atmosphere of disorder in which carelessness and danger breed. There is little to no incentive to fix a particular broken lock until that lock becomes the point of entry for a rapist. The incentive is directly related to a calculation of the likelihood of successful lawsuits. (Even our roads today evidence this: "road rage" is in part a response to lawless, aggressive, race-track driving styles that only infrequently are ticketed or become lawsuits). A narrow view of causation facilitates danger, disorder, and irresponsibility.

. . .

The law has been presented with a serious challenge which implicates the future of college, its present, and the lives and well being of students. Law, colleges and universities, and students are in the in-between times. Again, we do not believe that altered legal rules are a panacea for all college problems. In fact, the increasing legalization of university life has brought with it some profoundly ambiguous results. On the one hand, public universities can no longer capriciously expel students for protesting civil rights, and colleges must provide basic security measures like serviceable door locks, but, on the other hand, students continue to be raped, injured, and killed in situations that are the direct result of changes in legal rules which overemphasized student rights and freedom.

The almost total student freedom in *Bradshaw* is radically overinclusive, when judged by the limited constitutional freedoms defined by *Dixon v. Board of Education* and its progeny. The students of the 1960s fought the civil rights cases to secure speech, association and press, and due process prior to suspension or expulsion: they never sought total freedom from the orderly administration of the college's educational programs, extracurricular activities, or housing. The constitutional freedoms and rights won were still very deferential to college authority and did not grant students extreme rights to engage in disorderly conduct. The Supreme Court decided that discipline short of suspension does not demand a plenary hearing: a student must be able to meet with an appropriate college official prior to being disciplined to tell "his side of the story." Moreover, even in cases where students face suspension or expulsion, cases like *Dixon* do not require trial-like process at colleges but rather only the minimal fairness that any fair-thinking and responsible college would provide in any event.[38] Thus even the highly trained judges that saw the obvious need for *Dixon* rights on campus later confused constitutional rights (and the new "constitutional" adults) with much broader notions of student freedom. In this regard, the legal system also shares responsibility for how our campuses have evolved.

By its nature, the law is cumbersome and sometimes forceful and reactive; law can have difficulty in times of rapid transition. Nonetheless, the law does adapt and grow. And it is very powerful in terms of both reflecting and creating images of college life. College becomes, and mirrors, what law projects. Law, like students, parents, faculty, administrators, and culture at large, is a co-creator of and is co-created by university life. The types of universities we imagine define the parameters of acceptable risk and the extent of allocation of that risk. The law can facilitate a sense of efficacy, even though there have been times when it has had the opposite effect.

The legal model that can synthesize the best aspects of the competing images and reconcile existing case law is a facilitator model. Such a model is adaptable to the circumstances of college life and can work for higher education in transition and in its future states in the post industrial age. A facilitator model helps courts to better identify and describe their own trends and use familiar rules of decision adapted for the unique context of higher education. The model is descriptive, predictive, practical, and theoretical. It is also liminal and interdisciplinary in that it can be used to describe university and legal reality, and as a tool of communication between the two worlds.

A facilitator college balances rights and responsibilities—it is neither extremely authoritarian nor overly solicitous of student *freedom*. Importantly, a facilitator college seeks *shared* responsibility rather than allocating it unilaterally or not at all. Facilitation implies an appropriate and reasonable degree of risk—some students will be hurt by the inherent risks of rock climbing or even their own unreasonable actions (like "traying" down a snowy hill into a concrete post), but there is no reason for a woman to be raped in a dormitory by a criminal intruder whose opportunity for entry was the university's failure to repair a door lock that it knew was broken.

We believe that the facilitation model describes what almost all courts are expressing, often without a label, and is a clearer image of what it is that they are creating than other images (especially business/consumer im-

---

38. Remember, the due process mandates at public universities may never have been an issue had students not been arbitrarily suspended and expelled in the 1950s and 1960s for seeking an end to segregation of elementary, secondary and post-secondary education schools, bus terminals, lunch counters, and other places of public accommodation.

ages). What we offer is in the nature of regression analysis. As with any overview, some cases will represent only extreme viewpoints. (*See* for example, *Beach,* where the instructor facilitated a liquor suffused trip to a remote canyon with a student who was a known problem drinker.) Such cases are hard to reconcile with less libertarian, centrist positions. However, most cases (especially recent duty era cases) are easily reconciled using the facilitator model, and several legal paradoxes/problems are resolved as well.

B. Imagining a Facilitator University

When we think of a facilitator, we think of a guide who provides as much support, information, interaction, and control as is reasonably necessary and appropriate in the situation. A facilitator stands somewhere between a dominating parent and a pure stranger or bystander. The facilitator is not a parent, but does pick up on the idea that, for many students, familiar roles may be appropriate or even essential, particularly when it is the first time away from home at age seventeen or eighteen, and the student is thrust into an environment that is intellectually and emotionally charged. The many facets of college life are—for a seventeen or eighteen-year-old—potentially overwhelming if structure and guidance are not provided. A facilitator adapts to the student *body*; however *not all students* need special guidance, except perhaps in very particular ways (financial aid, course selection, etc.). And, older, non-traditional students at community colleges want and need much less than younger students at traditional four-year colleges.

Unlike parents, facilitators do not *choose* for students. Students must choose *for themselves* and shoulder significant responsibility for outcomes of their choice. The key is that the facilitator manages the parameters under which choices are made. Information, training, instruction and supervision, discussion, options, and, in some cases, withdrawal of options are all appropriate for facilitators. A facilitator (instructor or student affairs professional) is keenly aware of aberrant risks and risks known only to the more experienced. A facilitator is very aware of the types of students and the particular university community. Limited roles are fine for adult students who want "just classroom education." Greater roles are usually appropriate for less mature tweenagers, particularly those in full-time on-campus living arrangements. In other words, a facilitator *adapts* and varies the level and nature of involvement.

The facilitator university is different from a fiduciary in all but very unusual circumstances. A fiduciary is usually just involved in financial/economic affairs; a facilitator engages the full range of relevant experience. A fiduciary enjoys a position of trust; often a facilitator will do so too, but it is not always necessary or appropriate to require a facilitator to have such a relationship. For example, an honor code system facilitates the fairness of the academic setting but does not act as a fiduciary. It would be ludicrous, for example, for an honor code prosecutor or honor court members to be in a fiduciary relationship with an accused cheater—they could not perform their duties fairly or appropriately. Moreover, a fiduciary typically can exercise too much control and take on too much responsibility. A facilitator plays a role but is not a legal guardian or trust officer. Trust officers often facilitate choices made by others over their charges; a facilitator honors the choices of the student.

A major form of university facilitation is to offer services uniquely tailored to each community that are in the nature of traditional business services. The university can pose as dormitory landlord, education-mall superintendent, activities director, security force, or health services coordinator. Indeed, many universities provide a range of services that individuals not in school would avail themselves of in the private business sector. The range of services is more like a package or bundle.

Yet in the context of college life, these services have a special feel to them: nothing is exactly the same as in the private sector (just walk into any college bookstore). Intercollegiate athletics or field trips are not like the pay per use gym; dormitories are rarely configured or managed like apartment complexes for working twenty-somethings. A campus rarely looks like a shopping mall. It is meaningfully different. College offers a bundle of choices and services that serve to offer a lifestyle and a training ground for future patterns in life.

Students are not children to facilitators nor are they typical consumers. Part of facilitation is teaching how to "consume" university life safely and consistently with overall educational goals. Noise and alcohol restrictions facilitate studying. Co-ed dorms, properly managed, can facilitate safer living for female residents and greater socialization for young men and women. College sponsored activities and athletics can teach students cooperation and offer skills that can lead to a lifetime of fun, health and safe recreation. The facilitator is not like the rude waiter in the snobbish French restaurant who will not assist you to read the French-only menu. The facilitator would help you read the menu, but the choice is yours. The facilitator will remind you that escargot is snails but will serve them to you. Consumers often enter a world of *caveat emptor*, a very poor social world for college life. Facilitators help students make intelligent, fair, and reasonable choices; the primary goal is not to make money at the expense of relatively weak consumers subject only to minimal legal constraints of fairness. College is not an arms-length bargaining process. Most students are in-between pure consumers and those under fiduciary care.

To be sure, it is important that a college "do business" with its students. But this business should be done in light of the unique objectives of the college. Education (in the broader sense, not just classroom instruction) is the primary focus of the college, and all of its operations can either facilitate education, or not.

Admittedly, as the college offers limited programs to more experienced and mature students, the need to facilitate transition from childhood into full adulthood wanes. However, facilitating the improvement of the "bottom line" does not fulfill the scope of the traditional resident student/college relationship. A facilitator college in its business role does not simply give consumers what they want; left without guidance, students may desire grade inflation (which arises in complex ways) and a party-till-you-drop campus. In sum, the facilitator college must consider intergenerational equities and interests; education is a "product" for a lifetime. As Dean Wormer observed in *Animal House*, drunk and stupid is no way to go through life, and although it may seem appropriate in the short run, it is cheating the consumer student to sell this product. (Don't forget that students often say later on "that teacher was hard, and I liked that.")

A facilitator *is sometimes* a bystander—but a bystander who chooses to be in that role as a way to facilitate student education and student development. Control dominated management is ultimately inconsistent with the objective of helping the free choices of young adults. Thus, much like relatives, friends, and others who must watch with dismay as a student chooses a course of action, the facilitator too must be willing to stand down at times. However, this does not mean abdication of authority or appropriate duty. In this sense, the college that accepts responsibility for instruction, counseling, residence life, student activities, etc. cannot simply stand by like a stranger. Deliberate non-intervention is very different from indifference.

If students and/or faculty wish to canoe on dangerous Lake George in New York state then the college can choose to facilitate reasonably safe excursions or field trips through appropriate warnings and precautions. As the students set out, the college must then hold its breath and allow the students to choose—upon full knowledge and in reasonable safety—to take the *inherent* risks that for many make life worth living. A proper line of facilitation draws at what is reasonable. A facilitator cannot and does not eliminate all risks, but neither does it ask students to assume those unreasonable risks that would arise from lack of proper university planning, guidance, instruction, etc. A facilitator university would allow students to assume the inherent risks of rock climbing but would not allow an instructor to abandon the responsibility to see that inexperienced students did not exceed the scope of their ability. A facilitator university would acknowledge that a faculty member has a responsibility not to actively participate in alcohol consumption with students in a way that openly violates university policy and endangers students. A facilitator university would allow a student to visit a family services center on her own, but it would not assign her there as an intern without making some determination that it was a reasonably safe place for her to be and that she would receive proper orientation at the facility.

And a facilitator does not accept the idea that students are "uncontrollable." For one thing, this view misses the point of the college/student relationship. Under all but the most extreme situations, why would a facilitator want to "control" a student in a strong sense? A facilitator desires to be a guide and a source of positive influence but also trusts in the inherent wisdom of students. If a college is concerned about the risks of certain student activities, it can offer alternatives to the less desirable activities, thus minimizing risk. The facilitator is creative and practical not stifling and reactive. Only the most extreme forms of student misconduct need control in a strong sense.

There is an important analogy to law and jurisprudence. In legal theory, the so-called command theory of law, often attributed to jurisprudential writer John Austin, has been very influential. The Austinian idea is that law exists only when there is a command—a threat backed by sanctions—issued from a supreme commander. Dean Wormer is this commander but fails precisely because he knows only the more extreme forms of control and power. Modern legal theorists like H. L. A. Hart believe that law is not just a series of explicit and hidden commands but often consists of powers and opportunities conferred. The legal power to associate and create a corporation is not a command in any ordinary sense if at all. Modern law commands less and facilitates more. Over-emphasis on control is a reactionary model of what law is and can be. A modern transitional and transitory world requires *pro*-action. For every problem that might or might not be solved by control, the facilitator believes until proven wrong that there exists an opportunity to fix that problem by facilitating positive actions. A facilitator is not a zero sum game theorist. Pro-action is not about loss but possible gain.

On the other hand, a facilitator is not averse to controlling disorder on campus, especially activity of any nature that compromises student safety and security. Indeed, by leaving locks unrepaired or looking the other way while students parade to fraternity hazing events, a college facilitates bad behavior, disrespect for rules, and the unreasonable physical danger that follows. A facilitator college can embrace the ideas of Kelling, Coles, Wilson, and Bratton: disorder breeds crime, danger, and fear. Their views have relevance in many aspects of college life. Society must seriously question why any college would tolerate students who will abuse alcohol to the point of endangering themselves or others and then violently riot for "beer rights." These acts of disorder should not be left to government authorities to remedy. Credible threats that students who engage in such behavior will at the least receive permanent notations in their records will cause them to think twice before participating in dangerous activities that threaten others. Those who do not think twice should be dealt with seriously.

Unlike any other paradigm, the facilitator model *works* to provide proper legal guidance in cases of alcohol-related student injury or death. *Synthesis,* perhaps the most important law and policy newsletter in higher education, reported in the Spring of 1998 that the Harvard School of Public Health has called for initiatives and programs designed to limit alcohol abuse by students; a U.S. News and World Report Article observes that students drink more because college officials are less strict than they should be.[39] Society expects colleges to confront student alcohol abuse. Some prior legal models resisted duty for fear of a new *in loco parentis* and saw students as "uncontrollable" drinkers or radically empowered consumers. These models have clearly failed because they place little to no responsibility on the university to address student safety. These "all or nothing" models also have failed to define the proper role of students. Peer influence is critical to any successful attempt to minimize the risk of alcohol-related student injury or death. This means that college alcohol abuse programs must engender student support.[40] The college or university is in the best position to provide this structure to student life programs.

Facilitator models are already taking shape in this context. At the University of Delaware—which learned from its experience in *Furek*—Dr. Timothy F. Brooks has led the development of a new alcohol policy aimed at changing the culture of student life by drastically reducing high risk drinking and the illegal service of alcohol to university students by commercial establishments. The University of Delaware's program includes tougher disciplinary action, notifying parents of disciplinary sanctions, increasing appropriate student activities, and developing evaluation mechanisms to change fraternity culture.[41] Dr. Brooks reports that the program has been implemented with little additional funding and no increase in staff. Dr. Brooks' initiatives and programs are sufficient evidence that legal rules that see abusive college drinking as uncontrollable miss the mark. We do not have to revoke basic constitutional and fairness rights, nor act like Dean Wormer, to facilitate positive change.

A university as a facilitator is *not* an "insurer" of student safety. First, there is a risk that insurance facilitates unreasonable behavior by creating a "moral hazard." Without consequences, students cannot learn responsibility. Moreover, it is unfair to ask a college to shoulder all responsibility for all risks. We think that when courts say that a college is not an insurer, they mean this. Here, for example, comparative negligence is criti-

---

39. SYNTHESIS: LAW AND POLICY IN HIGHER EDUCATION, Vol. 9, No. 4, p. 687, citing, *Plugging The Kegs: Students Benefit When Colleges Limit Excessive Drinking,* U.S. NEWS AND WORLD REPORT, Jan. 26, 1998, p. 63.

40. *Id.*

41. *Id.* at 689, 692-696.

cal. A student whose own unreasonable conduct has significantly contributed to her/his own injury should not profit from that conduct or escape responsibility for it. The student's recovery should be diminished or barred—upon proper jury findings—according to principles of comparative negligence applicable in the college's jurisdiction.

Yet, the university can learn a great deal from modern risk management—insurance strategies—in loss avoidance and loss spreading. Looking for innovative ways to stop injury stops legal liability *before it ever starts*. And, a facilitator is conscious that a catastrophic case disproportionately allocates loss to some (a few) students when many others engage in similar risky behavior with more fortunate consequences. The college is in a unique position, along with its insurers, to assess this type of risk and find creative and fair ways to reallocate it. For example, professional football has found creative ways to deal with catastrophic injury to players. Do parents realize that if they send their son off to play at State University that he may suffer a crippling injury and that the family may face financial ruin for lack of resources to manage the costs of injuries? Is there no way consistent with the financial integrity of a college and the maintenance of equivalent levels of safety to protect the next family? The facilitator model recognizes that students and parents may systematically discount low probability events, yet statistically certain numbers of injuries inevitably occur. It is particularly appalling when a college runs a multi-million dollar "amateur" football program with enormous fund raising implications but fails to provide adequate protection for predictable catastrophic game-related injuries that may require years of expensive managed care. No business can run like this. Workers compensation was developed for businesses to create the appropriate social net. Do not forget that a ruined family turns to the taxpayers for support, so society as a whole has an interest in this facilitation of loss spreading.

A facilitator is an educator but not just in a pure sense (except in circumstances where that is reasonable and appropriate, as in a correspondence course). Education is the central mission of college and university life in much the way profit maximizing is for a corporation. A college with a large endowment and a positive income and expense statement may be a huge failure because these are not the appropriate benchmarks of success for an institution of higher learning. All aspects of the college balance sheets operate to promote educational goals. Curricular activities, co-curricular activities, physical plant, dormitories etc. function in interdependent ways. Students who drink heavily in dorms cause disruption for students who do not: grades and class performance falter for *both*. Poor security keeps students in their rooms and away from libraries or study groups at night or uncomfortable when they use a computer or art lab or laundry room after dark.

Sense of community suffers—isolation increases—and this causes greater risk (no one asks the stranger who he is; not knowing the other students, everyone assumes the stranger (Theodore Bundy?) is someone's guest).

A facilitator model embraces appropriate opportunities to manage and supervise student activities and affairs and interact with students. By following a no-duty paradigm and intervening only after injury occurred, the modern university increasingly distanced itself from students in the day to day ways that prevent danger—in much the ways that police left the neighborhood beat for police cars and rapid response 911 calls. Modern police strategies focused upon responding to crime rather than preventing it: so too the college and danger on campus. As such, the college became out of touch. The lesson of *Beach* should not be to become uninvolved but to foster strong involvement with students in ways that can prevent harm. For example, there was no need to handcuff the student in *Beach*: someone should simply have made sure she got back to her tent in one piece once she had been drinking so that she did not wander off alone; or, if she had a known drinking problem that in the past rendered her incompetent, she should not have been included in a potentially dangerous field excursion. Extreme fears of assumed duties have led colleges to be reticent in situations that demand proper college-student/interaction.

A facilitator model also reacts to notions of charity, contract, and government. Colleges are special mission organizations and are too invested with public interest to pretend to be golf clubs and the like. Moreover, college dangers are increasingly being exported to the community at large. A facilitator formulates the greater public interest into the equation. As campus risks move off campus and as students integrate more with the community, the connections to the greater community good will be more and more apparent.

The facilitator model also reflects the fact that colleges have a strong flavor, as Pavela writes, of being voluntary associations. A college feels something like John Locke's social contract, and the large university often provides all the basic services of any municipality. To some, college can be like city/state Athens filled with Socrates, Platos, and Aristotles. It is a free and socio-contractual political society unto itself. As such, the facilitator model respects the power of the collective community to define itself. An obsessive control-oriented dean at a commuter college for non-traditionals is out of step with the nature of the association. On the other hand, a Dean at a traditional four-year college must be sensitive to the need for appropriate housing, recreational facilities, and a wide array of positive student activities structured in large measure by the college but with meaningful student involvement. Such involvement teaches participatory values and citizenship—key components of a secure learning environment. Legal models that encourage the mutual disempowerment of students and administrations permit, and perhaps foster, disorderly and even dangerous behavior. Students do not aspire to run a college, but they are not 'inmates' in a prison or asylum, or purchasers of services who are to be left on their own in their community affairs.

The facilitator model accepts the idea that college/student relationships are unique and, in a sense "special." But the term "special relationship" is so loaded with legal imagery in the university law context that to make our point it is necessary to put the law as such aside for just a minute. In general, a relationship to any higher education institution, whether commuter community college or four-year traditional college, is a unique and unparalleled experience in a person's life. Teaching is special. Learning in an organized program is special. Experiencing both among similarly situated peers is special. It is no surprise that graduates often look back at college years as the best times of their lives and as the most fortunate and challenging periods in life. Courts can say that there is nothing special about the relationship of student and university legally and complicate the law with business rules, but there will always be something different about college. It is a mixture of many things, a dash of family (that is a safe distance from childhood), of personal freedom, of a variety of quasi-commercial services, of a voluntary association (often with genuine governmental responsibilities), of the public good and public interest, of fellowships and friendships, and, of course, of unique educational opportunities. One can form oneself for the future in a place like this and set the tone for a lifetime of vocations, avocations, associations, friendships and activities (including further learning). The Supreme Court of Delaware is correct when it says that student life is university *guided*.

Moreover, the university is also special in that it is not a singular concept. Higher education is served up in a variety of formats with different expectations and different responsibilities. There is no way to avoid looking at the particular circumstances of a given college in balancing risk and responsibility. We would expect that a snow "traying" problem would be handled differently in Louisiana than in Massachusetts. A small college in Montana does not face the complexity of security issues that are relevant to a large, urban university like the University of Washington. And colleges themselves are constantly in transition as every few years a new generation of students enters with regenerated needs and expectations and new sets of dangers associated with their generation.

The non-legal special sense of college life is only heightened during times of social transition of the kind Levine describes. All of society will benefit or not according to how higher education responds during the period of transition. There are few legal/cultural/social issues of more long term significance. College is special in this sense.

Fundamentally, a facilitator university continues to search for the right balance between student responsibility and university responsibility—and the appropriate amount of *shared* responsibility. There will always be areas where student or college is more (or totally) responsible, but there are significant areas of shared responsibility. The facilitator model is not polar and prefers centrist and balanced approaches. In essence, the failure of bystander and *in loco parentis* paradigms is their extreme allocation of rights and responsibilities. In one system, students were forced to fight in the streets for basic rights; in the other they were encouraged to disconnect, drink, and turn their energies to fights over consumer style rights. Ultimately, even *in loco parentis* and bystander images facilitated a reality on campus, but it was the wrong reality. Universities should not be either police states or Gomorrah. As we recognize that physical danger to students and the security of their learning/living environment can be correlative to the images and legal rules we use, the facilitator vision can help to find the proper balance of responsibilities and tolerable levels of risks.

. . .

Duty and the Facilitator University

The current duty era caselaw contains ambiguities and paradoxes, yet the legal rules courts are using are readily adaptable to constructing legal rules that facilitate college life through a shared university/student responsibility for the security of the campus environment. Some courts, like *Furek*, virtually adopt the facilitator model as such. Duty (and special relationship) rules can balance university authority with student freedom and can adapt to changing circumstances and different college and university environments. As one recent decision stated:[42]

> Duty is not sacrosanct in itself, but is only an expression of the sum total of those considerations of policy which lead the law to say that the plaintiff is entitled to protection.... Accordingly, there is no more magic inherent in the conclusory term "special relation" than there is in the term "duty". Both are part and parcel of the same inquiry into whether and how the law should regulate the activities and dealings that people have with each other. As society changes, as our sciences develop and our activities become more interdependent, so our relations to one another change, and the law must adjust accordingly.... [r]elations perhaps regarded as tenuous in a bygone era may now be of such importance in our modern complicated society as to require certain assurances that risks associated therewith be contained.

---

42. *Estates of Morgan, supra*, 673 N.E.2d at 1322.

Duty in the broad sense of legal responsibility and in the narrow *prima facie* case sense is an organic and elastic legal concept yet is capable of generating very concrete legal results. Duty, special relationships, and legal liability are often used interchangeably to denote the same ultimate conclusion—whether under a given set of circumstances legal responsibility for harm should or should not attach to whom, and why.

The decision to impose liability or not is a function of a variety of factors, policies, and considerations. The following factors are basically the ones that modern courts have used in decisions from *Bradshaw* and *Beach* to *Furek* and *Nero*. In short, whether holding a college liable for physical danger to students or not, courts largely agree on the relevant factors to consider regarding duty and liability:

(1) foreseeability of harm;
(2) nature of the risk;
(3) closeness of the connection between the college's act or omission, and student injury;
(4) moral blame and responsibility;
(5) the social policy of preventing future harm (whether finding duty will tend to prevent future harm);
(6) the burden on the university and the larger community if duty is recognized;
(7) the availability of insurance.

These factors essentially draw their roots from the *Tarasoff*[43] case and have been frequently cited with little variation in most of the major university cases of the last twenty years. This may be the only undeniable point of consensus among all the disparate cases of the last few decades. In the confusion of transition, it is easy to miss the consensus of so many courts on such a fundamental level.

In applying these factors to the university context, courts have also formed some powerful agreements on how they work out in given scenarios.

For example, in basic dormitory and premises maintenance cases, duty era courts have been sympathetic to students' injury claims and are increasingly intolerant of unsafe campus premises. Basically safe conditions in a dormitory and other campus buildings and grounds are essential to successful education—a tenancy unreasonably vulnerable to foreseeable criminal intrusion is not a place to learn economics or poetry.

---

43. Fundamentally, these factors draw their roots to Professor William Prosser, the father of modern tort law. *See* Peter F. Lake, *Common Law Duty in Negligence Law: The Recent Consolidation of a Consensus on the Expansion of the Analysis of Duty and the New Conservative Liability Limiting Use of Policy Considerations,* 34 SAN DIEGO L. REV. 1503 (1997).

Courts especially consider foreseeability of harm as the key (but not only) factor. Notice (from earlier chapters) how a facilitator college prevents foreseeable risks with reasonable care but asks students to share responsibility via an open and obvious danger rule. If a premises defect/danger is as obvious to a student as it is to the university and the student can avoid it, the calculus shifts in favor of less to no university liability. Courts will consider the *nature of the risk* and how *preventable* it is. For example, an unstable bannister on a stairwell that looks safe is different from stone walls around a campus courtyard. The former presents some unusual (latent) risks, and rules imposing responsibility on a college would tend to deter unreasonable delay in maintenance. Courts have seen these rules work for shopping malls and supermarkets. However, the stone wall presents no unusual risks *per se* and imposing duty on the university as to a student who voluntarily scales the wall (knowing the risk) and falls would not likely prevent much future harm (what would change?).

And while students will be responsible to *use* their door locks, courts will not accept *morally reprehensible* arguments that there is no legal responsibility to fix broken door locks in women's residence halls after reasonable notice is given to a college that a danger exists. The student/college relationship is not *caveat emptor,* and courts will likely respond to these situations the way reasonable parents might. Again, there is a balance of moral responsibility to share in safety concerns. The facilitator is responsible to provide reasonable conditions of background safety in the interest of the student's educational pursuits.

A facilitator model envisions that the college is especially sensitive to the risks it creates when it aggregates students in collective situations. Placing students together in residence halls perpetuates an important aspect of the Jeffersonian institution and can create educational opportunities and life long associations. With the benefit, however, comes burden. Their *will* be "bad apple" students who endanger others; there *will* be off campus predators who see dormitories as opportunities to fulfill criminal desires. Aggregation facilitates education, but it also potentially facilitates crime and danger.

A facilitator will use reasonable care to prevent foreseeable risks. Notice again how courts allocate risks and responsibility to students *and* colleges. When a dangerous person is specifically or readily foreseeable to the college, the college must act to reasonably prevent danger (*Nero, Johnson,* etc.); but when the risk is the undifferentiated risk that someone may date rape or attack another student, courts will be reluctant to impose liability on a college unless a pattern emerges. The *burdens* on a university to prevent random or low probability attacks would be too great and would not likely *prevent* future *harm*. Moreover, the actions necessary to make a college campus 100%

free of peer assault or criminal intrusion, would necessarily be draconian—and courts should not and will not require that result. Moreover, courts have often suggested that after proper education, a student may be in the best position to avoid and foresee otherwise random violence.

The line of foreseeability will nearly always be drawn in fact specific, case sensitive ways. In all torts cases it is an element with an air of unavoidable uncertainly. Courts can do their part by being particularly explicit in their decisions as to what is expected or permitted and what is not. Specific guidelines will be heard by college safety facilitators and students; vague rules can disempower those whose judgment could save lives by making them determine what is or is not 'foreseeable' at their professional peril. Courts should be sensitive to the way in which information regarding university law is disseminated. Messages sent to campus police will likely be received more clearly and accurately if courts are clear and consistent. The failure to even advert to key cases weakens judicial guidance to colleges. The *Orr* decision, for example, is a failure of the judicial role (even though it is unpublished it will be spoken of in campus communities, and not just by us). Colleges have nearly had the luxury of making and disseminating their own law for some time and distortion of case law is not uncommon. As long as the dynamics of university litigation are in place, a court must remain sensitive to the possibility that the message it sends is at risk of distortion. Opinions like *Rabel*, that fail to seriously discuss significant precedent regarding the duty of the university as landlord, contribute to the distortion of legal rules that define the proper parameters of duty with respect to the security of the learning environment. Similarly, the failure of *Beach* to discuss earlier cases recognizing a university's duty to properly plan and conduct a student field trip, invites confusion about the parameters of university/student duty.

Now consider off-campus danger to students and non-students that does not arise from any university sponsored activity or action. Courts typically determine that a college has no legal responsibility for these kinds of harm. For one thing, there are a plethora of risks out there which are more or less equally foreseeable to student and college. Colleges typically warn naive first-year students about the special risks of their communities, as any good facilitator would, but a Hill Street Blues roll call every morning is not consistent with most campus realities. In addition, there is often a lack of *closeness* between the danger and the college: without a doubt, the more *remote* a danger is—in time, space, and relation to college activities—the less likely a university is legally responsible for the resulting harm if it occurs. When injuries to non-students off campus occur, courts have often been unsympathetic; except as in *Tarasoff* where there is a knowledge of a more particular danger that can reasonably be prevented by simple means.

Thus, the facilitator does not think strictly in terms of *on/off* campus liability as such but in terms of closeness, burden, the nature of risks to be prevented, foreseeability, and what could reasonably and realistically be done to prevent harm. For example, when a university assigns an intern to an off-campus facility owned by another agency and she is attacked there, the issue of the university's duty to her should not turn on the fact that she was off campus. The boundaries of a campus are more elastic than geographical. Commentators and colleges often look for a magic bright line to draw around the campus like a moat. The law recognizes a functional, factor driven equivalent, but there is not a chalk-line of liability as such. Statements like "the injury occurred off campus" or "students are adults" or "the university student relationship is not special" *beg the question of how these factors weigh, on balance, in a given context.* One advantage of courts not giving student injury cases to juries—which they do in other contexts—is that the case language provides guidance on how this balancing of rights and responsibilities through fact analysis should proceed.

The Facilitator, Duty, and Alcohol

There is no more difficult problem in colleges today than how to reduce the risks of dangerous college-aged drinking. The problems a facilitator faces regarding alcohol (and drug) use and abuse and the dangers it brings to campus are acute. Most cases involving alcohol related injury—on or off campus—have resolved favorably to the college, with notable exceptions like *Furek*. No duty/no liability results primarily have been the product of closeness, moral responsibility, and burden factors, and, given that background risks of alcohol dangers are often equally well known to the student and the college, the foreseeability factor often washes out (but not always).

Here is how the argument traditionally has gone: After the student "revolutions" of the 1960s, colleges became more distant from student life. Close supervision gave way to 'adulthood' and freedom. Students, like most drinkers, became legally responsible for the harms they caused and were the morally responsible parties; or, professional servers or vendors of liquor—or 'fraternities' playing similar roles—were responsible. A university was an innocent bystander. Students have consumed alcohol since the time of the earliest universities (as Homer Haskins relates) and will continue to do so. The *burden* on a college and the *consequences* to the college community would be intolerable if colleges were required to stop college drinking entirely. It would be the return of a police state on campus and/or the imposition of crushing financial responsibility. In particular, college-aged drinking is largely uncontrollable, and therefore college aged drinking risks are uncontrollable. Finally, students know the general risks of alcohol use and are usually more aware of specific risks (the drunk guy with an attitude, etc.). In terms of foreseeability, the argument proceeds, students are better situated. If courts continue to believe these arguments, then the law regarding alcohol use is likely to favor images that the otherwise facilitating university is help-less and morally justified in not significantly reducing campus alcohol risks.

However, each of these beliefs (which animate cases like *Beach* and *Bradshaw*, for example, and are rejected by *Furek*) are under fire today. Thus, there is a growing sense that permitting unregulated and unguided student freedom is too dangerous for a significant number of students. As community policing initiatives have shown, *communities* are safer than aggregations of individuals who are responsible for only their own safety. (B-17's and zebras know that safety increases in tight, coordinated forma-tions). There is a safety need for closeness.

As to *moral responsibility*, there is a growing awareness that much of the most dangerous college-age drinking is done on and off campus by *underage, unlawful* drinkers. Colleges have created, permitted, and in some cases sanctioned the entities and activities which facilitated such drinking. Indeed, simply bringing large groups of seventeen to twenty-two year olds with a known social propensity to drink together in tight quarters creates a known problem. While not children, these individuals are not fully mature adults (as *Furek* pointed out, they are *not* adults for purposes of drinking), and many students are problem drinkers. In a real fact sense, the college is increasingly less and less a bystander to an adult problem: more and more, abusive and dangerous college-aged drinking is becoming a *college* problem not a social problem for adults independent of the university. There is a growing opinion that colleges and others have created a system which is susceptible to and predisposed to dangerous and unlawful alcohol behavior. Consider the remarks of Dr. Richard M. Schwartzstein, M.D., the doctor who terminated life support for Scott Krueger, an eighteen-year-old student who died of alcohol poisoning at M.I.T. in 1997:

> To serve alcohol to minors is a crime. To coerce a young individual to drink excessively is morally reprehensible. Whoever purchases liquor to be served to minors, whoever organizes parties to circumvent the legal drinking age, whoever compels our children in subtle or not so subtle ways to ingest toxic quantities of alcohol must be held responsible for the con-sequences. Any university that finds reasons to look the other way at under-age drinking over the course of many years must be accountable for the tragedies that ensue. The society that continues to glorify the "party ani-mal" and the "amusing drunk" must also take a critical look at its values if we are to prevent similar disasters in the future.
>
> Virtually every weekend during the year when colleges are in session, teenagers are brought to our emergency department with alcohol poi-

soning. Most survive. But the difference between those who survive and those who do not is primarily luck. Someone brought them to a hospital in time. They were placed on their stomachs. Do we want to leave survival of our children to luck? Young people go to war and die, but we justify the loss because they are fighting for principles and for their homes. Young people die each day from cancer, but we acknowledge that this is part of the human condition. There is no mitigating logic that allows me to feel better about Scott's death.[44]

The new alcohol attitudes are in part due to a resurgence in conservative social values. It once seemed conservative to protect colleges from tort lawyers, but denying college responsibility is increasingly being viewed as an anachronistic holdover of a dangerous and libertarian student freedom model of campus life.

Perhaps most significantly, there is new evidence to contradict the long held assumption that college drinking is uncontrollable and inevitably dangerous. For one thing, recent trends have seen upswings in particularly bad drinking (e.g., binge drinking) and campus alcohol injuries. Alcohol problems (particularly abusive) problems are now at an all-time high. And there is a recognition that controlling college aged drinking may be possible. The root idea, argued by researchers like Joel Epstein of Educational Development Center, Inc., is that attacking disorder on campus can have the potential effect on alcohol-related danger that similar initiatives brought to major cities like New York with respect to index and subway crime. While there is no way to alleviate all danger and all drinking, there are ways to address abusive drinking and the most dangerous disorders caused by it. Simply addressing the root causes of alcohol abuse and providing education and alternative activities, while essential, will not be enough. Modern colleges can and should address the problems of alcohol danger and disorder directly. There are realistic, proactive steps that can be taken.

Consider *Beach* and *Bradshaw*, for example. In those cases, courts fought the idea that college drinking is controllable and saw drinking as an "adult" student problem. Yet many cases, like *Bradshaw*, involve individuals who are not adults for legal drinking purposes. Moreover, there were obvious and reasonable ways to prevent the injuries in these two cases. In *Bradshaw*, the college and staff provided the opportunity for an underage drinking party off campus. In *Beach*, the professor facilitated consumption of alcohol by an underaged student with a prior drinking problem and then did not see to it that she made it back to her tent while in a remote and dangerous location. It may be next to impossible to stop

---

44. Richard M. Schwartzstein, A Preventative Tragedy: Alcohol and the Death of Scott Krueger. The Doctor published a version of this Article in the Wellelsly Townsmen on 10/23/97.

a woman from answering the door for a "friend," as in *Rabel*, or to prevent off-campus escapades like those in *Baldwin*, but the results in *Bradshaw* and *Beach* were preventable.

There is a common argument that if colleges clamp down, drinking will just move on to other colleges or into the community. Kelling and Coles encountered the same argument about their approach to crime prevention: If we fix broken windows, the drug dealers will just move to another neighborhood. And Levine points out that drinking off campus is more common than ever. While no doubt there will be some of this displacement, the college and community still are not disempowered. Strict community enforcement of underaged drinking standards, with college involvement, can facilitate reducing the problem. And, the college is in the position to assess and discipline its problem drinkers, even those who drink off campus.

The unspoken assumption that underage drinking is a "personal lifestyle" choice if done off campus must be reexamined. Indeed, the college has become a venue for the aggregation of underaged drinkers. Even worse, college is an almost ideal stopover point for sociopathic alcoholism. Problem drinkers who tend to aberrant behavior can get loans, housing, food, fellowship, and little responsibility as a student. They also can find fellowship for their lifestyle in college and prey upon wannabes to facilitate the problems. Some of these people wear blue blazers and have short hair but are far greater social menaces than a typical homeless person. Ask *any* campus police chief in North America (we did) and they all recount stories of how these individuals elude the system. Of course, in this environment there will be many, many students who do not drink unlawfully or who do so infrequently and with reasonable safety. But there will also be wannabes who are easily influenced by "beer bullies" who push, cajole, and intimidate others into excessive drinking and dangerous behavior that injures themselves or others. These individuals are like drug dealers and have fueled the alcohol culture on many campuses. We tend to dissociate them from drug dealers only because they usually do not sell liquor and because they come from all walks of life. But selling and profit are not a drug dealer's only motive. Efforts must be targeted at these individuals in particular; mollycoddling will not be appropriate. A troublemaker with sociopathic tendencies to incite others to dangerous levels of drinking has no entitlement to a college education—no right to party in ways that present unreasonable risk of personal injury. These people often acquire cute monikers like "party-animal," but the consequences to the college community can be devastating.

There has been a tendency to misidentify the alcohol problem on campus. Fraternities have been given black eyes and are often the defendants in tort litigation. Fraternities, and certainly Greek life in general, are not the problem as such. Indeed, sororities may be very safe places for women to live. The problem with fraternities often lies in the fact that they were once easy targets for sociopathic-style personalities who lure wannabes and others with hail-fellow-well-met bravado and false charm. Boys will be boys. But whose idea is it to assault women in dorms, gang rape, pour lye on someone's head, or fast guzzle hard liquor? What kinds of persons encourage others to engage in such behavior? These persons are intelligent and dangerous personalities. And they are often dangerously clever.

One way they are clever is that they have sized up the college liquor scene and recognized that fraternities are only rarely willing to accept this type of personality into their leadership ranks today. Many beer bullies have moved on and out. Off campus drinking is on the rise and, according to Levine, is a top college avocation. Although much of this is legal, organized, and non-abusive, some of it is not. Alcohol ringleaders are present in these groups and often are the principals in arranging for illegal liquor sources. If the civil authorities and colleges do not act to control these dangerous persons, they will become "facilitators" who lead other students down the path with them. College campuses risk evolving into places of greater danger and disorder.

A facilitator college is aware that, even unintentionally, it may facilitate some socially undesirable behavior. Placing beer bullies in the midst of young adults and failing to create meaningful swift consequences for incitement of dangerous liquor related behavior actually facilitates and glorifies the disorderly behavior. The sociopath revels in beating the system and in martyrdom. Waiting for students to be raped or assaulted before action is taken overlooks the problem until it is too late and nets only a fraction of the small, but hard core, group. In fact, many who become legally responsible will not be the ring leaders.

The basic idea is that there are meaningful ways to control and manage alcohol risks other than root cause solutions, deliberate indifference, or draconian control. It is not realistic or desirable to enforce prohibition on most campuses. What is at issue is problem, dangerous drinking and the extreme risk of harm it can cause. This can be eliminated or managed with creative solutions and problem identification. Such programs of active intervention are already taking shape.

Finally, and relatedly, college aged drinking risks are increasingly viewed in different foreseeability terms. In the bystander era, students were presumed to be adults and were capable of understanding and assuming the risks of drug and alcohol use. Nowadays, there is a recognition that many students—particularly young freshpersons and sophomores who are away from home for the first time and relatively inexperienced with alcohol are like *Ward v. K-Mart* plaintiffs. These individuals encounter an obvious danger but by reason of experience, distraction, and social pressure many fail to have appreciation of the real dangers ahead. Alcohol impairs judgement:

beer bullies can ply the individual with a drink or two, reinforcing opportunities to diminish good judgment. *Beach* and *Bradshaw* called these young victims adults who chose their fate. We now see them as individuals who are foreseeably endangered by the circumstances of college life and people whom reasonable care might save. They are responsible, but they are not solely or even primarily responsible for college alcohol culture.

The facilitator is acutely aware of students who pose direct physical threats to students and others. Courts typically emphasize foreseeability as the key aspect of determining liability. Once a student becomes a known physical danger to others, that student has no place in higher education, at least not without proper supervision. At one time, some problem students were simply shipped off to other campuses or jobs, with little warning to the other institution of what was in store. A recent decision of the California Supreme Court[45] condemns this practice and requires that evaluations and letters of recommendation neither misrepresent nor conceal relevant information relating to known physical danger. There is little tolerance in the courts for unreasonable conduct regarding information about known dangerous persons. Failure to communicate facilitates attacks of students on campus (*Nero, Johnson*). As courts begin to recognize the existence of beer bullies, *Tarasoff/Nero/Johnson* logic could push universities to recognize and deal with persons who create physical danger indirectly through inciting students to abusive alcohol events.

A facilitator university also respects the voluntary association that is the core of the college community. A facilitator does not dictate policy or restrictions unless absolutely necessary. Building community requires *meaningful* interaction. Students are not stupid and will recognize *pro forma* involvement as opposed to true community involvement. Students will need to be involved in solutions to alcohol risks and in discussions and policy making with regard to the problems. Kelling and Coles, for example, consider genuine community involvement essential for restoring order and a sense of safety and reducing index crime. Citizens, like students, have concerns that must be addressed and a knowledge of risk and danger that is essential to effective order maintenance/safety strategies.

The Facilitator Model as Synthesis of Contract and Tort Law: Law as a Positive Tool

Universities still face legal challenges to the process afforded students and contractual rights. One of the paradoxes of the duty era has been the

---

45. Randi W. v. Muroc Independent School District, 929 P.2d 582 (Cal. 1997).

strange use of tort/duty and contract rules simultaneously. The facilitator college recognizes, however, that in balancing the rights and responsibilities of students and college, the legal system apportions remedies into contract and tort categories. Rights of economic, dignitary, and civil varieties are typically and appropriately allocated to contract style analysis; rights involving physical safety and injury are allocated to the tort (duty) system. It is true that ultimately even tort responsibilities are heavily influenced by the quasi-contract, voluntary association nature of the college contexts, but in general there are and will be divergences in the treatment of the different types of cases. Truly, college is unique and requires an adaptation of basic tort (and contract) rules to the legal role of a facilitator. Under the facilitator model courts will see the roots of college law in tort and contract law.

The facilitator model is, then, tailoring of basic rules of tort (and contract) that courts use generally in other contexts. The duty era has been a powerful time of *mainstreaming* university law while simultaneously adapting non-university legal paradigms to the context of higher education. The danger which a facilitator model addresses is that in mainstreaming college law courts will lose the 'uniqueness' of college and university life.

In particular, colleges often believe that courts should protect them from burdensome financial responsibility. As a mature industry, the courts are less likely to provide special protections for a college (during the 1970s, with the enormous growth of the higher education industry, such protection was granted *de facto* under bystander rules.) Yet, we do ask colleges to do more than ever today, and in some cases the strain on personnel and financial resources is acute. The burdens we place on colleges may reflect quickly into the students and their educational opportunities. Colleges are concerned—in many cases legitimately—that duty rules will mean that they will experience heightened litigation and liability exposure like other businesses. But overstated fears of the costs of doing business should not lead colleges to avoid responsibility for student safety. Fundamentally, facilitators are not litigators and do not seek courts primarily to redress grievances. However, facilitators will embrace law as a *positive* tool of bringing fair and reasonable solutions to campus.

A facilitator college recognizes that legal scrutiny is inevitable and opts for legal involvement on its own terms in cases that can often clarify the definitive legal rules they need to co-create safer campuses. No doubt, courts will continue to show deference to colleges by deciding cases as a matter of law (averting jury questions) and using interpretations of college reality that favor no-liability rules. Even these protections will, however, erode over time. To the extent that colleges lose these last bastions of legal protection, questions regarding protection from damaging legal judgments will continue to arise from the college community.

The deep rooted belief that the law should *protect* colleges by *immunities* or other special legal rules that block lawsuits is a vestige of the era of insularity in which law was seen negatively as the enemy on campus. It is easy to underestimate how deeply ingrained negativism towards law is in the psyche of the university. Law remains—to many—"other," bad, negative, dangerous, something to be resisted, and potentially costly. There is much less recognition that law is an integral part of a college campus, a positive tool to reduce danger that can promote campus safety and order, and a way to ultimately reduce costs, including litigation costs.

The perception that there is a need for *immunity* or *protection* arises from *negative* views of law (fueled by current anti-lawyer, anti-government sentiments to an extent). The facilitator college sees law through a different, *positive* lens. Laws can be the conditions under which true freedom and safety can exist. A well-ordered college community—using law as an ally—can obviate the need for special legal protections by cutting off the danger and disorder before it manifests into costly student injuries and expensive lawsuits. The best protection is to do what is reasonable and to continue to seek and to devise proactive strategies that prevent injury. Law can be empowering in the search for safety on campus.

The facilitator model then, unlike its predecessors, does take one important leap forward. The facilitator college imagines law (even student litigation against a college)[46] as a positive tool of empowerment in its efforts to increase safety and promote an educational environment.

Facilitators embrace law and the opportunities it provides. The facilitator college, then, in one important sense is a critical evolutionary step away from colleges of yesteryear. College is no longer an entity outside the law or above it. Colleges today should work *with* law to meet the safety and educational challenges of this transitional period and beyond. The phoenix of the facilitator university can rise from the fall of insularly and complexities of duty law. The facilitator college is a hopeful and positive place that does not look backwards to see what is lost but forward to see what is gained.

There is already evidence that colleges that look to the law for positive assistance have improved campus safety, the educational program, and the lives of everyone, especially students, on campus. Dr. Timothy Brooks, Assistant Vice President of Student Life and Dean of Students at the University of Delaware indicates that it is "possible to change the alcohol

---

46. The facilitator college will view the court system as a partner in the co-creation of legal norms for campus. Some legal rules will be ambiguous because of, *inter alia*, changing circumstances or unforeseen developments. In these cases, a university may wish to permit a case to proceed on the view that all parties will be benefitted by clarification of the legal rules. Sometimes forcing a court to provide a clear rule of law can be achieved by joining issue in a contested case.

culture on [his] campus."[47] In an interview with *Synthesis,* he responded that "the program is working. We have had a significant drop in hospitalization for alcohol overdoses, in vandalism, and in fraternity problems.... We will have to continue this effort for many years, but I am convinced it will be successful."[48] He also reported that there was no negative impact in admissions. The program instituted did not require additional staff (although existing staff worked harder) and involved only small increases in expense. Non-drinkers have rights to appropriate living areas and should be free from alcohol related vandalism: problem drinkers are identified, sanctioned and, if residents, potentially removed from the campus community. Alcohol violence is also dealt with strongly. And evaluation methods and procedures are in place to assess the efficiency of the program. By identifying areas of shared responsibility, students are empowered and involved—meaningfully—at every level and are not just instructed, lectured to, and disciplined. Cases like *Furek* have facilitated these much needed, positive, work-with-the-law strategies. The structure provided is designed to work with student constitutional freedom (*Dixon* style rights) and with privacy rights.

Strategies like these will be tested empirically and legally in the decades to come. In large measure, the success of the facilitator college in promoting safety will turn upon initiatives that see law as an opportunity to provide structure and freedom. More than ever, there is hope for the future of our colleges to be safer points of transition in life and to be the very best educational institutions that we can provide.

---

47. 9 SYNTHESIS, No. 4, p. 693 (1998).
48. *Id.*

VII

Conclusion

The story of the modern American university is one of the gradual emergence from legal insularity into the world of law. The central problem in this evolution has been how to balance university authority with student freedom to achieve a proper and fair allocation of legal rights and responsibilities that maximizes student safety and promotes the educational mission of the modern college. For a society in transition out of an industrial age, finding the right balance has not been easy: colleges have had to redefine themselves in terms of their social roles and in terms of legal image simultaneously. Since World War II, and particularly since the 1960s, colleges have experienced dramatic and sometimes extreme swings in both legal image and social mission. Facilitator colleges search for the moderate and reasonable middle roads. The facilitator model is both an adaptable social vision for modern universities and a legal model for courts and college administrators to work with. The facilitator university empowers campus administrators to do their jobs and promotes shared responsibility for safety on campus. The facilitator university turns to law for positive tools and solutions regarding campus safety.

The Fall of Legal Insularity: Resistance to Law

Until the 1960s, the American university operated almost entirely free from legal scrutiny regarding issues of student safety and regulation. This freedom—also once given to certain other major social institutions of the industrial age—was the product of the combination of insulating legal doctrines. Colleges were considered legally immune from lawsuits by way of family, charitable, and/or governmental immunities. Legal insularity was also augmented by specialized legal doctrines of proximate causation (whereby a college drinker, or a person who did an intentional, deliberate violent act, were considered the sole causes of harm), by all or nothing defenses based on student fault (and assumed risk), and by liberal rules regarding responsibility for the facilitation of alcohol use. Commentators often look to this period to try to define the legal image of the university. What is most striking is the absence of such an image. We, and others, often refer to this period of insularity as the era of *in loco parentis*, as shorthand. Yet the law of this period only defined the boundaries of protection for colleges and typically avoided the positive imagination of college life. The university formed a powerful image of itself then as a non-legal, non-juristic community—a community entitled, like other hallowed social institutions once were, to be free from legal scrutiny. As such, there was only a small body of "higher education law," even into the 1950s.

In the 1960s, students at public universities began to protest against segregation and endeavored to secure equal access to schools, transportation, and places of public accommodation and thus end racial discrimination. In many instances, these students were met with suppression by public universities, particularly in the Deep South. In shameful abuses of the protections granted to them, some colleges expelled and suspended students—often with little to no process—when those students sought to exercise basic constitutional rights of speech association, etc. for the purpose of protesting against segregationist laws and policies. Courts reacted strongly against the abuses of the privileges granted to colleges under law and revoked significant university insularity in the civil rights era.

The loss of an important type of insularity in the form of the fall of protective *in loco parentis* immunities came close in time when other protective legal doctrines were falling within law generally. Charitable immunities were largely abolished; governmental immunities were substantially reduced. In personal injury cases, rules of proximate causation were relaxed to reflect more modern ideas of shared responsibility, and comparative fault replaced all-or-nothing defenses. In short, partly due to abuses of power by certain colleges and partly due to exogenous social changes, the walls of university legal protection began to crumble.

The sense of loss of privilege and protection from law permeates higher education and higher education law even today. Attachment to insularity has led many American colleges to resist law and to view law in negative terms. Instead of facilitating the creation of a new image of the modern college under law, universities resisted the formation of an appropriate new image (other than perhaps the corrupt bystander image), creating confusion, some bad cases, and disempowering campus administrators. At the same time, American college campuses began to experience more incivility, disorder, and crime than ever before. The combination of increasing disorder, danger, and disempowerment led to disastrous consequences on campus.

In response to the civil rights cases of the 1960s, colleges began to refashion their relationship to students and in many instances endeavored to fight legal responsibility for student safety at every turn. In the immediate period following the civil rights cases—the bystander era—universities fought to defend and re-create privileges lost. In a prominent series of no-duty-to-student cases (*Beach et al.*), courts created a new set of protections for colleges based upon rescue law and doctrine, purported lack of (custodial) control over students, and the increasing distance between students and college administration. Universities actually convinced several courts that they could no longer manage student affairs and protect student safety. In cases involving alcohol use especially, universities were successful in casting students as uncontrollable "strangers." American courts of the bystander period were still sympathetic to institutions where alcohol was used, other than commercial bars. The bystander era occurred during a time in which the "social host" was broadly construed and largely protected. Universities, in search of protection from law, found some assistance recreating insularity in libertarian legal attitudes towards social drinking.

Yet, even in the bystander period, powerful crosscurrents in the case law were present. When the student safety issues did not involve alcohol, courts began to question whether colleges deserved any special legal protections. Courts began to treat universities like other institutions, particularly like businesses. Many cases during the bystander era began to cast students in more commercial roles vis-à-vis the college—as consumer or tenant. In particular, the legal role of duty became prominent, and that role has only solidified since the mid 1980s.

Even recently, as courts have increasingly mainstreamed college affairs into the legal world, universities have resisted the loss of privilege and legal insularity. For example, colleges have litigated recently for the right not to fix broken locks in dormitory entrances and have defended placing dangerous sexual predators in dormitories without warnings or other protections in place.

Since the fall of *in loco parentis*, the message to campus law enforcement and campus administrators has been dangerously ambiguous. The no-duty-to-students case law of the bystander era resulted in admonitions against "assuming duties" to students for fear of legal liability. The law sent some messages to college campuses that the best legal strategy to avoid liability for student injury was distance and disengagement; bystanders who got involved could be sued, so avoiding assumption of duty was a paramount objective. Confusingly, the law also sent messages that there were new legal responsibilities for residential life, student activities, etc. College administrators and campus law enforcement officers became motivated by fear of triggering legal liability and were encouraged to pursue strategies in their jobs that would minimize the risk of lawsuits but not necessarily reduce risk or injury. In short, the law encouraged the destruction of much of the student/university relationship outside the classroom.

In the current duty era, resistance to law is increasingly futile (as well as a wasted opportunity) as a college legal strategy. In light of teetering legal protections for social hosts and new social attitudes about college-aged drinking, even the bystander era protections for student alcohol use are in danger of being lost. For example, in 1998, for the first time in memory, a university (and its principals) was summoned to a grand jury regarding the possible criminal responsibility of that university relating to the alcohol poisoning death of a young student. The matter was a clear signal of public frustration over abusive, predatory, and out of control college-aged drinking.

The resistance to law and negative, avoid-legal-scrutiny strategies are typical of adolescent industries that are in transition. However, it is increasingly clear that such strategies are dangerous, counterproductive, and inconsistent with realities and missions of modern universities. Distance, of the kind Boyer has described, facilitates danger. As a community grows apart and distant from its officials and police forces, disorder and danger grows. Kelling and Coles have shown how this kind of distancing hurt our cities; a similar phenomenon has occurred on our college campuses. Fostering a sense of shared responsibility is essential to campus safety. Legal strategies that seek to turn students into uncontrollable strangers work against safer models based upon shared community responsibility.

Strategies of resistance are also counterproductive. If boards of trustees and college presidents believe that there's no duty regarding many student safety issues, there will be a tendency to allocate resources away from residence halls, campus law enforcement, and other departments that can impact safety. More resources to fix broken locks can prevent injuries that could result in large dollar litigation. Loss avoidance is often the best litigation avoidance strategy. Energies spent resisting legal scrutiny can be better directed to fixing problems that create disorder and danger on campus. Moreover, a campus that fails to adequately address danger and disorder is less educationally sound: students who are afraid in their dormitories and are frustrated in attempts to have basic maintenance performed on residential halls are distracted (at the very least) from educational pursuits. Colleges and universities that spend their time resisting student litigation on the grounds that their students are beyond their control, spend money on lawyers and lawsuits that could have been better spent remedying danger and disorder and preventing student injury. A college or university is better advised to avoid liability by demonstrating that it exercised reasonable care under the circumstances than to assert that it had no duty to a student regarding her safety on campus.

The resistance to law and the desire to avoid assumed duties to students is also inconsistent with realities in modern universities. Student affairs administrators study and are trained to be managers of student life and direct housing and student activities etc. Many campus administrators are professional counselors. Many campus law enforcement officers are specially trained to maintain order and reduce risks of criminal intrusion. Campus police easily understand that many strategies that involve far less than custodial control are highly effective for managing danger and criminality. Administrators and campus security officers have the professional training, experience, and judgment to do their jobs. Colleges have given them their missions, but the law has all too often disempowered them by telling them that proaction can be a source of legal liability. For fear of being the person who triggered litigation, many campus administrators and police have told us that they stand back and take the posture of a bystander, or avoid the right choice simply because of fear of litigation. This kind of disempowerment leads to dangerous decisions. Few college professors today would fail to provide the supervision that would have prevented the horrible injury that occurred in the *Beach* case. Campus security departments are appalled to think that broken entry door locks in dormitories would go unrepaired as in *Delaney*; a decision to let a dangerous person go on his way to kill someone, as in *Tarasoff*, was likely facilitated by fear of litigation; most campus police want *rules* to stop and question students like those fraternity hazing-bound students who roamed campus before the sad incident in *Furek*. These states of affairs are directly contrary to the missions of universities and the role of student life administrators. The facilitator university seeks to reverse the longstanding resistance to law and overcome the danger, disempowerment, and disorder that comes from unclear responsibilities and campuses where students and the college are disconnected.

Facilitating Shared Responsibility: Empowerment Through Positive Use of Law

To reduce danger on campus and enhance the educational program, we must facilitate shared responsibility for safety. In the rush to resist law and blame or distance themselves from students, colleges lost sight of important opportunities to build safer campus environments and close the distance between administration/faculty, students, and even law itself. In retrospect, it was bad social policy and a losing legal strategy to resist partnerships with law. The law can bring campus communities together and provide the structure in which student freedoms can flourish. Students can be free and safe and yet enjoy constitutional adulthood; students simply need structure and guidance to manage their educational and personal development opportunities in college. Some structure actually enhances the hard won student constitutional freedoms. Lack of structure undermines those freedoms.

A principal goal of a facilitator university is to identify and manifest shared responsibility. This means that students must acknowledge their critical role in protecting their own and other students' safety. Legal rules of comparative negligence, for example, can reinforce this message. The university also shares responsibility with students for their safety. The typical college has many tools at its disposal to manage and reduce risks, including control of maintenance and security, housing assignments, and the identification of activities that are promoted or discouraged, etc. A college can establish some circumstances of campus life and engender others. Appropriately applied legal rules regarding duty can facilitate understanding of what colleges can and should do.

Campus administrators and police can be more effective with the law as an ally. The law should allow and encourage them to do their jobs as best they can, and they should be able to look to the law for assistance in how to manage new and difficult safety issues on campus. In a world of law and litigation, lawsuits are a fact of life. It is better—all the way around—for campus officials to do their jobs as they know best and not to turn their job descriptions into "litigation avoidance." Empowerment is more reasonable, much safer, and makes good legal and practical sense. Law does not facilitate the proper dynamic with no-duty rules which discourage reasonable efforts at addressing campus safety issues. Duty rules—balanced with shared student responsibility rules—facilitate cooperative, proactive university administration.

The law also can be a positive tool on campus in other ways. When attempting to deal with problems associated with squeegeemen in New York City, Chief Bratton and Mayor Gulliani looked to law and litigation as a way to define lawful and effective ways to deal with a seemingly intractable problem. Lawyers and campus administrators can devise strategies both lawful and effective—and more effective because lawful—to combat safety problems. Initiatives (like those at the University of Delaware after *Furek*) to reduce dangerous alcohol use are examples of how law-like strategies can help to find the proper balance between structure and freedom on campus. The law can promote colleges to do the right, reasonable, and safe thing.

This does not mean that colleges will no longer face lawsuits and menacing legal problems from time to time. However, even in the face of hostile litigation a college can have the opportunity to use the legal process as a way to define parameters of safety and responsibility on campus. And viewing the law through a positive lens, the university can elect the conditions under which it will most likely encounter legal process and litigation. For example, in *Nero*, the university could have elected to eliminate the dangerous student from the summer dormitory. The attack presumably would not have occurred, thus avoiding an inevitable lawsuit from the victim or her family; the removed student may sue, and in a worst case scenario the university will learn the lawful conditions under which it may deal with the next student who arguably threatens the safety of other students. In that sense, even a losing case is a winner in that it offers guidelines for future conduct. Indeed, a college may deliberately risk one type of litigation rather than another. Sometimes only by making a court state a clear rule of decision can confusion and uncertainty of the margins of the law be cleared up. The courts have a heavy responsibility to decide these cases in ways that facilitate efforts to promote student safety. We have offered the facilitator model to courts as a way to work closely with rules and procedures that are already in place so as to promote safer campuses and to recognize the uniqueness of colleges.

We do not propose or describe a radical change in law or higher education administration. The vision of the facilitator university illustrates what is reasonable and positive in the relationships among students, universities, and the legal system. Perpetuation of extreme positions and paradigms guarantees failure. A legal paradigm that asks colleges to exercise reasonable care for student safety—and asks students to be accountable when they are at fault—is equitable, balanced, safer, and contributes to a sense of community. There is a historic opportunity to seize this moment in the history of higher education, to embrace this time of transition and create closer and safer campuses.

APPENDIX

Illustrations

The following illustrations are examples of how the facilitator model functions in particular scenarios. The illustrations sometimes draw upon cases that have already been decided; other illustrations reflect a composite of rules from several cases or represent still other situations that are typically encountered by colleges and universities.

It should be noted that, in several of the illustrations, parties other than the university might also be liable for the injuries described. Indeed, the conduct of other wrongdoers and the victim her/himself are always relevant where the issue is negligence.

Illustrations (Set 1)

(A) John, a graduate student in chemistry, is seriously injured when Joe, another student in the laboratory, turns on a flame during an experiment with ether. All students in the laboratory are graduate students in chemistry and all had been told by the instructor to perform the ether experiment. The students had all been instructed on dozens of occasions of the dangers of allowing a flame near ether. The professor was out of the room at the time of the accident. The university has a duty to provide appropriate reasonable instruction to students at all levels in matters of safety but was not negligent and is therefore not liable. In this situation, it is reasonable for the professor to assume that these informed students will not expose ether to a flame under usual circumstances. The professor would not have the responsibility to stand near each and every student constantly.

(B) Now assume that the students are freshmen taking their first chemistry laboratory course. These students had heard a lecture on the nature and uses of ether but had never before experimented with it nor were they aware of the risks associated with ether. Both the injured student and the student causing the injury are eighteen years of age. The university could be liable for the injury if the professor were out of the room. A standard of reasonable care would suggest that the professor should have personally supervised the experiment or had an experienced graduate student do so, but s/he should not have allowed inexperienced freshmen students to perform the experiment without more elaborate instruction and/or some in-room supervision. A jury should determine whether the professor's omissions fell below a standard of reasonableness, given his education, training, and expertise and the relative inexperience of the students.

(C) Now assume that the two students are 30 year old "second career" students taking their first course in chemistry. The result should be the same as in (B); the age of the students should not, alone, be dispositive. Their level of experience and knowledge would be factors to consider. Again, the question is one of negligence - and for a jury.

Illustrations (Set 2)

(A) Students call their residence hall advisor (the "R.A." is also a student) to report that the lock of the outer entry door landing to the hall is broken and the door cannot be fully closed or secured. The R.A. reports the matter to the Director of Student Housing, who, in turn reports it to the office of physical plant and building maintenance. Many requests for repairs and maintenance are pending, and maintenance is substantially deferred/delayed until previously scheduled jobs are completed. During the period of deferred maintenance, a criminal intruder enters the dormitory through this door and assaults a student. The university is arguably liable for the student's injuries, because it had a duty as a landlord to maintain the common entrances to student housing (the premises under its control), including locks that keep the entrances reasonably secure. Unreasonably long delays in making necessary safety repairs will strongly impact potential liability.

(B) At 2:00 a.m. a student resident of one of state university's dormitories props open the outer entry door to the second floor landing of the residence hall, to facilitate the entry of a friend who has come from out of town. The friend has told the student that the friend will be getting into town "in the middle of the night" and will just come to the student's room. The door is in proper working order and automatically locks if it is closed. Students enter after 9:00 p.m. by using a key issued to them by the campus housing office. Students have been informed in student handbooks, a "security tips" pamphlet (similar to those used by hotels), and in orientation sessions with their residence advisors that "propping" doors seriously compromises the safety of residents and that anyone proven to have "propped" a door will be disciplined including being suspended from campus housing for at least one semester. At 3:00 a.m. a criminal intruder enters the "propped" door and assaults another student. The university arguably is not liable for the injury if it had no reason to know, by virtue of the short interval of time, that the door had been propped open. This situation is different from situation (A) above. The fact that the university had a duty to reasonably maintain its residence halls for the safety and security of its student tenants does not mean that it is liable for the intrusion. To impose liability, it must be shown that some university negligence contributed to the attack. Although a university must perform reasonable security checks, it will not be required to discover and remedy every student attempt to circumvent safety practices instantaneously.

Illustrations (Set 3)

(A) A student attending a college basketball game approaches a campus law enforcement officer and points out another student some fifty feet away who, the student states, has threatened to get a gun and shoot him for dating a female student the suspected assailant "desires." The campus police officer assures the student that he will look into the situation. The officer approaches the suspected assailant and questions him. The assailant indicates that the matter was a harmless disagreement and leaves. Subsequently though, the assailant returns to the gymnasium carrying a small bag and wearing a jacket. The victim of the threat sees the suspected assailant and again asks the campus police officer to intervene. The officer assures him that all is safe. The officer turns his back, whereupon the assailant pulls a gun from the bag and shoots the victim. The university may be liable; it has a duty to take reasonable action to respond to the threat.

(B) A student is shot and wounded in the waiting room of the college financial aid office. His assailant is another student who has signed in to see a financial aid counselor. The assailant has exhibited no abnormal behavior (there are many witnesses) and has no history of misconduct while enrolled at the college or prior to enrollment. There are no facts apparent to the college or any of its administrators or other students suggesting that the assailant presented any danger to self or others. The college should not be liable. Reasonable security could not have prevented this spontaneous, unforeseeable assault.

Illustration (4)

State University hosts an annual fireworks display on its campus that is open to the public. The event has increased in popularity over the years and is attended by more than15,000 students, employees and citizens of the community. The university is aware of increasing gang-related activity among high school-age youth in the surrounding area and has assigned more than 100 campus and local law enforcement officers to the event pursuant to a detailed protocol on crowd control. There have been no prior incidents of assault; the only past injuries have been "slip and fall" injuries and one or two minor vehicle accidents. A gang member from a local youth gang comes to the event looking for a member of a rival gang. Thinking he has spotted the rival, he draws a gun and shoots, wounding two students attending the fireworks display. The university should be able to avoid liability. It has taken elaborate steps to develop a successful protocol to minimize the risk of dangerous activity and has successfully controlled crowd safety for several years. There have been no prior gang-related assaults on students and it is arguable that reasonable police efforts cannot prevent this type of random shooting.

Illustration (5)

A member of a college's staff observes a familiar homeless man in the lobby of a campus dormitory speaking loudly and gesturing wildly. It appears that he has a weapon tucked in the front of his jeans. The staff member approaches the homeless man who says that he is upset by lack of sleep and hunger. The staff member escorts the man outside, gives him ten dollars, and indicates politely that the dormitory is not open to the public. The homeless man proceeds to the college cafeteria where he shoots a cafeteria worker. The college had a duty to exercise reasonable care. The question whether the college was negligent - that is, whether the staff member should have called campus security or taken other action - is one of fact for a jury.

Illustrations (Set 6)

(A) A female student is approached by a young male as she stands in a public university parking lot at 10:45 p.m. She has attended a night class that ended at 9:50 p.m. and is waiting for her roommate who is on her way from their off-campus apartment. The two are planning to take a "red eye" flight home for spring break and the friend has been loading luggage in the car and is running late. The man displays a gun and forces the student to walk with him to a wooded area near the university's football stadium where he sexually assaults her and then runs off. The attacker is later apprehended as the result of another assault and is convicted of sexual assault. The student sues the university claiming that it was negligent in not employing more campus police officers. The claim may fail, as governmental immunity doctrine will generally not allow a court to determine how a public university police agency allocates its resources. A private legal action based essentially on an allegation that police have not adequately fulfilled their duty to protect the general public is not permitted. To succeed on a claim, the student would likely have to show that the campus police undertook to protect her personal safety or that the campus police had failed to follow their own policies on patrolling that area.

(B) Same situation except that the student has walked with other students to a university kiosk at 11:00 p.m. where she decides to wait for her friend to pick her up. The kiosk is contained within a gated courtyard entrance to the university. The student is waiting alone in the area because she has seen the officer there on many evenings. (As the student waits, she assumes that he is in the area somewhere). She is approached by a middle-aged man who displays a gun, and forces her to walk with him to an unlocked academic building where he assaults her. Unknown to the student, the officer normally assigned to this post has called in sick, and in violation of campus security rules, no officer has been assigned to cover his post, check locks, or patrol the area on this shift. The university will likely be liable on these facts. The student has relied upon the presence of the police officer at this kiosk in making her decision to use this area at this hour. The university has provided an officer at this location on a regular basis and has also failed to follow its own protocol regarding the security of the entrance gate. Governmental immunity will likely not protect the university in this situation.

Illustrations (Set 7)

(A) A college operates a number of academic and sport camps for elementary and secondary school-aged children. The camps are held on the campus of the college, and participants between the ages of ten and seventeen are housed in college dormitories. The college utilizes some of its own undergraduate and graduate students to supervise and coach or instruct participants. Some of these college students have no training or experience in dealing with or supervising young children. During a lunch break at one of these camps, a ten-year-old camper decides to explore, by himself, a wooded path near the college's music building. He comes upon a construction site and falls into a construction excavation, sustaining serious injuries. The college student responsible for the group of students that included the ten-year-old said that he thought the "kids were old enough to walk around a bit on their own after lunch." The college is likely liable for the injury. Although it may not have had a duty to supervise an adult student during the lunch break, it has a duty to provide competent supervision for elementary school-aged children. [Some courts have held that even high schools students must be supervised by an appropriate instructor or administrator, when they are in any peer group setting as at a camp during lunch, etc.] *In loco parentis* rules, as typically applied in K-12 education, do apply here.

(B) During a golf camp for eight to fourteen year-olds at the college's golf course, a graduate assistant coach pairs participants and tells them to practice iron shots from approximately 50 yards. While the assistant is taking a drink of water from a cooler at the golf course's clubhouse, one student negligently swings a club and strikes his partner who is standing behind him, causing serious head injuries. The students have received instruction on using irons, but have not been told where to stand. The college is likely to be liable for the injuries. Instruction of children of this age must give much more attention to matters of safety that might be obvious to adults. Also, the graduate student is likely to be found negligent in walking away from the children during a session to a place from which he could not adequately observe them and be in a position to timely intervene if he saw a dangerous situation.

Illustrations (Set 8)

(A)   Students on an extra-curricular outing with a student environmental club are picnicking at a picnic shelter within the state park in which they are looking for hawks. The students and faculty advisor are sharing sandwiches and iced tea as they reload their cameras and discuss their afternoon agenda. Two nineteen year old students ask permission to return briefly to the last trail hiked to see if any hawks have reappeared. The faculty advisor grants permission and the two are told to return to the shelter in twenty minutes. On the way, one of the students walks down an embankment of a lake which he knows is very cold. He loses his balance and falls into the lake. The other student runs for help, but by the time help arrives the student has drowned. The professor has a duty to provide reasonable supervision of the students and also to provide reasonable equipment, procedures, etc. for the trip. But he has not acted unreasonably and the university is likely to avoid liability. Even if the instructor is found minimally negligent (as in not questioning the boys more specifically, or knowing whether they could swim), the victim has been comparatively negligent in his own conduct and has contributed to his death more than did any carelessness of the professor. In most states, where the injured party's negligence has been equal to or greater than that of the defendant (here the professor), the comparative negligence rule bars recovery altogether.

(B)   Same facts except that the professor observes that the young men have apparently been drinking and they appear quite unstable. The professor now has a responsibility to intervene by denying them permission to leave the group, and perhaps to see to it that they return home.

Illustration (9)

Jane, an eighteen year-old sophomore student, is known throughout the college community to be a heavy drinker. She has shared the fact that she drinks heavily with many student friends. At the urging of several friends, she shared her problem with a psychologist at the college's counseling center and two of her professors. She began seeing the psychologist regularly and joined a student support group that met once a week. The faculty members talked with her frequently but discussed the matter with no one else, although they knew she was receiving counseling. As the term progressed, she was frequently absent from classes and missed several appointments with her counselor over a three week period. She remained socially active and attended parties frequently on and off campus. She always consumed alcohol and was usually escorted back to her on-campus room by friends.

On one such evening, after consuming a large quantity of alcohol in her residence hall room, Jane decided to walk across campus to see a friend in another residence hall. She was observed by a member of the residence hall staff as she left the lobby of her dormitory and by a campus police officer as she walked toward her friends's dorm. Both later indicated that she appeared to be intoxicated and both recognized her and knew of her problem with alcohol. Later that night, campus police received a call from Jane. She was hysterical and reported that she had been grabbed by four male students as she entered her friend's residence hall, taken to a room, and raped by the four men. Bystander era case law likely would have relieved the college of all responsibility in this situation as a matter of law. The facilitator college acknowledges responsibility in this matter: specifically, it would have a legal duty to use reasonable care when it knows or should know that a particular student has engaged in conduct that places herself in a position of unreasonable risk (incapacity, peril, etc.). Moreover, a facilitator will administer a program of active intervention as to the general problem of alcohol abuse on campus. The college should not argue that it was sufficient to generally advise students about the dangers of alcohol abuse; the college should make efforts reasonably calculated to lessen the risks of student injury as a result of alcohol abuse on campus. Whether the action or inaction of college faculty, the counselor, residence hall staff, or campus police failed to meet a standard of reasonableness would be a question of fact.

A facilitator college would face liability if that college's conduct fell below that amount of care that would have been exercised by reasonable college administrators/police/etc. in similar circumstances. Jane's own conduct would be relevant and would diminish her recovery against the college to the extent of her own fault. In most jurisdictions, if her negligence in the situation were deemed to be equal to or greater than the college's negligence, she would be denied recovery.

Illustration (10)

Several fraternities on campus have actively resisted university directives prohibiting all forms of hazing and the pressuring of pledges to consume alcohol at fraternity functions. The university has held repeated meetings with the officers of these clubs over a period of a year, and, at each meeting there have been heated discussions ending with promises of fraternity leadership to "work on the problem." Despite these meetings, the university has received six formal reports from campus police about excessive noise and alcohol-related disorder at events hosted by the fraternities during the year.

During the first semester of the following academic year, one of the fraternities advertises in the student newspaper inviting students to attend a pledge party. The ad described the event as "The Party From Hell." No university administrator attended the event, nor attempted to advise, intervene, etc.

At approximately 7:30 p.m. on the evening of the party, campus police encounter several students walking across campus in odd clothing. They ask where the students are going and are informed that the students are on the way to "that killer pledge party - we're just hoping to survive." Later, at about 11:30 p.m., campus police receive a rescue call and dispatch two officers to the scene of the event. Partiers are observed crowded around a student who appeared to be unconscious on a sofa. After determining that the student is in serious distress, EMT personnel are called. The student dies on the way to the hospital from severe alcohol poisoning. A later investigation discloses that the student, under apparent duress by members of the fraternity, consumed an extremely large quantity of hard liquor in a very short time during a "drinking contest for pledges." A facilitator college would not claim that it had no duty in this situation. Rather, the university would acknowledge responsibility to take steps beyond mere discussions with the organizations in question, especially where it had actual knowledge of their willful resistance to rules against hazing and alcohol abuse and records of disorderly behavior. Moreover, when campus police had actual knowledge of the intent of the students they encountered, a facilitator college would have authorized campus police to take appropriate action in such a situation through specific rules aimed to deal with such dangerous and disorderly conduct. Whether a university's inaction falls below a standard of reasonable care and was the cause of the victim's death will be a question of fact.

Bibliography

Texts & Monographs

AIKEN, RAY J., JOHN F. ADAMS & JOHN W. HALL, LIABILITY, LEGAL LIABILITIES IN HIGHER EDUCATION: THEIR SCOPE AND MANAGEMENT (Association of American Colleges 1976), *printed simultaneously in* 3 J. C. & U. L. 127 (1976).

AM I LIABLE? FACULTY, STAFF, AND INSTITUTIONAL LIABILITY IN THE COLLEGE AND UNIVERSITY SETTING (National Association of College and University Attorneys 1989).

BLACKSTONE, SIR WILLIAM, COMMENTARIES 441 (Oxford: Clarendon Press 1765).

BOYER, ERNEST L., COLLEGE: THE UNDERGRADUATE EXPERIENCE IN AMERICA (Harper Row 1987).

BRATTON, WILLIAM & PETER KNOBLER, TURNAROUND — HOW AMERICA'S TOP COP REVERSED THE CRIME EPIDEMIC (Random House 1998).

BURLING, PHILIP, CRIME ON CAMPUS: ANALYZING AND MANAGING THE INCREASING RISK OF INSTITUTIONAL LIABILITY (National Association of College and University Attorneys 1991, 1990).

FISHER, BONNIE & SLOAN, JOHN J., CAMPUS CRIME, LEGAL, SOCIAL AND POLICY PERSPECTIVES (1995).

FOSSEY, RICHARD, MICHAEL CLAY SMITH, AN ADMINISTRATOR'S GUIDE FOR RESPONDING TO CAMPUS CRIME: FROM PREVENTION TO LIABILITY (FALL 1996).

GEHRING, DONALD D., ED., ADMINISTERING COLLEGE AND UNIVERSITY HOUSING: A LEGAL PERSPECTIVE (Rev. Ed., College Administration Publications 1983).

GEHRING, DONALD D. & CHRISTY P. GERACI, ALCOHOL ON CAMPUS: A COMPENDIUM OF THE LAW AND A GUIDE TO CAMPUS POLICY (College Administration Publications 1989).

HALBERSTAM, DAVID, THE CHILDREN (Random House 1998).

HASKINS, CHARLES HOMER, THE RISE OF UNIVERSITIES (Cornell University Press, 1957).

KAPLIN WILLIAM A. & BARBARA A. LEE, THE LAW OF HIGHER EDUCATION, 3D EDITION (Jossey-Bass, Inc. 1995).

KELLING, GEORGE & CATHERINE COLES, FIXING BROKEN WINDOWS — RESTORING ORDER AND REDUCING CRIME IN OUR COMMUNITIES (Martin Kessler Books 1996).

KENT, JAMES, COMMENTARIES ON AMERICAN LAW (2d Ed. 1896).

LEVINE, ARTHUR & JEANETTE CURETON, WHEN HOPE AND FEAR COLLIDE — A PORTRAIT OF TODAY'S COLLEGE STUDENT (Jossey-Bass, Inc. 1998).

LEVINE, ARTHUR, WHEN DREAMS AND HEROES DIED: PORTRAIT OF TODAY'S COLLEGE STUDENT (Jossey-Bass, Inc. 1980).

LEWIS, LAURIE, CAMPUS CRIME AND SECURITY AT POST SECONDARY EDUCATION INSTITUTIONS (U.S. Dept. Of Education Office of Educational Research and Improvement: Nat'l Center for Education Statistics 1997).

OSTRANDER, CURTIS & SCHWARTZ, JOSEPH, CRIME AT COLLEGE : THE STUDENT GUIDE TO PERSONAL SAFETY (1994).

PALMER, CAROLYN J., VIOLENT CRIMES AND OTHER FORMS OF VICTIMIZATION IN RESIDENCE HALLS (College Administration Publications 1993).

PAVELA, GARY, THE DISMISSAL OF STUDENTS WITH MENTAL DISORDERS: LEGAL ISSUES, POLICY CONSIDERATIONS AND ALTERNATIVE RESPONSES (College Administration Publications 1985).

PROSSER, WILLIAM L., RESTATEMENT (SECOND) OF TORTS §§ 314, 322, 323, 324, 333 (1965).

RADDATZ, ANITA, CRIME ON CAMPUS: INSTITUTIONAL TORT LIABILITY FOR THE CRIMINAL ACTS OF THIRD PARTIES (National Association of College and University Attorneys 1988).

SMITH, MICHAEL CLAY, COPING WITH CRIME ON CAMPUS (American Council on Education/Macmillan 1988).

STEINER, HENRY J., MORAL ARGUMENT AND SOCIAL VISION IN THE COURTS: A STUDY OF TORT ACCIDENT LAW (University of Wisconsin Press 1987).

WEEKS, KENT M. & DEREK DAVIS, EDS., JAMES M. DAWSON INSTITUTE OF CHURCH- STATE STUDIES FOR THE CENTER FOR

CONSTITUTIONAL STUDIES, LEGAL DESKBOOK FOR
ADMINISTRATORS OF INDEPENDENT COLLEGES AND UNIVERSITIES
(2d Ed. 1993).

WILLIAMS, JUAN, EYES ON THE PRIZE: AMERICA'S CIVIL RIGHTS YEARS
1954- 1965 (Viking 1987).

YOUNG, D. PARKER & DONALD D. GEHRING, THE COLLEGE STUDENT
AND THE COURTS (Rev. Ed., College Administration Publications
1977).

Cases

Abston v. Waldon Academy, 102 S.W. 351 (Tenn. 1907).

Albano v. Colby College, 822 F. Supp. 840 (D. Me. 1993).

Albert v. Carovano, 851 F.2d 561 (2nd Cir. 1988).

Anthony v. Syracuse Univ., 231 N.Y.S. 435 (N.Y. App. Div. 1928).

Baldauf v. Kent State Univ., 550 N.E.2d 517 (Ohio Ct. App. 1988).

Baldwin v. Zoradi, 176 Cal. Rptr. 809 (Cal. Ct. App. 1981).

Banks v. Trustees of the Univ. of Pa., 666 A.2d 329 (Pa. Super. 1995).

Barr v. Brooklyn Children's Aid Soc'y, 190 N.Y.S. 296 (N.Y. Sup. 1921).

Barker v. Trustees of Bryn Mawr College, 122 A. 220 (Pa. 1923).

Beach v. Univ. of Utah, 726 P.2d 413 (Utah 1986).

Beta Beta Chapter of Beta Theta Pi Fraternity v. May, 611 So. 2d 889
(Miss. 1993).

Boehm v. Univ. of Pa. Sch. of Veterinary Med., 573 A.2d 575 (Pa. Super.
1990).

Bolkhir v. North Carolina State Univ., 365 S.E.2d 898 (N.C. 1988).

Booker v. Grand Rapids Medical College, 120 N.W. 589 (Mich. 1909).

Booker v. Lehigh Univ., 800 F. Supp. 234 (E.D. Pa. 1992), *aff'd* 995 F.2d
215 (3rd Cir. 1993).

Bradshaw v. Rawlings, 612 F.2d 135 (3d Cir. 1979).

Brigham Young Univ. v. Lillywhite, 118 F.2d 836 (10th Cir. 1941).

Carroll v. Blinken, 957 F.2d 991 (2d Cir. 1992).

Corso v. Creighton Univ., 731 F.2d 529 (8th Cir. 1984).

Crow v. State of California, 271 Cal. Rptr. 349 (Cal. Ct. App. 1990).

Cutler v. Board of Regents of the State of Fla., 459 So. 2d 413 (Fla. Dist. Ct. App. 1984).

Davie v. Regents of the Univ. of Cal. et al., 227 P. 247 (Cal. Dist. Ct. App. 1924).

Delaney v. Univ. of Houston, 835 S.W.2d 56 (Tex. 1992).

Delbridge v. Maricopa County Community College Dist., 893 P.2d 55 (Ariz. Ct. App. 1995).

Dixon v. Alabama State Board of Education, 294 F.2d 150 (5th Cir. 1961).

Duarte v. State, 148 Cal. Rptr. 804 *vacated*, 151 Cal. Rptr. 727 (Cal. Ct. App. 1979).

Eiseman v. State of N.Y., 511 N.E.2d 1128 (N.Y. 1987).

Estates of Morgan v. Fairfield Family Counseling Ctr., 673 N.E.2d 1311 (Ohio 1997).

Fraser v. U.S., 674 A.2d 811 (Conn. 1996).

Furek v. The University of Delaware, 594 A.2d 506 (Del. 1991).

Gay Activists Alliance v. Board of Regents of Univ. of Okla., 638 P.2d 1116 (Okla. 1981).

Gay Alliance of Students v. Matthews, 544 F.2d 162 (4th Cir. 1976).

Gay Lib v. University of Mo., 558 F.2d 848 (8th Cir. 1977).

Gay Students Org. of the Univ. of New Hampshire v. Bonner, 509 F.2d 652 (1st Cir. 1974).

Gay Student Serv. v. Texas A&M Univ., 737 F.2d 1317 (5th Cir. 1984).

Gebser v. Lago Vista Indep. Sch. Dist., 118 S. Ct. 1989 (1998), *aff'g* 118 S.Ct. 595 (1997).

Goldman v. State of N.Y., 551 N.Y.S.2d 641 (N.Y. App. Div. 1990).

Goss v. Lopez, 419 U.S. 565 (1975).

Gott v. Berea College, 161 S.W. 204 (Ky. 1913).

Gragg v. Wichita State Univ., 934 P.2d 121 (Kan. 1997).

Great Cent. Ins. Co. v. Insurance Serv. Office, Inc., 74 F.3d 778 (7th Cir. 1996).

Green v. Cornell Univ., 184 N.Y.S. 924, *aff'd*, 135 N.E. 900 (N.Y. 1920).

Greenhill v. Bailey, 519 F.2d 5 (8th Cir. 1975).

Hamburger v. Cornell Univ., 148 N.E. 539 (N.Y. 1925).

Hartman v. Bethany College, 778 F. Supp. 286 (N.D. W.V. 1991).

Healy v. James, 408 U.S. 169 (1972).

Henig v. Hofstra Univ., 553 N.Y.S.2d 479 (App. Div. 1990).

Higgons v. Pratt Inst., 45 F.2d 698 (C.C.A. 2d 1930).

Hill v. McCauley, 3 Pa. C. 77 (Pa. County Ct. 1887).

Isaacson v. Husson College, 332 A.2d 757 (Me. 1975).

Jesik v. Maricopa Co. Community College Dist., 611 P.2d 547 (Ariz. 1980).

John B. Stetson Univ. v. Hunt, 102 So. 637 (Fla. 1924).

Johnson v. State, 894 P.2d 1366 (Wash. Ct. App. 1995).

Joyner v. Whiting, 477 F.2d 456 (4th Cir. 1973).

Kline v. 1500 Mass. Ave. Apt. Corp., 439 F.2d 477 (D.C. Cir. 1970).

L.W. v. Western Golf Assoc., 675 N.E.2d 760 (Ind. Ct. App. 1997).

Leonardi v. Bradley Univ., 625 N.E.2d 431 (Ill. App. Ct. 1993).

Malley v. Youngstown State Univ., 658 N.E.2d 333 (Ct. Claims Ohio 1995).

Mead v. Nassau Community College, 483 N.Y.S.2d 953 (N.Y. App. Div. 1985).

Medical and Surgical Soc. of Montgomery Co. v. Weatherly, 75 Ala. 248 (1883).

Militana v. Univ. of Miami, 236 So. 2d 162 (Fla. Dist. Ct. App. 1970).

Millard v. Osborne, 611 A.2d 715 (Pa. Super. Ct. 1992).

Miller v. State of N.Y., 478 N.Y.S.2d 829 (N.Y. 1984).

Mills v. Stewart, 247 P. 332 (Mont. 1926).

Mintz v. State of N.Y., 362 N.Y.S. 2d 619 (N.Y. App. Div. 1975).

Motz v. Johnson, 651 N.E.2d 1163 (Ind. App., 1995), *transfer granted and opinion vacated* (1996).

Mullins v. Pine Manor College, 449 N.E.2d 331 (Mass. 1983).

Nallan v. Helmsley-Spear, Inc., 407 N.E.2d 451 (N.Y. 1980).

Nieswand v. Cornell Univ., 692 F. Supp. 1464 (N.D. N.Y. 1988).

Nero v. Kansas State Univ., 861 P.2d 768 (Kan. 1993).

New Times, Inc. v. Arizona Bd. of Regents, 519 P.2d 169 (Ariz. 1974).

Orr v. Brigham Young Univ., 108 F.3d 1388 (10th Cir. 1997).

Papish v. Board of Curators of the Univ. of Mo., 410 U.S. 667 (1973).

Parks v. Northwestern Univ., 75 N.E. 991 (Ill. 1905), *overruled in part by Darling v. Charleston Community Mem. Hosp.*, 211 N.E.2d 253 (Ill. 1965).

Peschke v. Carroll College, 929 P.2d 874 (Mont. 1996).

Peterson v. San Francisco Community College Dist., 685 P.2d 1193 (Cal. 1984).

Piazzola v. Watkins, 442 F.2d 284 (5th Cir. 1971).

Pitre v. Louisiana Tech. Univ., 673 So. 2d 585 (La. 1996).

Poulin v. Colby College and Maine Bonding & Cas. Co., 402 A.2d 846 (Me. 1979).

Prairie View A & M Univ. v. Thomas, 684 S.W.2d 169 (Tex. App. 1984).

Pratt v. Wheaton College, 40 Ill. 186 (Ill. 1866).

Rabel v. Illinois Wesleyan Univ., 514 N.E.2d 552 (Ill. App. Ct. 1987).

Ramsammy v. City of New York, 628 N.Y.S.2d 693 (N.Y. 1995).

Randi W. v. Muroc Joint Unified Sch. Dist., 929 P.2d 582 (Cal. 1997).

Regina v. Hopley, 2 F & F 202, 175 Eng. Rep. 1024 (1860).

Rhodes v. Illinois Cent. Gulf R.R., 665 N.E.2d 1260 (Ill. 1996).

Riss v. City of New York, 240 N.E.2d 860 (N.Y. 1968).

Robinson v. Washtenaw Circuit Judge, 199 N.W. 618 (Mich. 1924).

Rupp v. Bryant, 417 So. 2d 658 (Fla. 1982), *superceded by statute as stated in Rice v. Lee*, 477 So. 2d 1009 (Fla. App. Ct. 1985).

Savannah College of Art & Design v. Roe, 409 S.E.2d 848 (Ga. 1991), *overruled by Sturbridge Partners, Ltd. v. Walker*, 482 S.E.2d 339 (Ga. 1997).

Scheuer v. Rhodes et al., 416 U.S. 232 (1974), *abrogated by Harlow v. Fitzgerald*, 457 U.S. 800 (1982).

Shannon v. Washington Univ., 575 S.W.2d 235 (Mo. Ct. App. 1978).

Slaughter v. Brigham Young Univ., 514 F.2d 622 (10th Cir. 1975), *cert. denied*, 423 U.S. 898 (1975).

Soglin v. Kauffman, 418 F.2d 163 (7th Cir. 1969).

Stanley v. Magrath, 719 F.2d 279 (8th Cir. 1983).

Tanja H. v. Regents of the Univ. of Cal., 278 Cal. Rptr. 918 (Ct. App. 1991).

Tarasoff v. Board of Regents of the Univ. of Cal., 551 P.2d 334 (Cal. 1976).

Taylor v. Phelan, 9 F.3d 882 (10th Cir. 1993).

The Regents of the Univ. of Cal. v. Superior Court of the County of Alameda, 48 Cal. Rptr. 2d 922 (Ct. App. 1996).

Tinker v. Des Moines Indep. Community Sch. Dist., 393 U.S. 503 (1969).

University of Denver v. Whitlock, 744 P.2d 54 (Colo. 1987).

Ward v. K-Mart Corp., 554 N.E.2d 223 (Ill. 1990).

Weller v. Colleges of the Senecas, 635 N.Y.S.2d 990 (N.Y. App. Div. 1995).

Williams v. Junior College District of Central Southwest Missouri., 906 S.W.2d 400 (Mo. Ct. App. 1995).

Woods v. Simpson, 126 A. 882 (Md. 1924).

Law Reviews/Journals

Adler, John M., *Relying Upon the Reasonableness of Strangers: Some Observations About the Current State of Common Law Affirmative Duties to Aid or Protect Others,* 1991 WIS. L. REV. 867 (1991).

Bhirdo, Kelly W., *The Liability and Responsibility of Institutions of Higher Education for the On- Campus Victimization of Students,* 16 J.C. & U.L. 119 (Summer 1989).

Bickel, Robert D. & Peter F. Lake, *Reconceptualizing the University's Duty to Provide a Safe Learning Environment: A Criticism of the Doctrine of In Loco Parentis and the Restatement (Second) of Torts,* 20 J.C. & U.L. 261 (Winter 1994).

Bickel, Robert D., *Tort Accident Cases Involving Colleges and Universities: A Review of the 1995 Decisions,* 23 J.C. & U. L. 357 (Winter 1997).

Carrington, Frank, *Campus Crime and Violence: A New Trend in Crime Victims' Litigation,* 17 VA. BAR ASSOC. J. 4 (1991).

Cohen, William, *The Private-Public Legal Aspects of Institutions of Higher Education (Part of a Conference on Legal Aspects of Student-Institutional Relationships),* 45 DEN. L.J. 497 (1968).

Curry, Susan J., *Hazing and the "Rush" Toward Reform: Responses from Universities, Fraternities, State legislatures, and the Courts,* 16 J.C. & U.L. 93 (1989).

Dodd Victoria J., *The Non-Contractual Nature of the Student-University Contractual Relationship*, 33 U. KAN. L. REV. 701 (1985).

Fowler, Gerald A., *The Legal Relationship Between the American College Student and the College: an Historical Perspective and the Renewal of a Proposal*, 13 J. L. & EDUC. 401 (1984).

Giles, Molly, Comment, *Obscuring the Issue: The Inappropriate Application of In Loco Parentis to the Campus Crime Victim Duty Question*, 39 WAYNE L. REV. 1335 (Spring 1993).

Goldman, Alvin L., *The University and the Liberty of its Students — a Fiduciary Theory*, 54 KY. L.J. 643 (Summer 1966).

Griffaton, Michael C., Note, *Forewarned is Forearmed: The Crime Awareness and Campus Security Act of 1990 and the Future of Institutional Liability for Student Victimization*, 43 CASE W. RES. L. REV. 525 (Winter 1993).

Hauserman, Nancy, & Paul Lansing, *Rape on Campus: Postsecondary Institutions as Third Party Defendants*, 8 J.C. & U.L. 182 (1981-82).

Hirshberg, P.M., Note, *The College's Emerging Duty to Supervise Students: In Loco Parentis in the 1990's*, 46 WASH. U.J. URB. & CONTEMP. L. 189 (Summer 1994).

Hogan, John C. & Mortimer D. Schwartz, *In Loco Parentis in the United States 1765-1985*, 8 J. LEGAL HIST. 260 n.4 (1987).

Jackson, Brian, *The Lingering Legacy of In Loco Parentis: An Historical Survey and Proposal For Reform*, 44 VAND. L. REV. 1135 (1991).

Kobasic, Dena M., Elizabeth R. Smith & Linda S. Barmore Zucker, Comment, *Eiseman v. State of New York: The Duty of a College to Protect Its Students from Harm by Other Student Admitted Under Special Programs*, 14 J.C. & U.L. 591 (Spring 1998).

Lake, Peter F., *Common Law Duty in Negligence Law: The Recent Consolidation of a Consensus on the Expansion of the Analyses of Duty and the New Conservative Liability Limiting Use of Policy Considerations*, 34 SAN DIEGO L. REV. 1503 (Fall 1997).

Lake, Peter F., *Recognizing the Importance of Remoteness to the Duty to Rescue*, 46 DEPAUL L. REV. 315 (Winter 1997).

Lake, Peter F., *Revisiting Tarasoff*, 58 ALB. L. REV. 97 (1994).

Lewis, Darryll M.H., *The Criminalization of Fraternity, Non-Fraternity, and Non-Collegiate Hazing*, 51 MISS. L.J. 111 (Spring 1991).

Little, Joseph W., *Erosion of No-Duty Negligence Rules in England, the United States, and Common Law Commonwealth Nations*, 20 Hous. L. Rev. 959 (1983).

McKay, Robert B., *The Student as Private Citizen (Part of a Conference on Legal Aspects of Student- Institutional Relationships)*, 45 Den. L.J. 497 (1968).

Miyamoto, Tia, *Liability of Colleges and Universities for Injuries During Extracurricular Activities*, 15 J.C. & U.L. 149 (Fall 1988).

Munch, Christopher H., Comment *(Part of a Conference on Legal Aspects of Student-Institutional Relationships)*, 45 Den. L.J. 497 (1968).

Note, *Common Law Rights for Private University Students: Beyond the State Action Principle*, 84 Yale L.J. 120 (1974).

Richmond, Douglas R., *Institutional Liability for Student Activities and Organizations*, 19 J. Law & Educ. 309 (Summer 1990).

Schwartz, Gary T., *The Beginning and the Possible End of the Rise of Modern American Tort Law*, 26 Ga. L. Rev. 601 (Spring 1992).

Silets, H.L., *Of Students' Rights and Honor: The Application of the Fourteenth Amendment's Due Process Strictures to Honor Code Proceedings At Private Colleges and Universities*, 64 Denver U. L. Rev. 47 (1987).

Smith, Michael Clay, Commentary, *College Liability Resulting from Campus Crime: Resurrection for In Loco Parentis?*, 59 Ed. Law. Rep. 1 (1990).

Snow, Brian A. & William E. Thro, *Redefining the Contours of University Liability: The Potential Implications of Nero v. Kansas State University*, 90 Ed. Law Rep. 989 (1994).

Spaziano, Jennifer L., Comment, *It's All Fun and Games Until Someone Loses An Eye: An Analysis of University Liability For Actions of Student Organizations*, 22 Pepp. L. Rev. 213 (1994).

Stamatakos, Theodore C., Note, *The Doctrine of In Loco Parentis, Tort Liability and the Student-College Relationship*, 65 Ind. L.J. 471 (Spring 1990).

Stewart II, George L., Comment, *Social Host Liability on Campus: Taking the 'High' Out of Higher Education*, 92 Dick. L. Rev. 665 (Spring 1988).

Szablewicz, James J. and Annette Gibbs, *Colleges' Increasing Exposure to Liability: The New In Loco Parentis*, 16 J. L. & Edu. 453 (Fall 1987).

Walton, Spring J., *In Loco Parentis for the 1990's: New Liabilities*, 19 OHIO N.U. L. REV. 247 (1992).

Walton, Spring J., Stephen E. Bassler & Robert Briggs Cunningham, *The High Cost of Partying: Social Host Liability for Fraternities and Colleges*, 14 WHITTIER L. REV. 659 (1993).

Wright, Charles A., *The Constitution on the Campus*, 22 VAND. L. REV. 1027 (1969).

Zirkel, Perry A. & Henry F. Reichner, *Is the In Loco Parentis Doctrine Dead?*, 15 J. L & EDUC. 271 (Summer 1986).

Zirkel, Perry A., *The Volume of Higher Education Litigation: An Update*, 126 ED. LAW. REP. 21 (1998).

Synthesis

PAVELA, GARY, DESIGNING AN ALCOHOL ABUSE PROGRAM, 9 SYNTHESIS 685, 687 (1998); *Plugging The Kegs: Students Benefit When Colleges Limit Excessive Drinking*, U.S. NEWS & WORLD REPORT, Jan. 26, 1998, p. 63.

PAVELA, GARY, THE POWER OF ASSOCIATION: DEFINING OUR RELATIONSHIP WITH STUDENTS IN THE 21ST CENTURY, 7 SYNTHESIS 529 (Winter 1996).

SHUR, GEORGE, A RESPONSE TO PROFESSORS BICKEL & LAKE, 7 SYNTHESIS 543 (1996).

Other Authority

Amy Argetsinger & Valerie Strauss, *Educators Wary After Overseas Attacks Boom in Foreign Travel Poses Risks, Colleges and Missionaries Say*, WASHINGTON POST (Jan. 20, 1998 at B1).

FLORIDA STATUTES § 240.262 (1997).

Joint Statement on Rights and Freedom of Students (American Association of University Professors 1992).

Reisberg, Leo, *Some Experts Say Colleges Share The Responsibility for the Recent Riots*, XLIV Chronicle of Higher Education A48 (May 15, 1998).

Schwartzstein, Richard M., *A Preventative Tragedy: Alcohol and the Death of Scott Krueger*, WELLELSLY TOWNSMEN (Oct. 23, 1997).

Thomas, Nancy L., *The Attorney's Role on Campus — Options For Colleges and Universities,* 30 CHANGE AND HIGHER EDUCATION 34 at 35 (May 15, 1998).